TICKET
TO RIDE

TICKET TO RIDE

*Denny Somach,
Kathleen Somach, and
Kevin Gunn*

•

*Introduction by
Scott Muni*

*William Morrow and Company, Inc.
New York*

Library of Congress Cataloging-in-Publication Data

Somach, Denny.
    Ticket to ride / Denny Somach, Kathleen Somach & Kevin Gunn; introduction by Scott Muni.
        p.   cm.
    ISBN 0-688-08769-8
    1. Beatles.   2. Rock music—Interviews.   I. Somach, Kathleen.
II. Gunn, Kevin.   III. Title.
ML421.B4S65   1989
782.42166'092'2—dc20   89-12313
                                                                                        CIP
                                                                                         MN

Printed in the United States of America

First Edition

1 2 3 4 5 6 7 8 9 10

BOOK DESIGN BY JAYE ZIMET

To Teddy and Emily Kate, and future generations of Beatle fans everywhere . . .

FOREWORD

When I first conceived the *Ticket to Ride* radio series over five years ago, my intention was to pay tribute to the greatest musical group of my generation, the Beatles.

The series, and now this book, celebrate the impact and influence the Beatles had on all of us.

When the time came to choose a host for *Ticket to Ride*, one name stood out above all others. Scott Muni has been a New York radio mainstay for more than twenty years. His days at WABC radio are legendary and he is now known as the cornerstone air personality at the Big Apple's "Home of Rock and Roll," WNEW-FM. "The professor" was more than a disc jockey to the Beatles—he was, first and foremost, their friend. Scott has followed John, Paul, George, and Ringo through every step of their career, from their very first day in America right through their breakup, and he continues to keep the memories alive for us all.

I am glad to share these interviews with you. After all, it was the fans of *Ticket to Ride* who prompted us to compile the transcripts into book form.

The Beatles have given us so much pleasure—it is virtually impossible to imagine a world without their musical genius. I'm just glad they gave us a "ticket to ride."

—Denny Somach

ACKNOWLEDGMENTS

The authors would like to thank the following people for their assistance with this project:

Sheri Gillis, Sean McKay, Marc Schiffman, Tom Couch, and Sal D'Aleo for their help and support.

Ken Sharp for his work on several interviews.

And, of course, "The Professor" who made this whole "hookey dookey" work every week across the nation.

CONTENTS

INTRODUCTION

by Scott Muni

The date was February 7, 1964, and I was at JFK airport in New York. America's first exposure of Beatlemania happened before my eyes—and my WABC microphone.

The police and security at the airport did not expect the thousands of fans, mostly girls, who swarmed the terminal. There had been no precedent for this kind of reception. I mean, Elvis didn't do public appearances anymore. If you wanted to see Elvis, you went to a movie.

As the Beatles got off the plane, they were led through stanchions, poles with ropes strung between them, like there are in movie theaters. They were set up to lead the Beatles off the jet, down the ramp, through a hall, and into a little office building. There they had set up a foldaway table and four foldaway chairs. That was the stage.

As soon as the Beatles came through the door, the girls went berserk and made their move. They came through the main door, through side doors, and from places that you didn't even know existed. They were everywhere. They grabbed me and threw me out of the way on their dash to the Beatles. I was standing there with my microphone, wearing a comparatively new wool overcoat to fight off the February cold. Unfortunately, it was no match for the females and was ripped off my back as they surged by me.

I pleaded, "Please, I'm Scott, your friend. Don't do this to me, go after them." Well, they were going after them, I was just in their way. Folks, that was the "mania" part of "Beatlemania." I'll never forget how each one of those girls was screaming, but also crying with joy and sorrow. The joy was for the music and the boys who made it. The sorrow was because they couldn't get closer to something that drew them so strongly.

Well, they ushered the Beatles into this little room, and shut the door. And then they had the press conference, as they called it. The Liverpudlian charm and wit illuminated that first meeting between the press and the Beatles. They had this keen sense of humor and it proved the perfect foil to some of the questions the assembled media threw at them. Question: "Are you going to get a haircut?" Answer: "We just did." The press quickly became unwitting straight men for these four comedians.

In all fairness, I don't think anyone assembled really knew what was taking place. But at least the radio people didn't ask dumb questions.

I was also struck by how pasty and pale they all looked. Maybe it was the fact that the sun is rarely out in England for too long. Or maybe it was because they were young kids living a typical rock 'n' roll lifestyle. Whatever, they looked bad, not at all like their pictures.

That day, our station went from WABC to W-A-Beatle-C. The management of the station was a little hesitant about that nickname. It took a while for them to OK the fact that we would devote a lot of time and energy to the Beatles and their music. To them it was new and untested. But we did convince them. And once these guys went back to their neighborhoods and saw the reaction on the street, they knew we had done the right thing. Within a few weeks, there was nowhere you could hide from that word; "Beatles" was everywhere.

Five nights later, the Beatles conquered America with their appearance on *The Ed Sullivan Show.* I wasn't there. Most of the tickets were given to the kids of TV bigwigs. Like seventy million other Americans, I watched TV on that Sunday night as they went into living rooms across the country and changed our lives.

The Sullivan appearance was significant in many ways. But the one that has always struck me was how the females started to notice similarities and differences in each of the lads. And what began to happen was that one girl would zero in on Paul, others on John, some on George, and still others on Ringo. The pictures they had been seeing suddenly came to life, and they developed individual or collective crushes. The Beatles didn't look like any boy American girls had ever seen.

Even though I had grown to love music, and had worked in radio for a while by then, this reaction was different than anything I'd ever encountered. It was *total*. There had been other heartthrobs, other great songs, and great records. But there had never been anything like this.

Some of the young guys may have been jealous of the Beatles at first, because their females now wanted nothing to do with them. So the guys changed to keep up, and in the process, were won over by the great music. That led to changes in clothing and hairstyles all over America.

The Beatles' image was Brian Epstein's touch, and I'd like to say at this point that I think Brian was a genius in his own right. His maneuverings, his planning, and his execution with the Beatles was magnificent. Remember, he didn't have a role model either. He ad-libbed a dynasty.

The following year, 1965, the Beatles came back to New York and stayed at a swanky hotel on Park Avenue. Park Avenue is divided by a neutral ground, a median with flowers, plants, and trees. It's a very wide and classy street.

On this day, tens of thousands of fans, mostly young ladies, lined the middle and both sides of Park Avenue. They were singing and chanting "We love you, Beatles."

The Beatles pulled up and made for the hotel. When they did, a number of girls broke loose from the barricades and swelled toward the hotel entrance. One of them knocked over a six hundred-pound potted plant. It took four guards to stand this thing back up again. She was crazed. And as the Beatles ran by her, she reached out and grabbed Ringo. She caught a piece of his neck, taking his Saint Christopher's medal with her.

The boys got inside, and we followed them up to a suite that W-A-Beatle-C had rented to cover the event. Meanwhile, the females remained in the street, keeping a eye on every window, searching for any movement that might lead to a Beatle sighting. They were all listening to us on the radio, and they'd chant or sing whatever we asked them. It was like cheerleading practice.

Their presence, however, rendered the Beatles prisoners in the hotel. Can you imagine a Beatle trying to take to the streets with that mob waiting for him? But they had been here before and they knew what to expect. And they plotted.

Later that evening, a couple of sweet little old ladies were escorted through the lobby and out past the crowd, into the night. John Lennon and Paul McCartney turned up at a few parties in Manhattan a little later on, and the crowd never knew that two Beatle grannies slipped right through their hands.

Meanwhile, upstairs in our suite, I had scheduled an interview with Ringo. To me, Ringo seemed like a real character. He wasn't the spokesman of the band, but he was a funny man. Not that many reporters talked to Ringo at that time; he was still kind of a sleeper.

Ringo was ready for the interview, and he followed me into another room in the suite. I got the tape recorder out and turned it on. And Ringo fainted right in front of me. I was shocked. I opened the door and yelled for help. Everybody came running. I wasn't sure what had happened, but I knew that it was the end of that interview.

Eventually, Ringo was fine. However he was still upset over the loss of his Saint Christopher's medal. It was a family heirloom, given to him by his aunt. We decided we'd redo the interview, this time live on W-A-Beatle-C. We figured that the girl who had Ringo's medal might be listening. In fact it was a pretty safe bet. Where else would she be?

Ringo and I did the interview saying that if the medal was returned, whoever brought it back would get a hug and kiss from Ringo, would get to meet the Beatles, and get tickets to their upcoming Shea Stadium show. Well, the ol' Saint Christopher's medal found its way back to Ringo in a matter of hours.

I'm sure that even today, that woman tries to tell people that story and gets reactions like "Sure, I bet." But it's true. It's one story, and there are so many.

Changes abounded after the Beatles hit America. New bands made new music and it was seeping into the streets. At WABC we played a lot of Beatle music, but stuck pretty much to the Top Forty format. I grew tired of fighting for new songs and eventually left. I opened a club in New York and booked bands like The Young Rascals, The Vagrants, (later Mountain), and many others. It was a great way to stay in contact with many of the new bands that were emerging.

One night, this group of men came into the club dressed in suits and ties. They said they wanted to talk to me about a new kind of radio. Seems that the FCC had passed a law stating that FM stations had to separate from AM stations. At the time, a lot of stations broadcast the same thing on their FM and AM outlets. That was no more, and they needed something to put on the FM band.

These gentlemen wanted to put this new music on the FM band. They asked if I was interested. I asked them to come back for lunch the next day. I wanted to see if they had the same story in the cold light of day.

But the next day they were back with the same story. And I got back into radio, at WOR-FM, in 1966. One year later, I joined the air staff of WNEW-FM, 102.7 on the FM band. I'm still there.

By this point, the Beatles had graduated from the two-and-a-half-minute pop song into more extensive writing. *Rubber Soul* and *Revolver* were the beginning, and *Sgt. Pepper* blew the roof off of it. As always, other groups followed suit.

Everyone began to write, sing, and perform, based on their feelings. The music began to shape and reflect the feelings of youth in the society. And I was right there, on the radio in New York, lighting the fuse.

The diversity of the music was staggering. There was jazz, country, folk, psychedelic, and pop. There were the Stones, the Who, the Yardbirds, and of course the Beatles. It was like going from one or two flowers in your backyard to a botanical garden.

Progressive Radio, as we called it, devoted itself to playing anything and everything. The FCC edict opened up the airwaves to alternatives, and off we went. There were no rules. We played what we wanted, in stereo. It was a golden era in radio.

This glorious music made its own room on the air. And when something great came in, we thought nothing of playing it, all of it. One of the first times I did that was with *Sgt. Pepper's Lonely Hearts Club Band*. I got it in my hands while I was on the air. I described the artwork as best as I could, then I dropped the needle on Side One and shared the entire experience with my audience.

All of the great music that followed the Beatles' lead sustained progressive radio after the Beatles had decided to go their own separate ways. They all had enough of being Beatles. They wanted to express themselves individually. Their bickerings were over various things, but mostly I think they were just worn down by the enormous responsibility of being Beatles.

So in the days to follow, we followed four stories. They accomplished what they set out to do in a way. They did get attention individually, and they all got the credit they were due.

The next time I encountered any of them was a snowy February day in 1975. It was the day John Lennon came to WNEW-FM. He had been absent from the music scene for a while in the early seventies. He put out *Walls and Bridges*, in '74, and had a number one song with "Whatever Gets You Through the Night."

So less than a year later, he walked into the radio station with his *Rock 'N' Roll* record under his arm. For me, it was hard to believe, but there he was, wearing a coonskin cap.

When he sat down in the studio, he was nervous. It wasn't like going onstage, where everybody screams and you get instant gratification. It was nice and quiet in the station, and we were just playing records. He said, "I have a new album here, called *Rock 'N' Roll*." I said, "Can we play some of this?" And he said, "I'd like that."

So I told him that he was going to be the disc jockey and was going to play the cuts and talk about them as he wanted. It took about ten minutes before he calmed down and then he was ready. He went on the air, chatting about the music he loved, hawking his new record, reading commercials, and talking about Yoko. He told New York City that he and Yoko had ended their separation and were back together. It was a great afternoon because it was unplanned. It was pure rock 'n' roll.

You'll read the conversation we had that day, later in this book. But I'll tell you now that it was an incredibly special day in my life.

That day John Lennon also solicited public support for his immigration hearing. He wanted very badly to be a New Yorker. He fought long and hard for his U.S. citizenship. When he finally got that status, he enjoyed it more than any native. That's because he had to fight to get it. When you fight for something, you appreciate it much more than if it was just handed to you.

John and Yoko also wanted very much to be parents. They fought hard for that too, and I was on the air on October 9, 1975, when I got the news that John and Yoko had just had a son. Sean was born by cesarean section on John's birthday. We wished them all well on the air and played a few songs to commemorate it.

As it happened, my wife was pregnant with our second child at the time, and a few days later, while on the air, I got the news that she had gone into labor. I had made up my mind that I was going to be with her. And I was there when our daughter Tiffany was born. Anyone who's ever witnessed the birth of their baby knows what an incredible experience that is. If you've never seen it, it is truly unbelievable. So the euphoria of watching Tiffany being born, and knowing she and my wife were fine, was draining. After they went to the recovery room, I had an hour to kill.

When I left the ward in search of wine and Chinese food, I noticed a Pinkerton guard at the end of the hall. I thought it was pretty unusual to have a guard on a maternity ward. So I asked a nurse about it and she said, "Oh, that's John and Yoko's room; they just had the baby." They were three doors down the hall from me. I ran off to make phone calls about our daughter and pick up the food and wine.

I returned to the hospital and made my way back to the room. My wife and I were quietly celebrating when John wheeled Yoko by the open door I was facing. He went by, then he backed up. "Scott? Is that you? What are you doing here?"

"I'm doing the same thing you're doing here. We just had a baby girl," I said. "Congratulations. How's Sean?"

"Well, we're going down to the nursery to see him right now," he said. "But we'll be back up and stop in."

So they came back and we shared the food and wine. We talked about our experience. We talked about the miracle of birth and the fact that we had brought new life in to the world. We talked about everything but rock 'n' roll. We found something that we could share that was more universal and basic than music.

One last note about that. Not only was the world small enough to put us in the same maternity ward at the same time, but we also found out that our wives had the same doctor! John later found out, much to his chagrin, that he paid much more for his "special delivery" than I had! By the way, Sean still kids Tiffany about being four days older than she.

It's well documented that John took the raising of Sean very seriously and spent the majority of the next five years concentrating on his son.

At that time, WNEW-FM began staging a Christmas charity concert to raise money to benefit children with cerebral palsy. In 1980, the concert fell on December 8. As usual, I was playing "Santa Scott."

We made sure that all the acts were off the stage by 11:00 P.M. Doing that insured that we wouldn't have to pay the venue overtime, which would have cut into the money we were trying to raise.

It was a great night, a beautiful high. We had a big party planned for after the show. It was a party we looked forward to, not only to blow off some steam from having the charity show finished, but also to get us in the holiday mood. So I was in the dressing room, taking off the Santa Claus suit, just around 11:00 P.M. One of the show's assistants came in and told me that there was an emergency call for me and she showed me where to get it.

The call was from the station. John Lennon had been shot

outside the Dakota. We learned that he had been taken to Roosevelt Hospital. So I sent one of the newspeople to the Dakota and the other to the hospital. I then assembled the troops from the radio station, told them that there was no party, and that we were all going back to the station to go on the air. By the time we got to the station, John had died.

We went from as natural a high as a human being can have to one of our lowest sorrows. When you're up that high, you have farther to fall.

We took phone calls and played Beatles music all night. People who were alone in their apartments, or alone in their minds, reached out to the radio in those long dark hours. It was devastating. We used the airwaves for consolation. In trying to help the many fans of John and the Beatles, we were also helping ourselves. We shared the grief and we shared the music. I don't know what I would have done if I would have had to go back to my apartment alone that night.

I went on the air the next day at 2:00 P.M. and I started my show with a Beatles song. To this day, I continue to do that, playing something from John or something having to do with him.

I went to the memorial service a few days later in Central Park. Each year, the vigil happens again. People with their candles walk and sing. And John hears that.

Obviously, the Beatles' story did not die with John Lennon. George, Ringo, and Paul had their period of grief, and then they carried on with their lives and their work.

In 1984, I met with Paul McCartney in a New York hotel. The security that was involved was really frightening. I felt sorry for Paul. And I realized that John's death had, once again, changed the lives of the Beatles.

I was the last person to speak with Paul that day. He was promoting *Give My Regards to Broad Street* and you'll find that conversation later in the book. When Paul left the room he was surrounded by ten men, all bigger and taller than he. The circle made it impossible to see him. They took him all the way down the hall, around a corner, down another hallway, into a specially secured elevator. It was frightening. And I knew what that was about. I think it's a hell of a way to live your life, wondering if there isn't another nut out there looking for another Beatle.

The last time I saw Paul was at Abbey Road Studios for *Sgt. Pepper's* twentieth anniversary party. Again, the class was evident as he took the opportunity to mention that we have to continue to strive to help our fellow man.

Then in 1987, I met with George Harrison in Los Angeles. George would not come to New York and there is a reason for that. He would not be public in New York. I think he was afraid to be public in New York.

Our conversation concerning *Cloud Nine* was upbeat and reflective, much like the album itself. He had been busy with movies, but this record he did in private. You'll read about that and many other things in our conversation, which is also included in this book.

Ringo has managed to keep himself with us, either through his commercials, his occasional personal appearances, or his acting.

I'm thrilled that Paul, George, and Ringo have kept active. I thank God for the survivors.

One of my fondest memories took place on a stage in New York City in 1987. It was the occasion of the Beatles' induction into the Rock 'n' Roll Hall of Fame. On that stage was George Harrison, Ringo Starr, Yoko, Sean, and Julian Lennon. Paul McCartney was not there, and he had his own reasons for that.

But George went up in that grouping and spent a whole lot of time talking with Julian and Sean, and it was he who gave the acceptance speech. It was not like some of those publicized disagreements that we read about. They were all there for all the world to see, accepting an award for the Beatles. I remember Sean saying, "I want to thank you for having me here, but I really didn't do anything at all." Everyone was together, and it was fantastic.

In the past five years, I've been to Liverpool twice. I went there to see where the Beatles came from. I found a depressing town, occupied with tough, spirited people, much like I was told I would. Yet, in a place with over 40 percent unemployment, there seemed to be a sense of 100 percent optimistic humor.

I visited the Beatles' childhood homes, went to Penny Lane, Strawberry Fields, and the site of the Cavern. I even ran into John Lennon's Uncle Charlie on Mathew Street, outside the John Lennon Memorial Pub.

It was an opportunity to experience the sights, sounds, and smells that the Beatles wrote about. They were from middle-class Liverpool families, but that's not to be construed as middle-class as we know in America. They came from tough backgrounds and good homes.

My visits there were eye-opening and emotional. Seeing the

starting point, their accomplishments came full circle for a disc jockey who stood shivering at JFK waiting for their plane back in 1964.

All of these experiences went into the making of *Ticket to Ride*, the radio series.

We started it back in February of 1985. Our intention was to offer a radio series with the emphasis on "sharing." We're reminded of the Beatles every time we hear one of their songs. But that's not enough.

Ticket to Ride shares the stories of the artists who got their careers started after being inspired by the Beatles. More often than not, they'll credit the Beatles with convincing them to write a song, to join a band, or to pick up a pair of drumsticks. That kind of tribute is only fully grasped when you consider the talent that was revealed as a result of that inspiration. The Beatles' spirit is alive in the people who make music because of them.

Ticket to Ride also offers the tales of those who comprised the Beatles' inner circle. For as you know, people like George Martin, Derek Taylor, Pete Best, and others, all played major roles in the big picture.

Ticket to Ride enables millions of people to recount and share some of the most precious memories they have. There is so much to share, so many interesting slants, and the stories grow every year.

Then there are the young people. We get so many letters from the young ones who are anxious to learn the story behind the music. They've heard the Beatles on the radio or have seen the albums in their parents collection. Their reaction is the same as ours was. They have to find out more about that wonderful music and the men who made it.

And that's a family. A family consisting of generations who share the wonders of Beatle music and the Beatles' story.

In the pages to follow, you'll read a collection of the most evocative and informative testimonies that *Ticket to Ride* has featured in its first four years.

I'd like to thank all of these wonderful and talented people for sharing their stories with us.

I'd also like to thank John, Paul, George, and Ringo—four lads who shook the world. If you're like me, and know just how good a favorite song can make you feel, then you also know what a priceless gift that is. They gave us all so much.

We are truly blessed.

Scott Muni (holding microphone) inter-
viewing Ringo Starr upon the arrival of
the Beatles in America, 1964 *Courtesy of
Scott Muni*

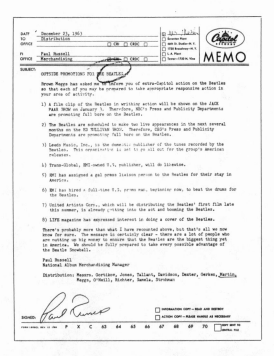

Capitol Records press release discussing promotional plans for the Beatles, received by Scott Muni, early 1964   *Courtesy of Scott Muni*

The official WABC Beatles Fan Club membership card, 1964   *Courtesy of Scott Muni*

Capitol Records reply to Beatle fans, received by Scott Muni, 1964 *Courtesy of Scott Muni*

CAPITOL RECORDS, INC.

Dear Beatles Fan:

First of all, we want you to know how much we appreciate your support of The Beatles. We wish it were possible for us to send each of you an individual reply, answering all the questions you ask. However, since we have over a quarter of a million letters to answer, this simply isn't possible.

The next best thing, we feel, is this letter, in which we attempt to answer to the best of our ability, the most frequently asked questions.

WHERE CAN I JOIN A BEATLES FAN CLUB? The only U.S. fan club authorized by The Beatles is: Beatles (U.S.A.) Ltd., P.O. Box 505, Radio City Station, New York, N.Y. 10019, Marjorie Winshull, Director.

WHERE CAN I WRITE THE BEATLES? Same as above. We have received thousands of requests for the Beatles' private addresses, but for obvious reasons, cannot give them out. The Beatles themselves have asked that all their American fans write them only care of Miss Winshull.

WHERE CAN I BUY WIGS, BUTTONS, COLOR PHOTOS, ETC.? A number of firms throughout the country have been licensed by The Beatles to produce these and other Beatles products. Most of these products are distributed through record, department and drug stores; others are available by mail-order and are advertised in many of the 'teen and fan magazines.

WHERE CAN I BUY THE MOVING-HEAD DISPLAY OF THE BEATLES? This was produced as a display piece and is not for sale.

WHAT ABOUT THE CARNEGIE HALL CONCERT ALBUM? Capitol had hoped to record this, but due to last-minute technical problems, was not able to. However, in addition to its first Beatles album, MEET THE BEATLES, Capitol has just released THE BEATLES SECOND ALBUM.

WHERE CAN I BUY "Roll Over Beethoven," "Please Mr. Postman," and "Long Tall Sally"? All three of these are contained in THE BEATLES' SECOND ALBUM.

IS PAUL MARRIED? IS RINGO ILL? Paul has told us he's still single and Ringo says he's feeling just fine, thank you.

/cont...

- 2 -

WHAT ABOUT THEIR MOVIE? This is being made by United Artists, 729 Seventh Avenue, New York, N.Y. Please contact them for information.

WHAT ABOUT THE BEATLES' AMERICAN TOUR? This is still being set up. As far as we know now, it will start in San Francisco August 19. If they will be appearing in your city, we have no doubt that you'll know about it before we do through your local papers and radio stations.

CAN I SEND THE BEATLES A PICTURE (OR ALBUM, OR BOOK ETC.) AND GET IT AUTOGRAPHED? This would be risky and we suggest you don't.

WHEN THE BEATLES COME BACK CAN I INTERVIEW THEM FOR MY SCHOOL PAPER? Chances are extremely remote since they will be traveling constantly and time simply won't permit it.

RELEASE OF VARIOUS SONGS AS SINGLES. If every request were to filled, every song on both of Capitol's Beatles albums to date would be out as a single record. Marketing problems, of course, make this impossible. Just keep in touch with your local record dealer and we're sure he'll let you know whenever a new Beatles record, single or LP, is available.

HOW MANY RECORDS HAVE THE BEATLES SOLD? As you know, some Beatles records are out on labels other than Capitol and we can only speak for ourselves, but to date:

        "I Want to Hold Your Hand" -- 3,500,000
        MEET THE BEATLES! -- 4,000,000
        "Can't Buy Me Love" -- 2,000,000 (in only three weeks)
        THE BEATLES' SECOND ALBUM -- 2,000,000 (in only two weeks--
            the fastest selling album in history!, thanks to you).

So that's about it. Again, thanks very much for your support of The Beatles and we're sorry we couldn't answer each of you personally, but we're sure you understand.

Very truly yours,

Public Relations Dept.
Capitol Records, Inc.

John Lennon and representatives of Capitol Records join Scott Muni in the WNEW-FM studios for world premiere of Lennon's *Rock 'n Roll* lp, February 13, 1975   *Courtesy of Scott Muni*

John Lennon on the air at WNEW-FM, February 13, 1975 *Courtesy of Scott Muni*

Scott Muni and Paul McCartney at the
New York premiere of *Give My Regards to
Broad Street*, 1984   *Courtesy of Scott Muni*

Scott Muni and George Martin at Abbey Road Studios at the party celebrating the twentieth anniversary of *Sgt. Pepper*, 1987 Courtesy of Denny
Somach

BILLY JOEL

BILLY JOEL

"They made it all possible, made it all conceivable. I said, 'That's what I want to do!'"

•

Billy Joel is one of rock music's most prolific and talented singer/songwriters. A tireless concert artist, Billy brought his piano-playing prowess to Russia in 1987 for a series of historic performances.

His long career has yielded innumerable Top Ten hits, not to mention two Grammy awards.

As you'll see, Billy's affinity for the Beatles rivals that of any guest *Ticket to Ride* has presented. He consistently features their music in his live act, including, most recently and most appropriately, "Back in the U.S.S.R."

Billy, how big a Beatle fan are you?

I tell you, if it wasn't for me seeing them that night on *The Ed Sullivan Show*, I wouldn't be doing what I'm doing right now. I might not even be alive. I credit them with creating a lot of my life.

I really had no idea that it was possible to be a rock 'n' roll star, until the Beatles. Before them, there was either soul music—and I was a kid from Levittown [New York], so what kind of soul did I have? I wasn't aware that I had any! I thought you had to be from the ghetto in Philadelphia. Then there was the manufactured rock stars, the Fabians, the Frankie Avalons, and the pretty boys who seemed to be put together by a Hollywood conglomerate, with a lot of money behind them.

I really had no idea that you could play an instrument, write your own music, go out and perform it, and be big at it. It looked like that wasn't in the cards. And then I saw the Beatles on *Ed Sullivan*.

Here were these guys—they didn't look like they came from the San Fernando Valley; they looked like these four working class scruffs. John Lennon had this wise guy look on his face, just like me and my friends were a bunch of wise guys, street kids.

They were playing their own instruments, doing their own arrangements, writing their own songs, on TV! on *Ed Sullivan!* next to Roberta Peters or whoever else was on.

It made it all possible; it made it all conceivable. I said, "That's what I want to do!"

They just had something totally different, and it changed a lot of things. But, most importantly, it opened the floodgates. And here, coming through the floodgates, is Billy Joel. Quite an influence for a band that wasn't together that long.

And the amount of output they came out with! Amazing, to be able to pump out those albums like they did, and they were all incredible albums too.

And then there was the changes, the evolution that went on with the Beatles. I mean, I grew up with them. And as I got older, they got older, and as I changed, they changed. And it was a big part of our lives, that was a big deal about the sixties.

There were no limitations to them. They did everything: ballads, rock 'n' roll, country, and blues. They covered the spectrum, which is the best way, I believe, to be a musician—to be eclectic, a renaissance person.

Being eclectic has its pros and cons. Part of the mantle of "pace setter" is to absorb criticism from the established society. After Lennon's "bigger than Jesus" quote flared up in 1966, the next big problem to haunt the Beatles was their public admission of drug experimentation. What did you think of that?

There was a period with the Beatles where their words got very obscure, and it was attributed to psychedelics or drugs or whatever it was. I remember the time in the mid-sixties when a lot of my friends were sitting around smoking banana peels going "Crackalaka fishwife, polyester whatever." [Saying], "That means, that's a reference to..." And I said to them, "C'mon, it's just nonsense; it's creative nonsense."

Everybody was trying to figure out the deeper meaning. But an important thing about the Beatles is for people not to get hung up in this whole drug thing. Their music was eminently listenable without any kind of psychedelics or anything like that. That's not what they were about. I did not do drugs then; I didn't know from none of that stuff. But I enjoyed listening to them immensely.

In Long Island, you lived near John Lennon, didn't you?

He lived near Cold Spring Harbor, and I lived by the same body of water. I could see his house, and I thought, "Gee, wouldn't it be great just to meet him, just to say hello. Maybe I'll go by there and just knock on the door." But I really respected the man's privacy, and I know he was hounded by a lot of people. So I decided not to do that. I'd just admire him from afar.

After his death, a guy who had worked with him told me that John used to like to row a boat, and he used to row past my house. And [that] John wanted to come say hello to me. And that John had told him he liked my music, which absolutely knocked me out. I didn't even know if he was aware of me. Now I really kind of regret not having met him, because I think it would have been nice.

Billy, where were you when you heard the news that John Lennon was killed?

I was in my house, and there was a quick news flash. And I just didn't believe it. I thought it must be some kind of joke or something. I thought that this can't be really true. It was late at night, and it was later confirmed on the evening news.

I remember I jumped on a motorcycle and just drove. I didn't put a helmet on, or glasses, or nothing; I just drove. I was crying. And I just drove and drove, trying to get as far away from the news as I possibly could.

I ended up in a bar somewhere, which is not the smartest thing to do when you're riding a motorcycle. But I just had a beer or two. People were kinda just going on like nothing had happened.

But there was a little, old, beat-up piano in the corner, and I had to do something. So I played all the John Lennon songs I could think of that night. I played "In My Life," which is an especially moving song that John had written. And people started to gather around the piano and sing John Lennon songs with me. It was a very moving evening. That's the one thing I could think of to do, was to make music. That's what the man made me do.

Billy, you've stated in interviews that The Nylon Curtain was sort of a tribute to the Beatles. Could you explain what you meant by that?

I probably said that after the fact. I think it was more a catharsis for me after the tragedy of John Lennon's murder. There's a lot of Lennonesque vocalizing going on. There's a number of tracks where I didn't realize I was doing it, but I was almost singing exactly like John Lennon. I was phrasing like him. I was very traumatized by his death. And I think subconsciously it was a tribute to John Lennon that the arrangement and production were couched in a Beatlesque form.

I wasn't aware I was doing it at the time. I came in, and Phil [producer Phil Ramone] would say, "You know you sang that exactly like John Lennon. Is that what you want to do?" I said, "That's the way I felt." And I went out and did it again, and I didn't feel right, except for the way I'd done it originally.

When you say Phil, you mean Phil Ramone, the producer. Were you thinking of George Martin to produce that album, or was that just something that was in print?

Oh no, I was going to do that album with Phil. But I wanted what I considered to be a real "FM" album, something that you'd put headphones on for, the way I put headphones on to listen to *Abbey Road, Sgt. Pepper, Magical Mystery Tour,* and *Rubber Soul.* I missed those albums. There was something very much missing for me in not being able to listen to an album on headphones, where you could really hear different textures.

That album was really built layer by layer. It wasn't a complete record until the final, final mix. We didn't really know what the songs were and it was built from the inside out, instead of the outside in. We just layered it.

In your stage shows, and I'm sure going back to early days too, you've done some Beatle songs.

They were fun to play. If you were in a band, you know how everybody starts out in a garage band or a bar band, and in those days, Beatle tunes were in the Top Ten all the time, so you played whatever the popular songs were. But you liked playing Beatle songs, because they were so melodic, so musical. They were fun and they never really leave your system.

Anybody who's ever been in a bar band to this day at sound checks still does Beatles songs. Everyone from Led Zeppelin, the new wave groups—I know Sting has mentioned it a number of times—everybody still has those songs in their systems. When we do sound checks, we do Beatle medleys. We do *Abbey Road* and sometimes it's better than the show.

Did you ever see them in concert, at Shea or Carnegie Hall?

No, I didn't get to go. I didn't have the money. It seemed to me that the Shea concert was going to be a lot of screaming.

It was.

And Carnegie Hall, you had to have an in, you had to be Jackie O. or somebody, so that was the end of that.

It was enough for me to see them on *Ed Sullivan*. I had a sneaking suspicion that they may not have been *that* great a live band. They were probably great doing the earlier stuff, but when they got to the more complicated stuff, I don't see how they could actually pull that off.

I think they probably kicked butt in the Cavern. I mean when they were just a straightaway bar band, they must have been something to see. Like in Germany. I know, in the early days of every band, when you go through rough times, you really do get your act together. You have to, or else they're gonna drink their beers and not look twice at you.

If right now, you decided to do three of their songs, what ones would you like to do?

One would be "In My Life." Another would be one of the extended ones because it gets a little bit of everything in there, and that's "Golden Slumbers," off of *Abbey Road*. It's a good piano player's song.

You obviously noticed their use of piano. Did that change your outlook on rock 'n' roll?

Oh, sure. The piano is a melodic instrument, not nearly as hard rock or raunchy as a guitar. And the Beatles made it an important instrument, they made it hip again. See, you'd have to be Jerry Lee Lewis, Fats Domino, or Little Richard, and rock the heck out of the piano, without really playing it in a melodic way.

The Beatles brought back a certain amount of orchestration to music. They used the piano in a melodic way, in a beautiful way, but not in a wimpy way. It was a very strong instrument. They did it on "Hey Jude." "Let It Be," same thing. A lot of that was probably McCartney because he has such a melodic touch.

But "Golden Slumbers" is for piano players, because you can play it all the way through.

And the third song, and really one of my favorite Beatle songs, is "She Said She Said," on the *Revolver* album. Ringo is not given enough credit. The drumming on that song is so phenomenal. We do that at sound check, my drummer does it, and it's so much fun to play if you can pull it off.

What did you think of the movies?

I liked *A Hard Day's Night*. *Help!* looked a little "Hollywood" to me. I liked hearing the soundtrack and watching them kind of go through the motions doing them. But in *A Hard Day's Night*, the Richard Lester production was great.

Earlier you mentioned "Golden Slumbers." I think that one of my favorite things about the Beatles was that they made the ballad accessible, without abandoning their rock 'n' roll roots.

They made them all work. They proved that a ballad—even though it's soft, even though the lyric can be gentle, and the instrumentation isn't CRASH BANG BOOM! and it's a strongly felt emotion—a ballad can be just as strong a statement as a rocker.

There were no limitations to them. They did everything. Ballads, rock 'n' roll, some country, and some blues. They covered the spectrum.

PETE TOWNSHEND

PETE
TOWNSHEND

*"That becomes a tragedy in itself—the
fact that ordinary people need other people
to not be ordinary."*

•

As the visionary for the Who, and a generation of rock fans as well, Pete Townshend
seized on the tensions of youth to make his
mark as a leader of musical dissent.

With fellow bandmates John Entwistle,
Keith Moon, and Roger Daltrey, Townshend
revolutionized the music scene in 1968 with
the release of the first successful rock opera,
Tommy.

The Who's first encounter with the Beatles actually took place two years before that
landmark recording, when they were among
the bands opening for the Beatles at the New
Music Express Winners Poll concert at
Wembley Arena.

More recently, Townshend played with
Paul McCartney and Wings on *Back to the
Egg*, and joined Wings onstage at the Ham-
mersmith Odeon during the concert for
Kampuchea.

In recent years, Townshend has devoted
his creative energies to solo projects, both literary and musical. A deeply analytical and
introspective artist, a conversation with Pete
Townshend is always an extremely enjoyable
and revelatory experience. And he proved
true to form when he joined *Ticket to Ride* in
London to talk about the Beatles.

Pete, you recorded a record as early as 1964. So you were active at the time of the Beatles and long after. Over those years, have you followed their career?

I know the Beatles' recording career is very interesting. There are a lot of secrets, especially if you work at a studio over here called Air Studios. That's where Paul McCartney does most of his recording.

What you find is that a lot of the guys who work at the studio there have been through Abbey Road [studios]. Geoff Emrick, who actually worked on *Sgt. Pepper*, comes out with these odd little gems of information that you just want to scribble down and send to somebody. But in the end, so much went on, so many fascinating things happened.

I suppose one of these days the story will get told. I just read a book by an English writer named Philip Norman—he wrote that famous book about the Beatles called *Shout*. And I thought I knew all there was to know. And then you read just a regular book some good researcher has put together, who's talked to somebody's uncle, or a road manager's friend of a friend, or a girlfriend from Hamburg, and the kind of stuff that you realize happened to a band like the Beatles is just incredible.

And they had quite a short career, that's the interesting thing. As a band, they had a short career.

In your book, Horse's Neck, you have a story called "Winston." In it, you wrestle with the issues of homelands, and I presume that is about John Lennon.

That's right. It's a short piece really. In the story I say that we all feel implicated in some strange way. You know the thing about Lennon's life, although he was in a private time, he was an open book, wasn't he? We all felt part of him and I tried to deal with that in that story.

I didn't know him that well, so if anybody thinks I'm speaking out of turn, I'm sorry. But I think he felt free in New York. He felt at home there, as I do. I've been to New York hundreds of times. When I come to New York, I stay in hotels, and I walk the streets as though I belong there. I walk them night and day, sometimes going alone, sometimes in a crowd. I use the cabs, although I never use the subway, and I've never been stopped, abused, held up, or mugged. I've never seen a gun on the streets.

A lot of people might just say, "Hey, you've been lucky." But that's been my experience and I'm sure, up to the time of his death, that was John's experience too.

He was happy there. It was his home. If his home had been Liverpool, or if his home had been London, that's where he would have been. He was a New Yorker. And I think if you would have asked Lennon what he was, he would have said, "I'm a New Yorker." And that's the end of the story. We [England] have no claim on him.

You've got to look at the system, the star system. We all need heroes, and sometimes we think that since our heroes have been able to work miracles in their own lives, that they can work miracles in our lives.

I'm afraid the tragedy is that most of us know the truth. Most of us know that people like me or John Lennon, people who've become famous, film stars, even politicians, presidents, it doesn't matter who they are—they're just ordinary guys. And if you fire a gun at them, they drop dead. They bleed, and they suffer all the same things that everybody else suffers.

That becomes a tragedy in itself—the fact that ordinary people need other people to *not* be ordinary. It's kind of weird, but it seems like one of the things that make the world go round. It's been like that since the dawn of time, and I don't see why it should suddenly change today.

I was talking with Paul McCartney not long ago and he told me a story about a time when you and Ronnie Lane turned up for a rehearsal twelve hours early. I think you were told that the session was for nine [o'clock]. And no one specified whether it was A.M. or P.M.

Paul's organizer told Ronnie Lane and I that we should get there at nine o'clock in the morning for a run-through. So Ronnie and I got to the Hammersmith Odeon at nine o'clock in the morning. The place was shut. So we waited for a while and then some guys showed up with some stuff. So we said, "What's happening?"

They said, "We've come to build the stage. Where should we put it?" I said, "I thought there was a rehearsal starting at nine A.M."

Anyway, we finally waited and waited, and Paul and Linda and company arrived at four or five o'clock in the afternoon, by which time Ronnie and I had been to every pub in Hammersmith and we were kinda loaded. And by the time it got to doing this particular piece, around midnight, Paul had the sudden notion that we should all wear these silver jackets for the video.

And I said, "No. I've been here since eight o'clock in the morning, wearing this brown suit. I slept in it at lunch time, I had my dinner in it, and my tea, and I'm not taking it off."

He said, "Oh, come on Pete, be a sport, put on the silver jacket." I said "No, I'm not wearing it."

He said, "Everybody's wearing it, we've got fifteen people up here." And I said "No, I'm not wearing it," and I didn't wear it. But we did have a great time—there must have been about forty people up there.

If I'm not mistaken, there was a time when you were quite close with the Beatles, early on. You also played some gigs with them. You knew them, right?

Yeah, we supported the Beatles. They were already quite big. They were on their second record. And we, with the Kinks, went out on a package tour in the UK, and we supported the Beatles for a few shows.

Later on, around the time that we first visited the States, we played the Murray the K show in '67. Our manager then, Kit Lambert, and the Stones' manager, Andrew Loog Oldham, Robert Stigwood, and Brian Epstein were going to form this big management monopoly. So we used to have lots of wonderful dinners up at Brian Epstein's.

I remember John coming in, sitting down, and he was eating with his then-wife Cynthia. I came in and was a bit nervous about meeting him properly for the first time. I knew Paul and Jane Asher quite well. But John could see I was uncomfortable so he says, *[in Pete's best Lennon accent]* "Pull up a food!"

JOE COCKER

"And sure enough, a couple of weeks later it was a phenomenon that came all around England. We all realized that, at last, someone had broken that sacred barrier."

•

Joe Cocker, with his trademark white soul vocals and quirky stage presence, is perhaps best known for his passionate renditions of Beatle classics.

A veteran of the British rock circuit, one of Cocker's very first recordings was a 1964 cover version of the Beatles' "I'll Cry Instead."

From his legendary performance at Woodstock through his more recent Top Ten hits like "You Are So Beautiful" and "Up Where We Belong," Cocker defines the term "rock and roll survivor."

Joe, your latest album includes a song from the Plastic Ono Band's first LP entitled "Isolation." Why did you choose to perform that one?

That was a great album and I've loved that song for a long time. I'd sung it to other producers who didn't hear a place for it on a record. So I sang it one night for [piano player] Jeff Levine, just sitting around the piano at the end of a date and Charlie [producer Charlie Midnight] came flying out of the studio saying, "Joe, that's great, let's cut it!" And we did it just about in one take, live vocal and all.

Did John [Lennon] have any effect on you in terms of vocal style or attitude?

Well, his vocal range was a lot sharper than mine so I don't think he had that much influence on me vocally. But his spirit and his soul did have an effect on me.

When was the first time you heard the Beatles?

All music had gotten stereofied at the time they came along. There was Cliff Richard and the Shadows and all, but it had gotten very "nice."

I was up late one night and I heard "Love Me Do." I remember thinking, "I wonder who the hell that was?" You know that little bit of soul that Paul sings, "Whoa, love me do"? I'd never heard any other singer do that on a pop record.

And sure enough, a couple of weeks later it was a phenomenon that came all around England. We all realized that, at last, someone had broken that sacred barrier.

Did you ever see them live?

I did actually. They came to Sheffield and they were a really good band then. They were so tight. They'd been working a bit by then. And that's what impressed us—they were really tight.

Your version of "She Came in Through the Bathroom Window" may be your best known Beatle cover, but it was not your first, was it? It was "I'll Cry Instead."

Yeah, but that wasn't by choice. I got this one-shot record deal, a single-record contract. And I made a record of "Georgia on My Mind," that [song] Ray Charles did.

Anyway, it cost a lot. I remember them bringing an orchestra in and we did this lavish arrangement. And when they had their board meeting, Dick Rowe [Decca chief who turned down the Beatles] said he hated it.

So I had to go back to the studio and do an instant cover and it was "I'll Cry Instead." But it wasn't by my choice at all.

Was it your choice to cover "With a Little Help from My Friends"?

JOE COCKER

Yes. I had help with people putting the arrangement together, but I did actually conceive the idea of doing it in three-quarter time.

And that was something very strange. See, back home in Sheffield at that time, we had one of those outdoor toilets. I remember just sitting there and pursuing life, you know? *[Laughs]*.

And it just came to me as I sat on the bowl. A few days later we went in and cut it and it ended up a number one in England.

Later I did it at Woodstock. I remember at the time I had a friend who went into Apple and played it for them. And a couple days later I got a telegram from the Fab Four, which I'm ashamed to say I've lost.

I can't remember the exact phrasing but it was something like: THE RECORD'S ABSOLUTELY GREAT. LOVE, JOHN, PAUL, GEORGE, AND RINGO.

How and when did you get to meet them?

That was a little after that. I think they were quite impressed with what we did with "A Little Help from My Friends."

So [producer] Denny Cordell got me an invitation and I very nervously went to Apple one afternoon. I met George and just sat with him. He's a gentle cat, George, very easy to get on with.

So he sang "Old Brown Shoe" for me and he ended up doing "Something." Of course, I ended up recording that one. I was so impressed at the simplicity, the changes were so slight. What a beautiful song with just these four little chords.

Another thing about your treatment of "Bathroom Window" was that you made it very much your own song.

I try to, when I mess with arrangements like that! And again, that was part of that same afternoon. Paul finally showed up and he just sat around the piano. He played a couple of songs, although they're vague to me.

But I always remember him playing "Golden Slumbers" and me saying, "Oh, I'd love to do that one!" And he said, "Well, you can't have that one." *[Giggling]* But then he said, "But you can have this one," and he played "Bathroom Window." And I said, "OK, I'll settle for what I can get." I mean, it's a Beatles' tune, right?

GERRY
MARSDEN

*"There was a lot of rivalry and fun
because we were great friends. There was
no animosity. We respected each other's
musical capabilities and we used to pinch
songs and try to get American records
before the Beats did."*

•

It was a magical time in Liverpool in the
early sixties. And sharing center stage with
the Beatles as one of the major creative cata-
lysts on the scene was a young man named
Gerry Marsden, leader of Gerry and the
Pacemakers.

Another Brian Epstein discovery, Marsden and the Pacemakers scored big at the
time with such classic hits as "Ferry Cross
the Mersey," "How Do You Do It," "You'll
Never Walk Alone," and "Don't Let the Sun
Catch You Crying."

Do you remember the first time you heard your music on the radio?

I think it would have been 1963, after we just recorded "How
Do You Do It." Basically, we hadn't even heard ourselves on tape
until we made the record. And the first time we heard it, George
Martin said, "Right, that's what you sound like." I thought,
"Bloody Hell." I was quite shocked. But the first time on the radio
was pleasant actually. It was nice to hear.

Let me ask you about the Liverpool/Mersey Beat explosion. Could it have happened anywhere?

I don't think it could have happened anywhere because there were so many bands in and around Liverpool. I don't think there were as many bands in London, Birmingham, or Newcastle. So when we made the records and came out, there were lots of bands to follow. So I think that the reason was there were loads of bands playing in Liverpool.

Can you define the Mersey Beat sound?

I think it's a very simple answer. The music itself was very happy, very pleasant. We didn't all sound the same, but we all had the same ideas about the writing of the music.

It was all nice and light, with not too many messages. Even the slow ballads were pleasant, no moaning, all nice romantic things. We've always been a bit romantic in Liverpool. To come from Liverpool—you've got to be a comedian or a romantic.

(MICHAEL OCHS ARCHIVES)

GERRY MARSDEN & THE PACEMAKERS

The first time you met John Lennon was when he was in the Quarry Men. What were your impressions?

Yeah, the Quarry Men weren't as good as the Gerry Marsden skiffle group—no way at all *[Laughing]*. Even though they had John Lennon and Paul McCartney, we were always competing in skiffle and in rock and roll.

I first met John and Paul when they were thirteen or fourteen, whatever, and we became very good friends in those years and stayed very good friends until John's death. Paul is still a very good friend of mine. Always two talented guys, John and Paul, excellent.

What were the Quarry Men like at the time?

Crap. Terrible. Rubbish. John and Paul had talent, but the band was terrible.

What were your memories of Stu Sutcliffe?

Stu was a very quiet, nice guy. Nothing wrong with him— never offended anybody. Maybe too quiet to the stage of boring. Stu would play with his back to the audience because he couldn't play the bass, basically. I just know that Stu was a nice guy, but couldn't play bass. But that's all I can say about Stu.

Tell us a little bit about Bob Wooler, the Liverpool Cavern DJ. What role did he play in town?

Bob was the first DJ in Liverpool. He didn't actually invent the Mersey Beat, but had a hell of a lot to do with it. He was into the young bands and he helped us a great deal, old Bob.

Weren't the Pacemakers involved with a contest in Mersey Beat, the magazine started by Bill Harry?

Sure, just like the Beats [Beatles] sent more of their own [votes] in than we did. But we had the competitions every year. I think we won it one year, the Beats the next year. It was all good fun. We didn't actually send our own, that was just a joke that Paul McCartney and I tend to tell people. People actually sent them in, you know; the fans sent in who they thought the best bands were.

We couldn't afford to buy all the copies because we were skint [broke].

Now, if I'm not mistaken, the Pacemakers played with the Beatles at one show, thereby making the "Beatmakers." Is that right?

It was actually at Litherland Town Hall, which is just outside of Liverpool. We were doing the gig and we decided to make the first big rock and roll band. So we joined forces and had a great time. Sure, it was great fun. My pianist, Les Maguire, played sax, and we took turns playing guitar, piano, and singing. And we ended up underneath the piano singing. It was a great night.

The competition sounds like it was healthy.

Sure, there was a lot of rivalry and fun because we were great friends. There was no animosity. We respected each others musical capabilities and we used to pinch songs and try to get American records before the Beats did. And they'd do the same as us and we'd swap 'em. We were very very good friends and still are, thank God.

Were you surprised when the Beatles exploded like they did?

No, not at all. As a matter of fact, I told Brian Epstein that he must devote more time to the Beatles because he was the manager, and I saw the Beatles being huge. I told Brian, "You cannot choose between the two. You must spend more time with the boys," which he did. So that was well expected.

How did you meet Brian Epstein?

We met in his father's record shop. We used to go and get records from Brian. Over a long period of time, Paul McCartney, especially, would say to Brian, "Come down and see the band." He [Brian] would say, "Why are you asking for these obscure records?"

So we took him down to the Cavern and he fell in love with the whole scene. He realized that was his forte and decided to take over. He had great charisma, a very charming, very elegant, good guy. A great fellow.

You also were associated with George Martin. How did he contribute to your career?

George was a nice guy. Before we met him, George was recording people like Shirley Bassey. And the Beats went down and George saw the potential and helped them, but not a great deal. I mean the boys knew what they wanted to do anyway.

George got us to record "How Do You Do It," which was our first record that went to number one. George was a great help, a lovely guy, very pleasant. We respected George, let's put it that way, and I think the Beatles respected George. I don't think George actually ran the sessions. He just helped.

George Martin also presented the Beatles with "How Do You Do It," yet they turned it down. What's your reaction to that?

I'm very pleased they did turn it down, because we got the hit with it. It was written for a guy called Adam Faith [a British teen idol] and, basically, Adam didn't like it. The Beats didn't like it. The only ones who liked it were George Martin and myself, which was great.

Have you ever heard the Beatles version?

Yes, it sounds like a very late Everly Brothers song.

The Everly Brothers were a big influence, weren't they?

Sure, on all of us. Along with Little Richard, Fats Domino, and Ray Charles.

Do you remember recording "How Do You Do It"? How long it took, etc.?

In the studio? About an hour and a half. [There were] only four tracks, anyway. So everything was miked up. . . . So you just went in and hit it. You didn't sort of retape or change or go onto other tapes. It was just straight in and straight out.

In those days we made LPs in twenty-four hours. That's why they sounded so bad *[Laughing].*

There was magic in those early recordings, in that style of record mak-
ing.

Sure. That's what it was all about, and I think George Martin
could see the earthiness of the Liverpool sound and Liverpool
bands. And to capture that he basically said, "Get in and bleedin'
do it"—which the punk people tried to do like twenty years later.
So they used to go in and do the same thing basically.

Maybe your most famous song in America is "Ferry Cross the Mersey."
Tell us about that one.

"Ferry" was written for the film *Ferry Cross the Mersey*. Basically, in those days, we didn't have videos you could send all
across the world. So the Beatles did *Help!* and that movie was like
a video.
   What you did in those days was make a film and let the kids
see you were doing it. And our film was *Ferry Cross the Mersey*. It
was a very pleasant video, and the kids across the U.S., Australia,
Canada, and Singapore could see what we were doing.

Then came a great song, "You'll Never Walk Alone."

Not a hit in the States—"Walk Alone"—though, was it? It was
a hit in England; yeah, it was number one in England. We redid it
last year for the dreadful fire disaster in the Bradford football stadium. I decided to redo it and give the money to the people who
lost relatives in the fire and people who were badly injured in the
fire.
   We also started a burn research unit because we found that
most of the people actually died because we didn't have the facilities [to save them]. So we started this whole new burn unit which
will go on forever to learn the techniques.

Gerry, what do you remember most about the Cavern Club?

The Cavern was a small, smelly cellar that looked like a train
tunnel, basically. It was great. All the kids came down and it stank
of disinfectant because they used to clean it out with thirty-ton
liquid fuel disinfectant.

But it was a great place to play in. But there were another one hundred places in Liverpool that was just the same.

You probably saw the Beatles at the Cavern. What were those times like?

Sure, as my impressions always have been of John and Paul—tremendous. They had Pete Best on drums, and he used to drive like crazy. He was great. And the boys were a nice, earthy Liverpool band.

I played with them for so many years, we didn't really look constructively at each other and say what our faults were. They were always a good band.

What kind of drummer was Pete Best? His story is often misunderstood.

Pete played what they wanted at the time. You know, this lovely driving rhythm they used to get. I think Pete was put out of the band on orders actually. I don't think it was anything personal. But he had to go. He was great with the band, you know, good drummer Pete. I think the problem was that he was too good-looking *[Laughing]*.

The Pacemakers and the Beatles toured Britain on a Christmas package in 1963, right?

It was a holiday and a party. It was just eight guys who were playing together and who were mates. We never considered ourselves stars, nor did the Beatles. We were just having great fun and getting paid lots of money for it. It made it very good. We never realized we could make so much money playing guitar.

Did you ever attend any Beatle recording sessions?

The Beats were very funny in recording sessions really, because everybody knows that sessions are sessions. You don't mess around in a recording studio. So we'd go down and sit for an hour or so, but it's work. You don't go down and fool around. The boys weren't into recording, but it was nice to be at the sessions, of course. Always a pleasure.

What Beatles song would you have liked to have written?

"Please Please Me." That was a great song. I heard the record when it had just been recorded. And I said to Brian Epstein that this is going to be a number one on the charts, because "Love Me Do" got to eighteen or nineteen on the charts, which we were all proud of. It was the first Liverpool band to get on the charts, basically. The first time I heard the tape of the session of "Please Please Me," I said, "That is a number one song." I would have liked to have written "Please Please Me."

WALTER CRONKITE

Actually the first place that the Beatles ever appeared on television in the United States was on the *CBS Evening News* with Walter Cronkite. We had a report from London and did a feature story on these four way-out guys who were singing in Liverpool and making a big splash in the Midlands. So we sent a reporter up, I think it was Morley Safer who did the first piece, and we had it on the air. And Ed Sullivan was such a superb showman that he called me almost before I was off the air. He said, "Who were those four guys?" And I said, "I don't remember. I'll have to look it up in the script!" So I told him the name and he said, "I'm going to have to try to get them over here." And that was the beginning of their coming to the States. I think they would have come here eventually, but that was the historic record of how they came here.

STEVEN TYLER OF AEROSMITH

STEVEN TYLER OF AEROSMITH

"I go backstage, around the other side of the stage, and I take a leak. And I'm in the stall and I look over to my right and there's McCartney."

•

The heavy metal pride of Boston, Aerosmith has been creating classic back-to-basics rock and roll for close to twenty years.

Aerosmith's considerable recording success in the mid-seventies landed them a spot in the film version of *Sgt. Pepper's Lonely Hearts Club Band*. Their version of "Come Together" proved to be one of the movie's few highlights.

Despite numerous personal and personnel problems, and overwhelming competition, Aerosmith has managed to stay on top of the heavy metal heap. And their success is in no small part due to their howling whirling dervish of a lead singer, Steven Tyler.

You recorded "I'm Down" on your latest album, Permanent Vacation. *Tell us what went into that decision?*

Joe Perry [Aerosmith guitarist] had a band in New Hampshire called The Jam Band. He was working with [bassist] Tom Hamilton and those guys, and I was working out of New York. I was trying to get a contract with MGM and I came up to my parents' resort in New Hampshire.

Joe was playing and I said, "If I have to be up here I might as well make a demo." I asked Joe and Tom and those guys if they would let me sing and do a demo, and we did. It was "I'm Down."

Consequently, when we were doing this album and they said, "Let's do a cover tune," I said, "Naa, we got enough tunes of our own." And Joe said, "Let's just try 'I'm Down.'"

There was a Beatle memorabilia store in Vancouver. We hit it, found the record, brought it in, listened to it about four times, and said, "That's it!" No more dissecting.

We went into the studio and put the digital on. We went live, direct digital, listened to it, and the next morning said, "It's going on the album."

Aerosmith's version of "Come Together" is the highlight of the Sgt. Pepper *film soundtrack. What was it like working with George Martin?*

Spectacular. He came in and I was buzzing because [he's] the guy that did the Beatles. Are you kidding? Doing Aerosmith? I'm getting to meet him. Phenomenal! He sat there and we were rehearsing it in the studio in the record plant in New York City.

We decided it was the perfect song because upon working it up—I played so many Beatles' songs with all the groups in Yonkers that I have it down. That's all one needs is to think you can do something. When he attempts it, nine chances out of ten it'll be a lot better than if he says "Well, I don't know." I always knew I could do Beatles songs great. I took pride in that.

We worked it ["Come Together"] up in a strange way, [which was] no way at all. We just did it a la Aerosmith. Trying to copy it, as the Beatles did it, was impossible. It was close, maybe.

But, once we had our Aerosmith sound down—we'd been together three or four years when we did this—it was just magic. George Martin said, "That's it. Don't touch another thing. Don't change it. Leave it, that's good." He left, and that was it.

I heard that you met Paul McCartney. Tell us how that came about?

I went to see him. I have a friend named Jojo from Boston. I used to go out with her sister. She moved over to England and married Denny Laine. So I went over to see her—we were doing something, I forget what—and I went to Denny's house and saw Jojo and rode the horses and da da da da—and he [Denny] said, "Hey, we're playing tonight, Wembley Stadium. Want to come? You'll get to meet the Governor." And I went "Ahhh, the Governor? Paul?"

He said, "Yeah. Let's go. We'll have a great time." They played a great show. McCartney was great with Wings.

It was a little silly, but for the most part it was fantastic because it was McCartney. When I say silly, that's because Wings is not the Beatles, never will be, never tried to be. So I don't even try to put the two together. My love was for the Beatles, not for Wings. But because McCartney was with Wings, [there was] major love there.

So after the show, we're back in this room and there's drinks and everything and I'm looking around and seeing the guys from *A Hard Day's Night;* the grandfather, he works for Paul, Mal Evans, and all these people are on Paul's road crew. I'm in heaven, walking around flipping out. I get bummed out because I don't see Paul anywhere.

I go backstage around the other side of the stage and I take a leak. And I'm in the stall and I look over to my right and there's McCartney. "Steven," he says to me—and I never met him—"I love your music."

So him telling me this and it was just phenomenal. That feeling from somebody that I looked up to as "The Lord High Doodle-dum of Music," my God!

MAY PANG, CYNTHIA LENNON,
MIKE McCARTNEY, AND SID
BERNSTEIN, 1987

SID
BERNSTEIN

*"I, as a promoter, thought, 'It's time to
strike.' Nobody knew them here, and I
just had a feeling that the timing might
be right. It was just a hunch."*

•

Sid Bernstein has gone down in Beatle history as one of the greatest gamblers of our
time. A New York concert promoter, Bernstein booked the Beatles for their very first
U.S. concert, at Carnegie Hall no less, without hearing them play even one note. Call it
foresight, call it extraordinary vision. But
quite simply, Sid Bernstein was the first to
see the potential of the Beatles from the other
side of the Atlantic.

Not one to rest on his laurels, Bernstein
went on to promote the band for two wildly
successful shows at Shea Stadium—the first
of the "ballpark concerts."

*Sid, start from the beginning, and tell us how you first heard about the
Beatles?*

I first heard of the Beatles in 1962. I was taking a course at the
New School for Social Research [New York], where I now teach a
course on the pop music business.

One of the requirements of this course was to read an English
newspaper every week. So in October of 1962, I began to read
English newspapers.

I began to read about a group making noise out of Liverpool. By the time the course ended in February of 1963, the headlines ran right across pages one, two, or three in most of the newspapers: BEATLEMANIA SWEEPS GREAT BRITAIN.

I, as a promoter, thought, "It's time to strike." Nobody knew them here, and I just had a feeling that the timing might be right. It was just a hunch.

At this point, had you heard any of their records?

No, I never heard a record until long after I made the deal. I searched for a couple of weeks to get their manager's name, and I finally got his number at home: "Liverpool 6512." I shall never forget it.

I made the call in February, made the deal, after some objections.

He [Brian Epstein] said, "Nobody knows us in America. We don't mean anything." I said, "We don't have to do it immediately. We can do it six months from now or twelve months from now."

He chose twelve months. We made the deal for February 12, Carnegie Hall, Washington's birthday. It fell on a Wednesday.

So with the deal in place, you must have been one interested party once they began to break in America?

They broke in the fall of 1963, which insured my bet. I'd been sweating it out. Ed Sullivan, who had gone to Europe in the summer of '63, had seen a huge group of kids with Beatles signs: WE LOVE YOU, BEATLES, BEATLES FOREVER. Ed asked an airport attendant what this was all about—was it an animal act? Sullivan's head was into animal and acrobatic acts, as well as entertainment and show business acts. The attendant laughed and said, "It's the most popular singing quartet Great Britain has ever had."

When he came home, it didn't take him as long as it did me to locate Brian Epstein. He found that a New Yorker by the name of Sid Bernstein had booked them a few months earlier for Carnegie Hall. So he booked them for February 9, right before my date, and February 16, right after my date. He later added a third show.

This totally insured my bet. The power of the Sullivan show was just incredible and exposure on that show meant you were important, especially if you played it two weeks in a row.

Did Ed Sullivan ever try to contact you?

Yes, he asked me whether I'd heard them. I said, "No, Ed, I haven't, but I've been following them in the newspapers and they're a phenomenon, so I took a chance." He said "So am I."

And after that, you got them for Shea Stadium.

Shea Stadium was the following year, the summer of '65. That was the first of the ballpark concerts. We turned so many people away at Carnegie Hall in '64 that I just thought that they could fill a stadium. And I was right.

Brian Epstein wasn't too anxious to do Shea Stadium. I offered to pay him for every seat that was unsold or empty. That turned his head around. He said "Let's do it, Sid." Then we did it again in the summer of '66.

Just wondering, did they both sell out?

The '66 one wasn't completely sold out, because they were playing too many dates in close proximity.

As I recall, there was an afternoon show at one of the Carnegie Hall dates, wasn't there?

It was two shows in the same day. It was Lincoln's birthday, a holiday for the kids. We did a show at 2:30 P.M. and one at 7:30 P.M.

Actually, they had already booked the Sullivan show and then they did a break-in date prior to my date, in Washington. I'd been offered the date but turned it down. My wife was pregnant and I didn't want to leave town, or I would have had them in Washington. But they did that break-in date because they were a little worried about New York.

What was it like backstage for you? Did you get to interact with them at all?

Yes, we got to say hello. They were fun guys, absorbing it all, curious, even amazed at all the attention they were getting in America. They didn't expect it. They were kind of overwhelmed by it all.

We had heavy security so they were in good shape. We had tremendous security for them. They got here February 7, so they had a couple of days to get their feet on the ground and get a feel of what they were allowed to see of New York. I then saw them on the Sullivan show on the ninth.

I was prepared for almost any eventuality at Carnegie Hall. We had almost twenty thousand people behind wooden horses, because Carnegie was blockaded from Fifty-seventh [Street] all the way around to Fifty-sixth. The police estimated that there were at least twenty thousand people waiting to get a glimpse of them. It was history in the making.

What did you think of their music when you heard it? Did you think it would sell?

I loved it. I prayed that it would sell. I don't know that I *knew* that it would sell. I don't have a crystal ball; I just prayed that it would sell.

That's a pretty fortunate discovery from reading English newspapers. Speaking of which, didn't you also place an ad asking them to get back together in 1979?

That was in the fall of '79, I believe. It was to get them to do a concert that would have raised, I estimated, five hundred million dollars around the world for the children of the Boat People. They were adrift at sea with no place to go, no food, no medicine, no clothing.

I just couldn't reach them individually, so I figured this was a way to go over the heads of their managers, advisers, agents, theoreticians, politicians, and every other person who wanted to have a say in what the Beatles do and don't do.

So I wrote the ad because I couldn't get to them individually. The only response I got was from John Lennon.

What was his response?

He wanted more details on how the money was going to be raised, how the concert was to be conducted. After giving what I thought was enough information on the phone, I was then asked to put the details down in writing. So I typed it all out, rushed over with a secretary to his apartment at the Dakota.

I told the doorman that Mr. Lennon was expecting this package and he said he would get it right to him. But we never heard [from him] again. That was it.

What were your feelings the night of the tragedy?

I felt that half my world had caved in. Despondent, lonely, lost. Tragically unhappy in that I'd lost a great friend.

Prior to John's death, did you ever feel that there was a chance that the Beatles may have gotten back together for some reason?

No. I could see by the nonresponse. I had placed a similar ad [in 1976], that you may not be aware of, for what I thought was a good purpose.

There had been an earthquake in Italy with a lot of people left homeless and lives lost. There was also a war going on in Africa—Biafra. I placed another ad asking them to do this, with *all* funds, everything, going to either the victims of the earthquake or the homeless and parentless children in Biafra.

I read some months later when Paul McCartney did a benefit to save the city of Venice from sinking, and he raised fifty thousand dollars. A reporter from the Paris *Herald Tribune* asked Paul what he thought of Sid's ad in the Sunday *Times*—which I also did in the *Herald Tribune* which reaches all of Europe. McCartney responded that the responsibility for saving the world should not be on their shoulders. So I knew that there was no hope then, and I just gave it one more try three years later.

How did the kids act at the first show?

Not violent, but very exuberant, a very good crowd. Tears—a lot of tears; a lot of screaming. But Carnegie Hall didn't have to worry about its sacred property or paintings on the wall. They shook a little bit, you know, and they asked me never to come back again after the February 12 concert, but it was a good crowd.

I had heard that they brought the Beatles into that show in an armored truck. Is that true?

Yes. These were our logistics and we spent weeks drawing up plans, as if they were battle plans, trying to insure their safety.

You're not allowed to land on the field at Shea Stadium, which would have been the best way. So we had the helicopter bring them into a marina. The armored car picked them up at the marina and brought them in the back door of the stadium. The doors opened and closed real quick and it was just when it was time for them to go on.

They got out the same way. The minute they'd finished, off they went, into the car, and out the back door, without incident.

Now I know, and I'm sure you'll confirm, that those early shows were almost inaudible. Mostly, you just heard the females screaming.

That was true. You could barely hear the band. Even at Shea, the first year, I guess we didn't lick the audio problem, because you could not hear too much of what they were singing, over the screaming. There was so much screaming and heightened emotion.

But just being there was important. For the kids, for those of us associated with the concert, it was an historic moment. Just being there was being part of history.

SMOKEY
ROBINSON

*"I was very proud of the fact that the
Beatles had said that they liked Motown,
and that they recorded some of my songs."*

•

As an infinitely talented singer, songwriter,
and producer, William "Smokey" Robinson
is one of the most influential and important
artists to figure in the history of pop music.

Since Smokey began his recording career
with the Motown label back in 1957, as the
lead singer of Smokey Robinson and the
Miracles, he has influenced a generation of
pop, rock, and R & B performers. In fact,
the Quarry Men included Smokey's "Shop
Around," a number two single in 1960, in
their set while performing in Liverpool.

The Beatles recorded a cover version of
Smokey's classic "You Really Got a Hold on
Me" for one of their early albums. And later,
George Harrison paid tribute to his idol on
his solo LP, *33 and a ⅓*, with a composition
entitled "Pure Smokey."

*Smokey, talk a little bit about Motown in the early years—What
Berry Gordy intended the label to be and its significance in entertainment.*

We started Motown with Berry's idea of making music. We
were the first black company and the first black music manufac-

turer that started to cross over into the white market heavily. I mean, we sold more records to white kids than to black kids.

You were established when Elvis and the Beatles hit. What did you think of them at the time?

The one thing that I loved about the Beatles and Elvis Presley was—being big white artists as they were, the fact that they were the first ones to ever admit that they even listened to black artists; that they'd even been into listening to the music of black people— that was a wonderful revelation for them to come out with, be- cause the world was two-sided at that time. Much more so than it is now, especially musically.

I don't see why it's necessary to label music, especially nowa- days, but it was worse back then. Most black people were never even played on white stations. So for Elvis Presley and the Beatles to admit that they had listened to black people's music, and that they patterned their style or whatever after some black people that they had enjoyed, was a wonderful admittance to me!

So I was very proud of the fact that the Beatles had said that they liked Motown and that they recorded some of my songs.

Paul McCartney tells a great story about getting requests for "Shop Around" during lunchtime sessions at the Cavern Club. Then on one of their earliest albums they covered "You Really Got a Hold on Me." What was your reaction to them covering one of your songs?

I loved the fact that they had recorded my song, man. When people record a song of mine, I don't really critique them; I just love the fact that they've done it. You see, every time somebody records one of my songs, that's a dream come true for me.

That's why I write them. I just don't write them for me or whoever records them, I write them so they can be songs, so that people can record them. So when they recorded that, it was one of the most flattering things that ever happened to me. I love the fact that they recorded it and I listen to it over and over again, not to criticize but to enjoy it.

On George Harrison's 33 and a ⅓ album, he wrote a tribute to you called "Pure Smokey." What did you think of that?

I had the pleasure of meeting the Beatles. And George, I spent

SMOKEY ROBINSON

more time with him than any of the other guys, who I met briefly.

But George for a time was living in Los Angeles, and I had the pleasure of being in his company a few times. And it was, once again, a wonderfully flattering thing he did. To feel like that and write about it so the world would know he felt like that. I was very flattered by that.

JOHN
LENNON

"They've been saying rock will die, or it will never last, ever since I first heard about it. It's always written in the paper like 'It's dying . . . it's this, it's that.' People are so busy writing about it [that] they're not listening to it."

•

February 13, 1975, was a snowy day in Manhattan. Scott Muni set off to do his shift at WNEW-FM, figuring it would be yet another relatively normal day on the radio.

Shortly after going on the air, Scott received word that John Lennon was at the station and wanted to come in to the studio to say hello. That hello lasted three wonderful hours—and provided some of New York radio's finest moments.

John had brought along his brand new album, *Rock 'N' Roll*, and he and Scott proceeded to spend the afternoon debuting tracks. John also read a few commercials, lamented his immigration problems, and most importantly, broke the news of his reconciliation with Yoko.

As long as you're here, we have enlisted you to play the role of the air personality, or le Jacque de disc, because you have a brand new album coming called Rock 'N' Roll. *And since you're going to play the album, cut by cut—*

[Mock horror] Ooooohhhhhhh!

There are about a million people out there wondering about this new John Lennon album. So what's it all about?

Well, it's a rock 'n' roll album which the title suggests, none of which I wrote. You might call it "oldies but goldies," although I was calling it "oldies but moldies" when I was making it.

Quite a lot of the songs are ones I was singing when I was fifteen, which was 1955. Some of them are the first songs I ever learned that were rock 'n' roll. Some of them were the first I ever learned to play on guitar, even banjo originally. They're some of my all time favorites.

There are about fourteen of them on the album and I could have gone on forever. I had to stop.

Did you do a whole bunch of them and then decide on these, or did you just do these as you could?

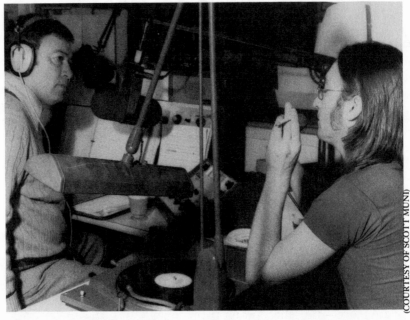

(COURTESY OF SCOTT MUNI)

JOHN LENNON ON THE AIR WITH SCOTT MUNI AT WNEW-FM, NEW YORK, FEBRUARY 1975.

Well, it was in two phases, as it were. It started in '73 actually, when it was a brand new idea. I started with Phil Spector, and the tracks that I did with him, he produced. I just wanted to be a singer.

And to put it simply, there was some psychodrama and it fell apart. So there was a long spell, for one reason or another, that I couldn't get hold of the tapes. I got these tapes back the day I was to go in and start *Wall and Bridges*.

So I did that, and afterwards, started sorting through the tapes I did with Phil and I chose the ones I thought were good enough. Then, after a few weeks rest, I went back into the studio and cut enough to make a full album. And here it is!

Let's start with the first cut. Here's John Lennon's new album, Rock 'N' Roll.

[Music—"Be-Bop-A-Lula"]

That was my version of Gene Vincent's "Be-Bop-A-Lula," one of the first songs I ever sang. And the first day I sang it live with a real band was the day I met Paul.

Really?

It was at a garden party at the church hall in our little town of Liverpool. I was performing with a friend of mine and a mutual friend who brought Paul along introduced him to me saying, "I think you two will get along."

And I was doing "Be-Bop-A-Lula" that day. And it's always been one of my all-time favorites.

Sooner or later, Gene Vincent moved to England, didn't he?

Yeah. The first time the Beatles met him was at the Cav [Cavern Club] in Liverpool. Brian Epstein, the Beatles' first real manager, used to bring rock stars who really weren't making it anymore—no reflection on them, but they were coming over for that reason—and he would put us on the bill with them as second billing. We'd use them to draw the crowd and then they'd see us!

So we met Gene Vincent backstage—backstage, hah! It was a toilet—and we were thrilled. Later, we were with Gene Vincent in Hamburg, with Little Richard, and there's still many a story going around about the escapades, especially with Gene! He was a rather wild guy.

It's hard for people to realize just how thrilled the four of us were just to see any great American rock 'n' roller in the flesh. We were almost paralyzed with adoration. And a side note is that Little Richard's organist was Billy Preston! He looked about ten, but he was good even then.

Didn't Roy Orbison come over there too? After the million sellers?

That was later, when we had begun to make it in England a bit, when we began selling records. And one of our first big tours was second on the bill to Roy Orbison. It was pretty hard to keep up with that man, he really put on a show. They all did, but Orbison had that fantastic voice.

On the Rock 'N' Roll *album, you have selected things that you remember so well from the past. And they're just your favorites, done your way.*

It's a *new* album of oldies. The ones we did with Phil, we spent more time changing them. So to finish it up I did it quickly, because I felt like we were lagging behind. I felt like I was constipated with the album.

So with the stuff I finished off, I left pretty much variations of how the originals did it. In fact, I would have done this years ago but I was always so in awe of the records, I wouldn't cover them.

And when I came to the end of this album, I realized that there were so many I hadn't touched. I didn't touch Jerry Lee [Lewis], Carl Perkins, early Presley, and so many people that I could go on forever.

How about a volume two?

Well, we'll see how this one goes *[Chuckles]*. This one's been such a drama and it took so long. I'll be glad when it just gets out and I can get on with my next album, whatever it is.

If my memory serves, Ben E. King had a million seller with this next cut.

Yeah, "Stand by Me" was one of my big ballads. I used to score a lot of groupies with that one and it's rather one of my favorites. So let's go with that one!

[Music—"Stand by Me," "Ready Teddy," "Rip It Up"]

[As the music fades, John says:] Are we doing this now? *[Changes to exaggerated and loud radio-announcer voice]*

Hi. Korvettes, the world's largest seller of records and tapes, is offering super special prices for the holiday. Choose from the top stars like Minnie Ripperton, La Belle, Elton John (goodie!), Neil Diamond, and Carole King. Plus Stevie Wonder, Temptations, Barry White, Love Unlimited, Jackson Five, Chicago, and many more!!! All LPs from Columbia, A and M, MCA, Motown, and 20th Century labels series at five-ninety-eight are sale priced at just three-twenty-seven, and series six-ninety-eight are just three-eighty-seven. Korvettes, now through Saturday. My own new album will be there this weekend, latest Monday. *Go get it!*

Is it going to be there?

Yeah, I asked Capitol and they said it would be there maybe this weekend and, latest, Monday or Tuesday. So go get it, folks. *[Announcer's voice again]* It'll be in *the stores!*

We're under the influence of a brand new album called Rock 'N' Roll, *which contains great oldies, redone. John, you can pick it up from here.*

OK, the next one is the first one produced by Phil on this album. You'll probably notice the Spector touch on it. This one is "You Can't Catch Me" by Chuck Berry, but the arrangement we came up with is quite different. It might ring a bell to some people, but we'll let them find where it came from.

[Music—"You Can't Catch Me"]

There's something about Chuck Berry's music that is so infectious.

He is one of the all time greats. I've said this many times, but he is the first rock poet. That song came out a long time ago, I don't even know the date, but I think it was one of his first cuts, almost.

Chuck's music has an identifiable tag which is almost immediate. Everybody has tried to do Chuck Berry songs and some have done it well. But he really has an identity thing. And that's the case with the dude who did this next song on your album. This is one of his umpteen-million-sellers. Antoine—

Ah, Fats! Antoine "Fats" Domino. He's been cutting big sellers since 1948, so he was [active] before rock 'n' roll even.

I saw him last year in Vegas and it was good to see him. I was a bit sad that the audience was as drunk—as me, I guess *[laughs]*. It didn't seem like the right audience, but he was still great.

This song has a lot of special meaning for me. I cut "Ain't That a Shame," and there's many a "Fats" that I would have liked to have done. I did "Ain't That a Shame" because my mother, who died shortly before I made it, taught me to play banjo. She also bought me my first guitar and this is the first song I ever learned.

I used to sing Johnny Ray, and whoever else was around, before there was rock 'n' roll. But this is the first song I could accompany myself on. It's a pretty simple song and that's probably why I learned this one. It has a lot of memories for me and I thought I'd do it for that reason.

[Music—"Ain't That a Shame"]

This album has got a great cover.

Oh yeah, that was a picture taken of me in Hamburg in '63 or '62. I've had it around for a long time and I thought that this was the perfect time to use it. And there are some mystery people on the front of it and we'll have to guess who they are.

I have to laugh. On the wall [in the photo] is graffiti and that was in 1962. And I guess it's come back into its own here in New York.

Graffiti has been with us a long long time and it's here to stay. I like it myself.

[Commercials. The final commercial is about a film, and when they resume, the subject is films]

There's a great hoopla about the film version of the Who's Tommy. *I understand it's coming.*

Yeah, everybody's in it. It's worth going to see just for Keith Moon as the dirty old man. I want to see that!

I think some of the movies and documentaries that are done about the folks in music today are excellent. I don't know whether you've had the chance to see Stardust *yet. But Keith Moon, David Essex, and Dave Edmunds all are in it.*

There was a screening the other day but I missed it. I've heard good reports though. And I've also heard that it's modeled after the Beatles life story. They've even got their own Brian Epstein.

There's no question. The story concerns a group from the beginning up through its tremendous success. The only thing that I saw that strayed from the Beatles was that one of the members develops a great solo career, only to lead himself down the road to destruction.

[Laughing] I wonder if that's supposed to be me.

It's not you. You definitely have to see the movie, but it's not you. David Essex plays the solo star—and Keith Moon, he just plays Keith Moon.

Yeah, I heard he scared Ann-Margret on the set a couple of times!

He probably scared everybody. I heard the director tried to give him an acting course and he told him, "No, I think I'll just be me today, thank you!"
John Lennon is with us and he's brought us his new album, entitled Rock 'N' Roll. *And there hasn't been a loser anywhere. They're all so familiar. The next song, Bobby Freeman wrote, as well as had the million-seller with—*

"Do You Wanna Dance" is the only one that I messed about with a bit more. I tried to make it reggae. We'd been doing some jam sessions on the West Coast and I'd always try to do this song with a reggae feel. This one makes you feel happy but I don't know if it makes you want to dance, and that's the problem. It's definitely different than the original.

[Music—"Do You Wanna Dance," "Sweet Little Sixteen"]
That was the dance hall version of "Sweet Little Sixteen," by the great Chuck Berry.

That might be the best and most-covered Chuck Berry song ever.

Yeah, "Johnny B. Goode" and that one. I mean, the first thing you learn is the guitar break on "Johnny B. Goode." That, and "Carol" is another one.

We have turned the album over to side two. Now some of these songs you completed on your own and some of them you did with Phil Spector, until Phil disappeared. There are so many records here that I remember getting on a little 45 RPM. And we'd play them, and we'd listen, and we'd love 'em.

Yeah, me too.
There's no question that Little Richard is a one-of-a-kind performer. His flamboyance, his "viva la difference" onstage, along with the selection of his material make him a joy!
Plus the fact that he was such an influence on James Brown and Otis Redding. They admitted it.

Is this your favorite Little Richard thing?

I could never pick a favorite. The first time I heard Little Richard, a friend bought it. He had it imported from Holland. It came out in Europe and the A Side was "Long Tall Sally," and "Slippin' and Slidin'" was the B Side.
I also liked Buddy Holly's version but I did this a la Richard, although it's not quite the same of course 'cause I ain't the great man!

[Music—"Slippin' and Slidin'"]

We're into the second song of side two, John Lennon's Rock 'N' Roll *LP. And John is doing a fabulous job, even reading commercials.*

I like doing commercials. I like them! Especially record shop commercials.

Do you want to do an introduction for the second song?

Yes! The next one on Side Two is the great Buddy Holly's "Peggy Sue." And what a cosmic joke! Paul McCartney has bought the catalog of the late great Buddy Holly, which is one of the best buys that one could make in this business. Now I wasn't sure if he had this song or not, but he'll be making more out of this than I will!

But this is virtually as Buddy Holly did it. In fact, when I was doing it, I had déjà vu. It came back to me. I didn't even have to read the words, which I did on most of them. And I was singing this one when I was around sixteen. It's virtually how Buddy did it. Well, not quite, but it'll have to do!

[Music—"Peggy Sue"]

Now we get to an old favorite and, also, one of the tragedies. Sam Cooke, along with Buddy Holly, and J. P. Richardson, known as The Big Bopper, all died within a few years of each other.

He's related to Muhammad Ali.

I didn't know that!

Yeah, he was his second cousin or something.

Did you have a particular reason for cutting this Sam Cooke song?

Yeah. This is one of my all-time-favorite songs. I always was going to do it but didn't do it. We always jam to it between tracks. And I almost didn't release it on this album because I knew that Rod [Stewart] had just done it, and Dave Mason had just done it.

But I've been so keen on the song, and I've been putting it off for so many years, that I thought, "I'm going to do it anyway—I love it, man."

I actually like the Carla Thomas version of "Bring It on Home to Me" better. That might have been because I got that version first in Liverpool. It was a long wait to get tracks and it's a very rare record; I can hardly find it now. I have it in the house, but we lost it the other day when I had it out to get the words on it.

This one segues into Little Richard's "Send Me Some Lovin'," which was also sung rather well by Buddy Holly. So this is like a medley, two in one.

Is that "L. Price" who wrote this, Lloyd Price?

Yeah, that's him. The great Lloyd Price *[laughs]*. They're all in there, aren't they?

Music—"Bring It on Home to Me"/"Send Me Some Lovin'"

Excellent. There's not a bad song yet. And the John Lennon arrangement is really something special.

Thanks. Somebody heard it and said, "Oh, he's doing it for real." I don't know if they expected [me] to camp it up or something.

But that's the music that brought me from the provinces of England to the world, and finally to America and New York. And I'll never forget it. It's what made me what I am, whatever it is I am. I don't know where we would have been without rock 'n' roll. And I really love it.

I think that once the Beatles established the fact that there was such a thing as a group making it large, it brought down the curtain on the solo performer. Guys like Fats, Fabian, Frankie Avalon—

Yeah, or else you had Buddy Holly *and* the Crickets, or Dion *and* the Belmonts—

That's right, and all were American. Then this group from England broke and that gave inspiration to a kid who liked to play the drums. He thought, "Hey, I can make it too." That led to the keyboard players, and the writers, and all the things that are so important. So when they ask if rock will last, I just point to all the things rock can be and say "Yes!"

It'll never die, as the old song says. It's been apparent in the music since rock began. And rock came from roots like blues, and rhythm and blues, and jazz—

And country! . . . What a blessing! One of the things I like best about sitting here every day is listening to some of the things that are said. You know, fifteen, twenty years ago, writers were very structured in what they did. Now any subject that a writer can imagine, he can write about! And that inspires more writers.

And I think it can only get better. I don't go with that bit that nothing's happened since—It keeps changing, and it never stops. It's getting better and better. The young musicians, with all the techniques, are far superior to the young musicians of our day. I mean, look at Average White Band. Who'd of thought such a soulful band would come out of Glasgow?`

There's just fantastic music going down and I don't go with the people who are knocking it. It's really happening.

They've been saying rock will die, or it will never last, ever since I first heard about it. It's always written in the paper like "It's dying; it's this; it's that." People are so busy writing about it, they're not listening to it.

Yeah, I've been playing it a long time. And that goes back to my early days when the station I was at actually took the chance and started playing the "ethnic" versions of some hits, instead of playing the remakes they used to do, for the mass audiences. The things Pat Boone used to do.

But that helped introduce it. See, it took a long time before I realized that "Money Honey" by Elvis was actually first done by Clyde McPhatter. And a lot of Elvis' pre-army material was very black.

And although I'd been listening to people like Leadbelly and blues singers, I hadn't really realized that a lot of the songs the early white rock singers were doing was black music. And that introduced me to a whole field of music that I wasn't really aware of before.

That period was full of people like Pat Boone, who'd hear a great record and then "pop" it. And, in so doing, take away a lot of the earthy feel of the original.

Well that's what prevented me from doing a lot of these things earlier. I had such great respect for the original versions that I wouldn't dare touch them. But then I thought, "Time's going on, boy. You'd better do them now, or never."

Boy, we're going back now, aren't we? Revealing our spread, as it were.

John Lennon is our guest and we're reminiscing about our musical past —which is what John has done on his brand new album of oldies, Rock 'N' Roll. *These recordings have been done from October of 1973 through October of this past year [1974]. And I understand that sometimes you used as many as twenty-eight musicians.*

Yeah, in the '73 sessions with Phil Spector we did have as many as twenty-eight musicians. Some of them out of their minds, and some of them not!

There's a great many names here, but I couldn't begin to tell you. It'll all be on the inside sleeve of the album, which we don't have with us.

It was enough just remembering who was there and getting it down on paper, never mind who played what! So we listed them all, and some of the all-time great names in rock who are still around are the musicians here.

I mean, Leon Russell was there. He played piano on "Da Doo Ron Ron," and all the early Spector records, which I didn't know. I learned a lot just hanging around these great musicians.

You've covered a lot of ground and territory since you started this project, including doing another album in between.

Yeah, I did *Walls and Bridges* in between this, because this sort of collapsed, as it were. So [after the delay] I started on *Walls and Bridges*, then finished that, and came back to finish this while I was still on a groove. So I virtually went right back in, with maybe a two week rest.

You are an excellent host.

Thank you.

And we also appreciate your commercial ventures. And by the way, you've passed the audition and you're hired.

We've already mentioned the next artist in passing, I believe, Larry Williams. He was sort of a la Little Richard, but he came after Richard. I sang a lot of his songs. I did "Dizzy Miss Lizzy" and "Bad Boy" with the Beatles.

And it was easier to do Larry Williams than Little Richard when we were doing these in the dance halls. He didn't have quite as an identifiable voice as Richard did.

But he also had some great songs. And this is one of them called "Bony Moronie."

[Music—"Bony Moronie"]

Another classic! We were reminiscing during the record—

Oh, yes, Ringo fainting!

There were a couple of things about the first time you came to America. There was this huge flurry of activity. You guys were emerging from your triumph over Britain and you were tired, confused—

And excited!

And excited. And the difference in each one of you from that time to now, in only ten years, is just amazing. I remember we were in the hotel room with you. And I also remember that John Lennon was the one who did have the nerve to sneak out of the hotel.

Yeah *[Laughing]*.

You went in disguise and you went around and hit a number of clubs.

I think I went with Paul.

Yes! I remember you discussing how you could sneak out of there and not look like John Lennon.

It was the nose that was always the giveaway! Whatever I did it was always the nose. I didn't have the glasses in those days because they weren't known.

But I could stuff cotton wool up it [the nose] like [Marlon] Brando did in his cheeks, but then I couldn't breathe. But if I had to put a beard on, or whatever it took, it was this nose that got me into trouble. That was always the case.

We just heard "Bony Moronie," a song from Larry Williams who comes from the same camp as Little Richard and Sam Cooke in the sense that they never had a huge record deal but their music still managed to find its way to you in England.

In those days we didn't know what size anything was. All we knew was what we could get our hands on in England and it was a luxury.

It was nowhere near what's going on today! During commercials we were talking about the Gay Peelaert [and Nik Cohn] book of rock art called Rock Dreams. *Now you're on the cover in the British version and the American version has you and another person has been added, David Bowie.*

Yeah, he's a good lad.

He was not on the European one that featured you, along with Elvis.

Me and Elvis! A dream come true. I took the cover off the British version and put it on the wall. I would like to have the one with David on it, but actually the British cover was larger. On the American one, they made the picture smaller which I think was stupid. So I took the British cover and framed it.

I got hold of one of the originals, which is the one he did of Beatles in Hamburg. It's from the same period of photographs like the picture on the cover of this album!

I'm surprised that Elton John wasn't in the book. Apparently, the first picture he did from this series was of Elton, so maybe it wasn't as good as the others. I was rather surprised. He should have spent more time on that and less on Cliff Richard and other unknown British artists.

But I understand that Elton's wasn't as good as some of the others. I tried to get hold of it and buy it for Elton, but I couldn't find anybody who had it. Somebody has it, somewhere in Germany.

I can think of two dozen that I would like to purchase.

I wanted the one with the Beatles and the queen, but I couldn't get hold of it. I thought it was so funny, with the teacups! And, of course, there was that great Stones one, with them in their S and M gear. That's a classic!

Yeah, he did the cover for the Stones album, *It's Only Rock 'n' Roll*, and David Bowie's *Diamond Dogs*, which was censored.

There have been a lot of weird things censored: Buffy Sainte-Marie, Roxy Music. But you, of course, have a classic album cover that was also censored!!

Yeah, the *Two Virgins* cover!

The classic album cover of all time.

But do you know the first one that got banned? It was the Beatles' "meat and dead babies" picture, which was on the album over here called *Yesterday and Today*. It's now fifty dollars on the market. I have one, but I had it from a long time ago.

It's rather like the Alice Cooper *Billion Dollar Babies* cover. We did it in '65 and Capitol printed up fifty thousand copies. It went out to the public and there was an outcry. So it was whipped back immediately and it was covered with this corny picture that made us look more dead than the meat we had on our knees!

I'd like to use that for the next Beatles package. It's really a classic. We look like monsters, ourselves.

That would wipe out the black market, though. I have a lot of that stuff. I have stuff from Beatles that I didn't even know existed.

I have one that is very important, and nobody knows how important it is. I'm not going to say what it is, until I can find the sources of this amazing bootleg. I don't know where they got it from. It's been out a few years, but nobody knows the story behind it, but I do! It's gonna blow a few minds when they find out what it is.

This is going to be a much talked about and very successful album. And I hope it is so maybe you'll sit down and think about John Lennon's Rock 'N' Roll Part II.

Well, it was hard to stop at one point. There's so many great songs and most of them I sang when I was fifteen or sixteen—and they just come back to you when you start doing them again. Even if you rearrange them, the words and inflections come back to you.

Just like yesterday—

[Sings] All your troubles seemed so far away!

Hey, there's a song title! What about "Ya Ya," the next song on the album. Where did that come from?

I did a joke version with my son Julian on *Walls and Bridges*. I liked the great Lee Dorsey, and there are other tracks [of his] that I prefer, but I knew "Ya Ya." It's just when you're sitting down to jam, everybody could just go, "Sittin in the la la, waiting for the Ya Ya . . ." I know the Stones did it too.

If I ever do another Lee Dorsey track, I know which one it is. I'm not going to say it because I know people will go and cover it right away. But there are some great ones.

[Music—"Ya Ya"]

While you've been here this afternoon, we've gotten a lot of insight into the oldies on your new album—but you do have some sort of news, I understand, that I'm sure our listeners are not really aware of.

Well yeah, really. I would like to dedicate this whole album to my very special friend, my wife, Yoko, whom you might not have heard I'm living with.

As I put it, our separation was a failure. Those two indomitable loonies are back together again, and we're very happy. This next song really has nothing to do with either one of us so I'll dedicate it, and the whole album, to her too.

That's my past, and there it goes.

When did the get-together happen?

About a week ago, although it's not really been out. I think there was a little news about it in England although I don't know how it got there.

But I'll say it again, our separation was a failure. John and Yoko are back in their bag, as it were, together. And rock on.

I know I speak for our audience when I say that I'm certainly delighted, if you and Yoko are. Two people are as close as they want to be, as together as they want to be, as often as they want to be. So this and the album are dedicated from John to Yoko.

[Music—"Just Because"]

That's Larry Williams, written by Lloyd Price.

By the way, somebody called and said that the current price of the Yesterday and Today *cover you mentioned is now two hundred fifty dollars.*

My God!

I've got an idea, John. I've got a printing press and I know a printer.

Yeah, I've got one at the house, baby!

If not we'll get one, it sure beats counterfeiting twenties! Speaking of rarities, the Christmas messages that the Beatles used to issue are also hard to come by.

Yeah, I have that set as well. That's why I'm schizophrenic about pirates. I'd get a copy of something and say, "I didn't know they recorded this in Sweden."

For those of you who did not get to hear some of the songs that are on the "Rock 'N' Roll" album, we'll be doing more of that in a little while. But, right now, we're just talking with John Lennon, playing some music.

I'm in the middle of a book on languages. A lady wrote it and it's on American English and all the changes in it from the Revolution, and pre-Revolution, up to now. It's fascinating.

And as you might have guessed, listeners, I'm a bit of a wordsman, so I really like to see how words came about. In fact, on the Carson show last night, they were talking about how the word "hooker" came from some American General in the Civil War. A General Hooker. So they called the girls who followed the army camp Hooker's Heroes. And that's where the word "hooker" came from.

So all you hookers out there, now you know how you got your name, on WNEW-FM.

See, if I wasn't here this afternoon, I wouldn't know the derivation of that word.

There was a lot of snobbery from Europe about the American culture, which the Americans believe and still believe today. They've got great writers like Tennessee Williams, etc, etc.

They still feel like they have no culture. But it's the greatest culture on earth. This is where the culture is now, folks. It isn't over there; it's here.

So this book is very interesting, showing how Europe reacted to America breaking away. The English were especially furious, so the only thing they could do was—it was like a kid leaving home.

It's like parents who say, "You'll get into trouble; you'll never manage on your own. You don't know anything about money; you haven't been educated; you'll never sustain it." And the poor kid, in fact America, was beginning to believe it. But they got over it. And, as we all know, here you are.

We're playing your new album, Rock 'N' Roll, *but you also wanted to go back to* Walls and Bridges *and Ringo's* Goodnight Vienna.

I spoke to him last night and I said, "Ringo, I'm going on the radio tomorrow. Shall I play 'No No'?" He said, "You better!" It's a great one.

Well, we better, then.

[Music—"The No No Song," "# 9 Dream"]

Hope you didn't mind me sneaking that in—

[Exaggerated rock star accent] I'm rather pleased with it and it's on the charts, folks, and it's still cooking. So if you want it, go get it.

We've spent two and a half hours together, and we haven't gotten to something that I definitely wanted to talk about. What is happening with your immigration situation?

It's pretty much the same. There's been a few appeals or something. We lost one appeal, on the phone tapping, because there's no real way you can prove your phone was tapped. We won the right to interview the ex-head of immigration and the ex-prosecution counsel, which we were denied for a period of time.

My legal people believe that there are papers there that we should have access to.

And other than those details, I'm still in the same piece of crap I have been for the last three years. Nothing's going on and they're still making me go through this.

Meanwhile, taking half a million dollars tax from me since I've been here with one hand and making me pay more in legal fees with the other hand.

People always ask what they can do, and I really can't say, except for their interest. That's welcome and it's shown by writing to anybody who's got anything to do with politics.

The radio station here would be kind enough to accept letters, if you don't know where else to send them. Write to your local guy, write to the White House, write to anybody. Say whatever you want to say about it.

If they get one letter, they think it represents fifty people, same as the commercial people. They want to know who's listening to a station or reacting to a commercial. One letter counts for twenty or thirty or more in a sponsors mind.

In this situation, the sponsor is the government or the politicians. You keep them aware of the problem by writing to your local rock paper, or any paper, or writing to the station.

Let's zero in and be more specific. Our friends on campus might do it with a petition, getting a number of names. And if any of you would like to localize it, write to John Lennon, care of WNEW-FM.

Whether it's an individual letter, or petition, send it here, and we'll see that it gets to the right hands.

Thank you. I'd like to thank a fellow artist, who I've only met once, who very kindly dedicated his follow-up single to me. And that's Neil Sedaka. He's been around this business longer than I have. And I met him once, and then I got a call from him about two weeks ago and he said he's dedicating his new record called "The Immigrant" to me!

Usually, when people call you, they want something. And I was very pleased to accept those good wishes from him. The only other artist who actually did something like that was the late Bobby Darin, who I never met.

He took an advert out in *Variety* or one of those trade papers, and it's heartwarming. That sounds corny, but whatever the expression is, it's very nice of people to do things.

It gets boring talking about it and I think the government's hope is that everybody gets so bored with it that nobody wants to know about it.

You're right. Apathy, or a we'll-let-things-take-care-of-themselves approach, is not going to work in this case. Your letters can make a difference. We'd appreciate it if you let your feelings be heard about the immigration proceedings being brought against John Lennon.

[Music—"Be-Bop-A-Lula"]

Rock 'N' Roll *is the title of John Lennon's new album, chock full of great oldies, all newly done.*

The cover is a Hamburg picture from 1961, in the leather jacket, looking like I quite don't know what's going on yet. And I didn't, that's for sure.

I know that you have to go, but it seems like these three hours were more like thirty minutes. It's been a sheer pleasure and a lot of fun. I know the kind of response that we get from our listeners and I know that they're going to help you with the immigration problem.

Thanks to all of them intending to or even wishing me well. Good wishes are useful too.

I thank them all and I'd also like to thank you, Scott. I enjoyed it. I like deejaying, and thanks for the exposure. You're always good to me at this station.

Will you come back?

I'll be back, yes!

God bless you and Yoko.

R O Y
O R B I S O N

On my first tour of England I went to this little theater where we were going to rehearse and there were Beatle placards everywhere. So I said to someone, "What's all this crap? What is a Beatle anyway?" And John Lennon tapped me on the shoulder and said, "I'm one." I said, "Sorry about that." In Europe it means a great deal to top the bill, to close the show. So they asked if they could close the show. And I said, "Let's wait 'til after rehearsal." So during rehearsal I was doing mostly ballads and they were doing everything up tempo. And they didn't sound all that good. So they came to me after rehearsal and asked if they could close the show again. I said, "Let me think about it." They said, "You're making all the money. Please let us close the show." But I had already decided to let them close the show, because everything I was doing was a ballad and they were doing "Twist and Shout" and all these fast numbers. So I let them close the show and it helped them internationally. But I always thought they would be as big in America as they were in Europe, and sure enough, the next February, it happened.

TOMMY SMOTHERS AND DICK
SMOTHERS

TOMMY
SMOTHERS

*"Oh my goodness! I'm being immortalized
with the Beatles!"*

•

American television has never been quite the
same since those two zany brothers, Tommy
and Dick Smothers, graced the airwaves
back in the late sixties. In fact, they are
widely credited with revamping the variety
show concept.

The Smothers Brothers Comedy Hour un-
loaded on "the Establishment" every Sunday
night, at a time when the American political
scene was prime comedic fodder. Their ex-
pertise in this regard eventually led to the
show's cancellation. But not before Tommy
and Dick introduced a nation to some of the
top musical talent of the period.

The brothers were ardent fans of the
Beatles and used their program to debut
video-taped performances of the band—a
real treat at the time. Both George Harrison
and Ringo Starr made rare guest appearances
and Tommy, in particular, experienced a tumultuous relationship with John Lennon.

*You had George on the program and you premiered "Hey Jude" and
"Revolution." But the Beatles as a group never appeared live, right?*

No, they never appeared live as a group. George did and also Ringo separately, but we never had them on live. We got the first premiere [video] of "Hey Jude" and the other song, which was a real coup. As far as Lennon goes, well we had a lot of strange, interesting—well, we'll get to that later.

Tell us about George appearing on the show.

Well, I had a very beautiful lady that I was living with at the time who was my production assistant on the show. He [George] came over and we spent a lot of time watching some of the old tapes and some of the newer shows together. He was very charming but a little uncomfortable by himself on the show. I look back, when I see some of the old shows, and I see he was a little self-conscious.

They're [the Beatles] not so used to talking as they are performing and singing, so we didn't put a lot of pressure on him to do any of the sketches like we did some of the other groups who were more adept at getting involved there.

Later on, when we had another television series in '74, '75, '76, Ringo came on and we did sketches with him. You've got to help him along. He's a funny guy, but he suffers through it. He tries everything. He's a good soul.

Now you were part of another episode in the story. You were at the bed-in strumming along to "Give Peace a Chance," right?

The Montreal Bed-In for Peace. [Dr. Timothy] Leary was there, as well as a whole group of people at the time who were hanging around. They were laying in bed, Yoko and Lennon, and we spent about three days up there, just partying and having a good time.

They had all these mikes set up there and they gave me a guitar. I remember this distinctly—he was playing "Give Peace a Chance" and we were all sitting around the bed singing. He was playing in a lower open chord formation, so I went up and did the next chord inversion and I was playing a couple passing chords. We were singing along and all of a sudden he stops and says, "Hey, play what I play. Play exactly what I play. I want it to sound that way."

I said, "Sorry, I thought I was filling in some of those chords."

Of course, he's a pretty good musician. I've been playing for a while, but he liked that doubling of the sound of the guitars on that particular song.

Then later on, a poster came out with Lennon, Leary and I and Yoko on the bed there and I said "Oh my goodness! I'm being immortalized with the Beatles."

Another time, there was a big party in Laurel Canyon. It was with, what was the name of the guy, my good friend—Harry Nilsson.

We were all hanging around together at the time. Lennon and Harry started hanging around together a lot. They'd drink a lot of brandy and get a little high, a little crazy. I'd stay with them for a while. But I was the only guy who had a regular job. They had done their albums and really weren't working at the time. This would be later on, in '74.

Around the time of the famous Troubadour incident?

Yeah, before then, things were pretty nice, but we'll get into that later.

What, if any, influence did the Beatles have on a musical-comedy actor?

The first time that the Beatles really got to me was *Rubber Soul.* It was the first album that impressed me; it was so acoustic and pure. Just about all the tunes on that album were—"Norwegian Wood"—all of them. They were played constantly.

The sixties were a very psychedelic and high period. There was a lot of hope in the country. Everybody was kind of radically liberal and peace oriented. I would say "Norwegian Wood." Let's see, what are the other tunes—I haven't played that album actually in such a long time. I've got to bring it out and play it again.

You mentioned that you'd elaborate on the Troubadour incident. Can you clear that up for us?

That was in '74 and my brother and I had just started working for a couple of years. We were ready to come back and play our first appearance at the Troubadour in many, many years. Actually, since the television show went off the air.

So, it was opening night and I mean it was a huge Hollywood

opening. During our first set I heard someone yelling something about pigs—it was fairly disgusting. It came from an area that was kind of the elite, raised area.

The Smothers Brothers have slow timing. I work kind of slow, not the rapid-fire, Robin Williams type of comedian. And I kept looking over, and every time I'd take a timing break, it [the yelling] would come in. I couldn't figure out who it was. I knew Harry was there and I know how Harry Nilsson gets because I've been out with him when we've been a little crazy. And I knew Lennon was there, but I didn't know who was doing it.

The heckling got so bad that all of a sudden—I couldn't see very well from the stage—but our show was going downhill rapidly. No one cared because it was just a happening anyway, but there was a scuffle going on and we stopped the show.

My wife, who I had just married, ended up with Lennon's glasses because of the punches that were thrown. Then he went outside 'cause he was still angry and kicked the car parker. I was pissed off 'cause here was Lennon, a pretty good friend of mine, and Harry Nilsson was a close—I mean we were very tight and had great respect for each other, but they were tuned up pretty good and drinking brandy.

Harry was very persistent saying "Tommy, I didn't do anything." "I know you, Harry," I said. "You were whispering to John to yell out those things." And he says "I didn't whisper it—I just made the suggestion."

I forget how it came about, but he denied having anything to do with it. But I knew he did. He admitted it later.

Flowers came the next day, apologizing. Those things happen. I looked at it then as the way I still do now. The Beatles weren't performing or recording anymore. Harry Nilsson was working on other things and wasn't recording a lot. And when you're that high-energy and that creative, and you don't have a job to focus on, it comes out somewhere. It's either in someone else's performance or jumping in.

It was another one of our highlights. A lot of our career has been based on accidents.

THE POLICE

*"I think the Beatles are the reason that
I'm a musician."*
—Sting

•

The Police emerged from the British punk
movement of the late seventies, sporting a
powerful blend of rock and reggae.

Led by charismatic vocalist Sting, the
Police took the world by storm, driven by
the innovative rhythms of Andy Summers'
guitar and Stewart Copeland's drum kit.

Recent years have seen band members
forego group projects in favor of solo endeavors. In fact, *Ticket to Ride* caught up with
Sting in Paris, where he was putting the fin-
ishing touches on his very first solo effort
and eventual platinum album, *Dream of the
Blue Turtles*.

STING

What about early Sting musical influences? Did the Beatles affect you?

I think the Beatles are the reason that I'm a musician. They are
from a similar background to mine, in that they are from a work-

ing class but they were well-educated. And I think the main influ-ence is that they wrote their own music. This was quite a new phenomena that I think the Beatles are responsible for. And my success has relied on being able to write my own songs.

The Beatles did open the door by having a producer and record company that let them write their own material.

Basically, they were in charge of their operation from the be-ginning because they provided the raw material, which is the songs.

I think before that we'd had artists who relied on teams of professional songwriters. And to take it out of that arena made it much more realistic to get involved in, from a creative point of view. It interested me much more.

ANDY SUMMERS

Andy, growing up in England, I wonder if you ever saw the Beatles live?

(A & M RECORDS)

STING

Oh, yeah, I saw the Beatles. It must have been 1963. They played in my hometown and I actually did go to see them.

I can remember it. They came out, and on two of the songs they played, they said "One of these is going to be our next single. Shout for which ever one you like the most." One of them was "She Loves You." And everyone shouted for "She Loves You," and that was their next single.

Yeah, I remember them. They were a huge influence on everybody and really, in a way, provided the blueprint for success in a rock group. Them and the Stones, but from two different schools, in a way.

As an accomplished student of the guitar, give us your impression of George Harrison's guitar prowess.

I think George Harrison is a very good guitar player, and he played everything that was right. If you go back to his guitar playing, it definitely stands up.

I know he's very down on his own guitar playing. He's not like a great virtuoso lead player. In that era, Eric Clapton became that. Harrison had a feeling for a song's form, and would play very nice and interesting guitar things.

I always thought his solo on "Something" was great, but he hated it. I know that he hated his guitar solo. And that bit he did at the end of "Help!," that kind of Chet Atkins run at the end of that song, was really good.

He was definitely a real player in the sense that he was dedicated to his instrument. He learned about Indian music, he liked Segovia, he listened to Chet Atkins. He was into the guitar, and you can tell. He's a sincere player.

Do you have any favorite Beatles songs?

There's so many out there. I love "Help!" I liked the melody, the kind of bittersweet quality of the whole song. The lyrics are great, too.

Looking back at the lyrics, they wrote some very good ones. They definitely hold up. "Fixing a Hole," "Tomorrow Never Knows," and almost anything off *Revolver* are great.

GLADYS KNIGHT

GLADYS KNIGHT

"I kept hearing these sounds and I kind of felt like something was about to happen. Having been around so many years before that, you can get a sense when things are about to happen. And they happened!"

•

Gladys Knight learned to sing in a church choir and, by the time she was seven, she had been a winner on the *Ted Mack Amateur Hour*. She formed the Pips with various members of her family and was on tour by the age of thirteen.

Since then, Gladys Knight has become a consistent hitmaker and remains one of the most respected and humble performers in the business.

You were already a veteran when the Beatles hit in 1964. Can you remember them coming to America and the first time you heard their music?

I remember them vividly. I was living in New York at the time the Beatles started to happen.

And this little group came out, talking about "I Want to Hold Your Hand" and all that stuff! [*Laughing*] As a matter of fact I was pregnant with my son at the time and I was just kind of stuck right there in New York. I kept hearing these sounds and I kind of felt like something was about to happen. Having been around so many years before that, you can get a sense when things are about to happen. And they happened!

It was a phenomenal thing. I was like what we called "swept." And that's exactly what they did!

You would go on to do your own version of "Let It Be." Tell us how that came about.

If I hear a song and it touches me—you see, I'm kind of a ballad person anyway. I like a lyric because you can emote with a lyric a little bit better when the tempo is slow, so I lean towards a ballad. "Let It Be" was one of those songs, just like "The Way We Were."

So, when we started in the studio, we were looking for what we called a name-value song to put on the album to help sell it. So the producer we were working with at that time said, "Hey, I think 'Let It Be' would be a great song for you guys to do."

I was appreciative of that fresh new sound, and I really loved the Beatles. As a matter of fact, the first theater we played in when we went to England belonged to the Beatles: The Saville [owned by Brian Epstein].

It was our first time over and Paul came to the show. We were kind of skeptical about playing over there because all we'd heard were that the people were sort of sophisticated. They didn't applaud; they'd just sit there, you know, real stuffy.

So we didn't know what to expect. Those people went crazy, scared us to death! I mean the show was over and they rushed the stage. I couldn't believe it.

I haven't had the opportunity to meet all of them, but it's really been something to watch their success.

PETE BEST

"He said 'Pete, I've got some bad news for you. The boys want you out and Ringo in.' That was my first warning of the dismissal."

•

Pete Best has the dubious distinction of being the "almost-Beatle."

Yet the story of Pete Best plays a critical role in Beatle history. Best's mother Mona ran the Liverpool nightspot, The Casbah, and often featured the Quarry Men in concert. Best, who was drumming for a local band at the time, was recruited by the Quarry Men when they set off for Hamburg.

Renamed the Beatles upon their return to Liverpool, Best was sacked by the band just prior to the signing of their first major record deal.

The reasons for Pete Best's replacement by Ringo Starr remain as murky today as they did more than twenty-five years ago—but the speculation continues.

Pete, can you remember getting your first drum kit?

My first drum kit was a Premier. Pearl blue. I got it around 1958–59. I finally persuaded my mother and father to go out and put the money down to buy me a full drum kit. Before that, I had a small snare drum and scissor cymbals, which was a normal way to start. But the Premier was my first real kit.

Tell us about the first time you saw the Quarry Men?

It was in my mother's club, the Casbah. I first met them when they came down with George Harrison. I'd met George before, simply because he used to play in this club called the Lowlands, so he was the first one I'd met. At that time, George was very much into his music, and before then, he was still sort of a baby-faced guy.

He turned around and said, "I got a couple of guys, friends who might be interested [in playing the Casbah Coffee Club]." They came down, and it was John Lennon and Paul McCartney.

At that time, John was very much into his art college image: black corduroy jacket, white "KDs," corky denims [pants], base-ball boots, dark shades, and long sideburns. He was the humorist, the funny guy. He had a devil-may-care attitude which won over a lot of people. As soon as you saw him, he started cracking jokes and messing about and your heart warmed to him.

Paul, even in those days, was more the impresario. He was the guy who wanted to be the PR man, even before the Beatles. He still wanted to be the negotiator. "What are we going to do? What are we going to play?" They were my first impressions of them.

There was a photo taken of you guys just prior to your first trip to Hamburg. It was taken in front of a war memorial that read: THEIR NAME LIVETH FOREVERMORE.

That particular photo that you're talking about was just one of those things; whether it was fate or not that we had our picture taken there.

The journey itself was hilarious. Right from when we started off in Liverpool, all the way through to Hamburg. The things we got up to, the way we amused ourselves, the people we picked up on the road, the things Allan [manager Allan Williams] did to get us into Germany. Well, even to this day, we went in without the right papers. We were smuggled in. Allan stood around the corner, as we were smuggled in as students. We didn't have the right papers to play over there, but that got sorted out.

When we were sitting in the van, the atmosphere was fantastic, simply because we had no impressions whatsoever about Hamburg. We didn't realize. We said, "Oh, it's going to be like Liverpool."

(STAR FILE)

PETE BEST IN 1964

We were playing away from home, and we were going to be the big rock stars in Germany. I mean the adrenaline was flowing. And even though it was a long trip, we still kept going. Hamburg was the golden pot at the end of the rainbow. And when we got into Hamburg itself, and saw the lights and the Reeperbahn, that was it as far as we were concerned. We'd made it.

The neon lights were like Broadway in America, or the West End in London. It was a case of "Everyone outside the van, quick." We charged into the Kaiserkeller club, and went downstairs to see what the atmosphere was like. And it was fantastic. We had never played a place like the Kaiserkeller club before. We had played in dance halls, coffee cellars and this type of thing.

But to actually play in a night club, so to speak, or "beer keller," as they were called over there, was fantastic. The place was jumpin'. German audiences were going wild and all of a sudden, people were saying, "I want to be a part of it."

When you went back to Liverpool, weren't you billed as a group from Germany?

Yeah. That initially started with the first booking we had when we came back. It was a lifeline from my mother because she had the Casbah. She billed us as "The Fabulous Beatles from Hamburg." So when we actually played at the Casbah, we came down the stairs, and everyone was waiting to see who "The Fabulous Beatles" were. And down the stairs came John, Paul, George, Stu, and in behind them, came Pete. And then, it was, "Hang on a minute, they're not the Beatles, they're the Quarry Men, who used to play here. And that's Pete from the Black Jacks. What's going on?"

The minute we started playing, that was it. The whole atmosphere changed. The place was going wild, and it was never the same.

It was fantastic. The girls who were sitting in the front row thought we were actually German. I mean, when I say "Sitting in the front row," I mean that they were propped up against the stage. There weren't seats or anything like that.

When they heard John, George, or myself talking in a Liverpool dialect, they suddenly turned and said, "Oh, these guys aren't from Germany." We said, "Yeah, we never said we were Germans. We'd been playing in Germany, we live in Liverpool."

George Harrison said the Beatles were never better than when they were in Hamburg.

Simply because of the fact that we played seven or eight hours per night. That did a lot to formulate and blend the group into that charismatic powerhouse, which took Germany and the rest of the world by storm.

Eventually, we were playing over there with no inhibitions whatsoever. We were playing things as we wanted to. We had the urge for it, and it was an adventure for us. It was freedom of music, and we played as we wanted to play, the way we felt it should be played. And I think that was part and parcel of the old Beatles charisma.

Why don't you run down each of the Beatles and assess their musical ability.

Let's take George first. He was very much into his guitar, but he was the lead guitarist, very much in the lead, compared to the rest of the guys. He was always out to improve his own ability, always working on it, listening to new sounds, new chords and riffs.

John was a good lead guitarist, even though he played second fiddle to George. But on many occasions, John had to play lead on the songs. He made a good job of it. But he would say at the time that his forte was mainly rhythm and vocals.

Paul was the unknown quantity at that time [*Laughing*]. That's a funny way of putting it, simply because we knew Paul could play trumpet, we knew he could play piano, and that he could play guitar. When I joined, I didn't know what ability he had. He used to mess around a lot. Sometimes, his guitar wasn't even plugged in.

Paul's musical ability came more to the fore when Stu left the band. That's when his bass playing came out, and he said, "Look, I'm a good musician." Plus the fact that we used to listen to him messing about, and he could play good guitar. But his role in that moment in time—because there were so many guitarists—was to sit down and either play the piano or the bass, as required. He was a good utility man.

Stu always said that he was limited in his ability. He didn't profess to be a brilliant musician, but he did the job. He did what was required of him and his character contributed an awful lot to the band.

I heard a tape of 1960 Beatles music from Hamburg, and on it Paul was toying with "I'll Follow the Sun" and "When I'm Sixty-Four." Not many folks know he was working up those songs so early.

Those were some of the songs Paul would mess around with. They were his two songs at that moment in time. Trying to impress people, he'd say "Look, I've written a song. What do you think of it?" That would give him a chance to play the piano and vocalize. It was a little bit different from what he was doing on stage.

With all the spare time we had in Germany, and with all the pianos available, we had the facilities to practice in the afternoon and mess around if we wanted.

You'd listen to Paul working out on those particular songs, and you knew the origin was there. It was just bubbling, and it was only a matter of time before they started writing their own material.

I'm going to ask you to describe what comes into your head when I say certain phrases. "The Exis" [short for Existentialists]

"The Exis." This is the nickname we put to the college students at the time: Astrid [Kirschner], Jurgen [Vollmer], Klaus [Voorman]—the people who were a little bit different from the Hamburg frau. They were a little more Art Nouveau than the others, more arty in their approach to things.

How about "Prellies"?

"Prellies" was short for Preludin, an amphetamine which kept most of the rock musicians going for many hours. It was something that was available. If you needed it, you took it.

"The Thing?"

[*Laughs*] "The Thing" was something that we nicknamed for an escapade, which George started by puking over the side of his bed one night after we'd been on a real bender. It was a nickname which we gave to the pile of puke, which grew and grew and changed into a hairy monster. We fed it cigarette butts, Preludin, you name it. And that was our nickname for it—"The Thing."

Describe the Bambi Kino, the movie house where you lived in Hamburg?

It was the back of a cinema that was concrete right the way through. There was one main living room at the back of the toilets, which had two beds and a sofa. And that was the palatial quarters that John, George, and Stu stayed in.

Twenty-five yards down the corridor, there were what we nicknamed "the Black Holes of Calcutta." They were two dungeons about eight by six. You could just about get a bed in there. There was no light. If you wanted to write a letter, you had to get a torch, a candle, or strike matches.

Now what happened when you guys got accused of setting it on fire?

The actual truth about the burning of the Bambi Kino was that over a period of time, we had played the Kaiserkeller for many months. By this time, we got to know Tony Sheridan and Peter Eckhorn, who was the owner of the Top Ten Club around the corner. He knew that we were going great guns, and he also knew that if the Beatles and Tony Sheridan played at the Top Ten, it would virtually put everyone else out of business.

So he said, "Whenever you want to leave the Kaiserkeller, you have the opportunity to play at the Top Ten." We'd been on with [Kaiserkeller owner] Bruno Koschmider for many weeks, and we'd been trying to put the price up. But he kept saying that he wouldn't.

There was a sequence of events that happened around that time. George had to go home. He was underage and didn't have the right papers.

[The] next thing was [that] we weren't working too well at the Kaiserkeller, in view of the fact that Bruno Koschmider wasn't going to do what we asked of him. And since Peter Eckhorn said we could play at the Top Ten, we turned 'round and said, "Let's go play there." Koschmider said, "If you play the Top Ten, you'll never play in Germany again."

Now, read into it what you want. He might have broken our legs, put us to sleep—that was for him to decide.

But we decided that we were going to play at the Top Ten, so that meant moving all of our equipment. John managed to get his away peacefully. Paul and I had to go back and pack whatever bits of clothing we had, the instruments, drum cases, etc., from the dungeons.

When we went back, we had to sneak into the Bambi Kino, but there was no light. The only thing we could find to give us light was condoms. Paul had some, so we stuck them into the wall, and lit fire to them. Well, they sparkled and blubbered and gave off black smoke. They just about gave us enough light to throw our things together, and disappear. We did a moonlight flit over to the Top Ten Club.

We were walking up and there happened to be two policemen. Paul and I were whisked off for an hour of being cross-questioned, sort of [having] thumb screws put to us. We finally found that Bruno had charged us with trying to burn down the Bambi Kino. Paul and I have always asked, "How can you burn down a cinema made of concrete with rubbers?" But that's the true story behind the Bambi Kino incident.

What was Stu's relationship with the boys like? Was there a rivalry with Paul?

Well, rivalry, I'd say no. I think basically things have been taken out of context there.

Stu was a fantastic artist and there was no bones about that. Forget him as a rock musician; as an artist, he was brilliant. His contribution to the band was brilliant regardless of the fact that he didn't have the same musical abilities as the rest of us. He was a powerhouse, simply because of his charisma on stage. He was the guy who looked like James Dean. He was smaller in stature than the rest of us, but stature didn't come into it. His contribution on stage was great. And he gave one hundred percent of what he could give. You couldn't take that away from him.

As the story goes, Stu fell very much in love with a darling girl in Germany called Astrid Kirschner. It was basically love at first sight. Before that, Stu wouldn't sing to anyone in the audience. He wouldn't even sing. But he made it a point, that whenever Astrid was in the audience, he would sing Elvis Presley's "Love Me Tender" to her. That was around the time that Paul was playing bass.

Now, typical Beatles, we used to take the holy mick out of

him, simply because there was this guy crooning "Love Me Tender" to his beloved in the audience. The remainder, us four Beatles, would be trying to put off his singing. He was trying to concentrate, and get his love ballad over to Astrid. It was something that we laughed at, but we saw he was sincere.

What happened this particular night, was that we were playing the Top Ten Club. As was normal, Paul came up to play bass, and again, Astrid was in the audience. Paul said something that went a little bit too over the top, and possibly, Stu was feeling a little bit down that night. But for some reason, Stu just turned around and he clobbered Paul. Imagine that, the smallest person in the band belting Paul, who was just about the tallest. He leveled him, knocked him back on the stage up against the piano. We were thinking, "What the hell has gotten into Stu?"

We split them up, and we could tell that Stu was absolutely livid. But we managed to placate him, and got things calmed down. That was the only time there was any fisticuffs between Stu and Paul.

Pete, tell us your impressions of Brian Epstein.

When he first approached us, we knew him, because he owned NEMS [North End Music Store], the record shop. He was very clean-cut and walked around in a suit all the time, which is something we never did. We never even thought of it.

As a person, he was very soft-spoken, very rarely lost his temper, even though there was the odd occasion when we broke his tolerance. But when we first met him, we knew that he was quite well-off, a businessman. He made it quite clear to us. He said, "Look, I'm interested in managing you. I've never managed a group before, but I'm prepared to have a go at it."

After we talked it over, we agreed that Brian would manage us. And for a while, his main aim was to try and be accepted by the Beatles—he still felt an outsider. The funny thing was, as he was converting us from leathers to suits, he was changing from suits to leathers, just to become one of the boys.

But again, a person who did an awful lot, initially. He was the guy who attempted to land us a recording contract with a major English label. We had recorded for Polydor in Germany. It took him a long time, but then there was that fateful day when EMI said, "Yes!"

And then you were summoned back to Liverpool by a telegram from Brian telling you about that audition. Unfortunately, this is where it got hard for you. Tell us about what happened in the end.

As a graphic description, I was called into Brian Epstein's office. I could tell that he was very apprehensive. See, prior to Brian, I had handled all the business for the group. So for me to be called into his office wasn't out of the ordinary. He'd call me in to discuss business matters in general or to get advice about a particular engagement. So this was no forewarning as to what was going to happen.

But this particular day, he was apprehensive. He talked around the subject for a while, but then he had to come out with it.

He said, "Pete, I've got some bad news. The boys want you out and Ringo in." That was my first warning of the dismissal.

It was cut-and-dried beforehand. Ringo had already agreed to join the band, and I was just completely devastated. I had been with the band for two years. We got the recording contract and were on the verge of releasing "Love Me Do," and I had been through the hard times. That was the fateful day, and I was just completely devastated.

But I was fortunate to know them before they got to be the Beatles.

Do you still live in Liverpool?

I'm still in Liverpool, Scott. I was born in India, but I came over at the end of the war. And since 1945, Liverpool's been my home. I still like the place. My friends are still there. What more can I say about it?

Well, you look amazingly well; you're taking care of yourself—

Thanks. I suppose it's contentment, a good, happy lifestyle. I'm enjoying myself. I'm not a nondrinker or a nonsmoker. I'm not a recluse. I enjoy life, and if this is the result, fine!

BRIAN
WILSON

The Beatles hit the music business so hard that it was kind of a weak feeling. I love the Beatles; I've always loved them. The Beatles and the Stones were a shot in the arm to the whole music industry. I put high stakes on the Beach Boys and figured that the Beatles were a bit of a threat to steal some attention away from us, but I figured it wasn't the end of the world. It's never the end of the world. [When I heard them] I got this impulsive feeling that you get when you hear something great on the radio like, "I didn't do that!" It was that competitive feeling. When I heard *Rubber Soul*, I said, "I have to top that." Then I did *Pet Sounds* and McCartney said, "I'll top that with *Sgt. Pepper*."

PHIL COLLINS

PHIL
COLLINS

*"I admire someone like George Martin
who, on four tracks—we have forty-
eight!—made some of the most marvelous
music and music that you still couldn't
actually get to sound that good today."*

•

Phil Collins was a British child star when he
appeared as an extra in the Beatles' first film,
the semidocumentary *A Hard Day's Night*.

While he enjoyed success as an actor in
his youth, and more recently on the big
screen in *Buster*, Phil is first and foremost a
musician. A noted session drummer in the
late sixties, Phil joined Genesis in 1970. Following the departure of lead vocalist Peter
Gabriel four years later, Phil became the
band's front man and guided Genesis from
cult stardom to tremendous commercial success. Phil has also scored big on the solo
front, consistently landing his efforts on the
top of the charts worldwide.

*Phil, let's go back to some roots. Some historians say that rock 'n' roll
started with Bill Haley's "Rock Around the Clock," which was released
in 1954. It didn't do much then, but the following year, it was included in the film* Blackboard Jungle *and, of course, went on to sell
millions of copies. And you, as a young tyke back in the old days,
probably had some sort of influence in there somewhere, didn't you?*

My brother and sister, who are marginally older than me, were listening to Radio Luxembourg which is the station we had for that kind of music over here. And I remember hearing things like "Rock Around the Clock" on the radio, and I remember *Blackboard Jungle* when it came out.

In fact, there was a cartoonist in England who, every day in the newspapers, would draw cartoons on the topical events of the day. And it was always Teddy Boys ripping seats up at cinemas after having seen *Blackboard Jungle*.

So I have recollections of that. But by the time I had started listening to music, it was people like the Shadows, the British version of the Ventures. And since it was the early sixties, it also was the Beatles.

What prompted you to pick up an instrument along the way?

Well, actually, my uncles made me a drum kit with bits and pieces of triangles, drums, tambourines, and things. They made it so that it could fit into a suitcase and then be erected into a drum kit. Then I started playing along in my Mom and Dad's living room along with television shows, variety shows.

I don't know why I took to that more than anything else, but it developed from there into getting rid of that and buying a proper drum kit. And all this was happening around the time of the Liverpool thing; you know, Gerry and the Pacemakers, Billy J. Kramer, and the Beatles.

Also at that time, while a teenager, I was going to dramatic school because I was doing some acting. So it was a natural thing to do, just keep playing music.

Were you into Motown?

Oh, Motown and the Beatles were the two big things in my teenage upbringing. Because, when I was in bands at school, we always used to play rearranged versions of stuff like "Reach Out, I'll Be There."

The early days of Motown, like up until '68 or '69, were really full of great songs. And it was a sound as well, just like George Martin had with the Beatles. You know, like there were records produced around the same time but [they] did not have the same sound as the Beatles.

And Motown bands like the Four Tops, Martha and the Vandellas, the Marvelettes, all had such a distinctive thing that I still, as a record producer, am very interested in how that was achieved. It was only through all the limitations of the studio equipment that they got what now you can't get! It's so sophisticated now that you really can't go back to basics.

I had never ever dreamed of using a computer to mix [a record] because, as far as I was concerned, *you* had to *do* it. There was a physical act of *doing* it. But now I've actually started using a computer on the mixing, and you can *listen* instead of actually doing it yourself. You do it first and put it into the computer, and the computer will remember it and do it again the next time you listen to it.

So you give your ears a chance. I've come around. If you use it in the right way, all these new technical things are great.

So I actually admire someone like George Martin who on four tracks—we have forty-eight!—made some of the most marvelous music and music that you still couldn't actually get to sound that good today.

I tried it with "Tomorrow Never Knows." I tried to get the drum sound that was there on *Revolver* and get the tambourine to sound the same, you know? But it's very hard and I admire all that stuff.

Phil, have you ever met or worked with Paul McCartney?

I've met him a few times. I bumped into him when he was doing *Tug of War*. I was producing Frida's album at Air Studios in London and we met there.

I got a phone call the first day I was supposed to start my second album. George Martin phoned me up and asked me to play drums. It was a great opportunity, and I'd love to do that, just to see how the man works.

But it was the first day of my record and I couldn't sort of blow myself out! So I had to carry on with what I was doing. So I never really worked with him.

I did a session on George Harrison's album, *All Things Must Pass*. I was about sixteen and I was in a very shabby band. I got a phone call: Would I like to go down to Abbey Road Studios and play percussion on George Harrison's new album?

Of course I leaped up in the air and got in my car and got to the studio. And there was Phil Spector, Ringo, Maurice Gibb, Badfinger, Billy Preston, George, Mal Evans, and all these notorious people I had heard of.

And I was asked to play percussion on this track and I had never played congas or anything like that before, since I was only sixteen.

Anyway, the way Phil Spector used to work would be to say, "OK, let's hear the keyboards, the drums, and the guitars play through the track." And every time he said "drums" I played, figuring he meant me. And since I'd never played congas, my hands were getting some pretty bad blisters by the time a half an hour had gone past.

And then he said, "OK. Let's hear the bass, the acoustic guitars, the guitar, and the drums." And he'd go through all these combinations from the control room. And about two and a half hours later Phil [Spector] says, "Right. Congas, you play this time!" My hands were almost bleeding by this time and he hadn't been actually listening to me at all. I had passed my peak by that point!

Anyway, having said all that, I went out and bought the album when it came out thinking that my name was going to be there. You know, "Eric Clapton," "Gary Brooker," "Klaus Voorman," "PHIL COLLINS!"—and I wasn't on it. It was a big disappointment to me.

Later, in 1982, I met George Harrison when I was doing a Gary Brooker album and I mentioned it to him. He did remember that I'd done it, but it was a big moment for me but not for him. That's one of my favorite stories to tell.

While we were doing the Brooker album at the Genesis studios, he [Gary] said, "Why don't we ask George to play some guitar?" And apparently, when Gary rang George up, he was so "over the moon" that someone had asked him to play guitar that he ran upstairs, changed all of his strings, and had to practice. He hadn't played in years.

He turned up with these two priceless guitars stuck in one case with gaffers tape around it. He didn't play much because nobody ever asked him. Now he's more involved with films; you know, he does all the Monty Python stuff.

KEN
TOWNSEND

*"In the beginning, their sessions ran on
specified three-hour periods. When they
became more famous, and were selling a
lot of records, they began using the studio
as more of a workshop."*

•

A success story in his own right, Ken Town-
send started as a tape engineer at Abbey
Road studios in the mid-fifties and is now
general manager of that venerable recording
facility.

Ken was the man George Martin asked to
assist him in recording the Beatles' first audition tape. He has been a part of Beatle history from the outset and has a grand scope of
how Abbey Road has figured in the band's
career.

His story is important not only for its
content, but for also understanding the devo-
tion of the many hard-working and talented
individuals who helped the Beatles create
magic.

*Do you still see the effects of the Beatles' presence here at Abbey Road
studios today?*

We do, actually. Abbey Road is quite a center for Beatles fans
who come from abroad. Most of them look at the zebra crossing as
a highlight. They get photographed crossing the zebra with their

shoes and socks off. They could be Japanese, American, what have you.

You've also probably noticed on the wall outside, the graffiti, as we call it over here.

Abbey Road studios was around for a long time before the Beatles made it famous. Could you give us a little background on the studio, pre-Beatles?

Abbey Road studios is one of the oldest studios in the world. It was actually opened on November 12, 1931. The official opening was [famous British composer] Elgar conducting *Pomp and Circumstance*. There was actually film documenting that, which has been on television quite a few times.

On June 6, 1962, George Martin asked you to help him record this new group from Liverpool. Is that how it went?

ABBEY ROAD STUDIOS, LONDON.
THE MOST FAMOUS RECORDING
STUDIO IN THE WORLD.

That's right. The sixth of June, '62 was a pretty famous day. As a matter of fact, it was D-Day in Europe, so it was D-Day for EMI as well.

But the fact was, George Martin was head of the Parlophone label and George had not been recording groups. It may sound silly now, but in those days each label had one group: Cliff Richard and the Shadows were on Columbia, Johnny Kidd and the Pirates were on HMV. Our other label was Parlophone, and there was no group on that label.

So this group called the Beatles, who George had heard a tape of, came along for an audition from six o'clock to eight o'clock in the evening on June 6, 1962. I had been working with George up in the Cambridge Arts Theatre recording [British comedy group] Beyond the Fringe the previous week, and he mentioned that this group was coming along.

You invented a machine called the artificial double tracking system, or ADT. That enabled you to lay one vocal on top of itself, which turned out to be a staple of the Beatles' sound. Explain how you came up with it.

Artificial double tracking was one of those mad ideas that I get every now and again.

I was driving home one night, after a Beatles session, in which we had spent all night double-tracking voices. It seemed to me to be a bit of a waste of time.

So I thought of this idea of electronically putting a voice on again. The following morning I came in and fixed up these bits of equipment and tried it on a [EMI artist] Cilla Black tape. And, in actual fact, it sounded quite effective. The following night, we used it.

I understand that Paul McCartney phoned you when he was recording Ram *to find out how you did that. Is that correct?*

Yes, he phoned me to say that they couldn't work out how to do ADT and asked me to explain it on the phone to him. I tried to, but they couldn't succeed.

We did it on the mixing board, not on pure recording. The way was to send off the J-37, the four track machine that we used in those days. It had a sync head and a replay head. You could take off either channel and it would be delayed about one-fifth of a second.

I thought that if we could take off the first one, pass it through something else, and put it back on again, we could actually have it in close proximity to the first one. And that was how it worked. Now of course that system is used electronically in most studios throughout the world.

Before the Beatles got to Abbey Road, things were pretty normal. You had specific recording periods that were treated like timed appointments. But when they were working here, especially later, they sort of moved right in. That changed life around here a lot, didn't it?

Yes, before the Beatles came along, we had sessions booked for specific times. Adam Faith was probably the first one to record at night. We did 12:00 A.M. to 3:00 A.M. sessions and 12:00 A.M. to 4:00 A.M. sessions with him probably two or three years before the Beatles came along.

In the beginning, their sessions ran on specified three-hour periods. When they became more famous, and were selling a lot of records, they began using the studio as more of a workshop.

They were really the first people, at least in my mind, to use studio time in what we now call open-ended.

I understand for the Sgt. Pepper *project you linked two four-track machines together. Is that true?*

That was a particular occasion on "A Day in the Life," where George [Martin] wanted to double the orchestra several times. We were only using four-track and he said, "Can't you lock these machines together in some way, Ken?"

So what I did was to put a fifteen-cycle tone on the first machine, and feed that to the second machine, and make that drive the second machine. So, in actual fact, we basically had seven tracks. That worked fine when we did it.

The problem came when we tried to mix it. Although it was fine on recording, locking the two machines together was very difficult. Again, that sort of technology now is commonplace. If you go into Studio One today, you'll find about two twenty-four tracks locked together. It's all very commonplace today, but I believe that was the first time it was done.

Would you explain the relationship between EMI and Abbey Road studios. Is it an exclusive relationship?

Well, the situation basically is that Thorn is the whole company and EMI is one of the companies within the Thorn group.

EMI Music is a worldwide company, each individual country has it's own record company. In America, it's Capitol. Here in England it's EMI Records. EMI Records is the record company of England; we have a factory, a distribution center, marketing, and a studio. That studio is Abbey Road. So we are part of EMI Records, which is part of EMI Music, which is part of Thorn.

So it is not exclusively an EMI artist recording studio.

Right. We're a profit center in our own right. We record for anybody. Sixty percent of all the work we do now is for third parties.

I read that there was an auction here a while ago. I think you called it The Sale of the Century. Tell me about it.

I think it was in 1981. A friend of mine wanted to have a sale of equipment, so I suggested we have it at Abbey Road and we auction off things as well.

It got a bit out of hand because the Beatles started getting mentioned. We weren't originally auctioning any Beatles material off.

But there were hundreds of people gathered out front thinking that we were auctioning off Beatles material, when in fact we were selling tape machines and mixing consoles.

What I did do was, I had in my drawer a couple of rolls of toilet paper that John or Paul had given me. They very rarely complained, but the one time they did, they said the toilet paper was too shiny and it had "EMI LTD" imprinted on it.

So we auctioned this and fetched one hundred twenty pounds, which we gave to a deaf school.

You were quoted as saying that you don't think any one studio could dominate like Abbey Road did in the sixties. Do you still believe that?

I believe that even more now because I'm on the executive of all the studios in this country. And whereas when Abbey Road was dominating, there were no more than seven or eight studios in this country, now we have well over two hundred twenty-four-track studios of real professional standards. The whole industry has gotten inefficient to the point that it takes now six or nine months to make an album sometimes. Before, we would chew out an album in two or three weeks. You could be doing a lot in one studio.

So no studio really has the physical capabilities of putting out as many hits as we did in those days. There will be the "in" studio, it changes every year. They will have a higher ratio of hits than the others, but no studio will dominate with one, two, three, four shots in a row the way that Abbey Road did.

TOMMY
JAMES

"They really did take us on a 'Magical Mystery Tour,' didn't they? They really took us on a trip that can never happen again."

•

Tommy James has had a hand in selling an estimated thirty million records over the course of his career as a solo artist and as the leader of that landmark sixties band, Tommy James and the Shondells.

A master of pop and production, Tommy first hit the top of the charts back in 1966 and eventually placed seven singles in the Top Ten before the end of the decade.

Tommy also exhibited a flair for adaptation, moving with ease from pop tunes like "I Think We're Alone Now" and rockers like "Mony Mony" to the more experimental and psychedelic "Crimson and Clover." His recording success influenced even the Beatles at the time.

Tommy, what were your early impressions of the Beatles and how did they influence you?

I think the Beatles had an influence on everybody coming up in the sixties. They changed everything; the way we dressed, the way we wore our hair, the way we thought, the way we approached music.

They were the first group who made their own records. Even though George Martin produced them, they basically produced their own records. They were totally self-contained, and that had never happened before. Buddy Holly came close but, up until that time, no group had ever been as self-contained as the Beatles.

It was a very good lesson for the people who were in the music business at the time. They wrote their own material; they recorded their own material; they performed their own material until it got to the point where they couldn't do it live anymore because it got so intricate and involved.

They really did take us on a "Magical Mystery Tour," didn't they? They really took us on a trip that can never happen again.

I remember seeing entire studios torn apart and put back together again because of a drum sound that the Beatles would get that American studios just couldn't get. What they did, everything they did, became state of the art. They had a tremendous influence on all of us.

Did you ever encounter them at any point?

I remember when they were just starting Apple Publishing—not Apple Records but Apple Publishing—they came to my house! Paul and John came to my apartment in New York.

"Mony Mony" had been the biggest song of the decade in England. It was bigger over there than it was here.

They had written a whole batch of songs, twelve to fourteen songs, with the idea of starting their own publishing company and having major artists do their work. The funny part was that I didn't like any of the songs that I heard. One or two were OK, but the majority were very contrived. It was like "Let's sit down and write a Tommy James record;" you could hear it all through the tape.

But anyway, now I have twelve to fourteen never-heard-before Beatles tunes at home. I was very flattered and honored that they took the time to do that.

Do you still have the tape?

Oh, yeah. I almost lost it in a flood in Jersey but I managed to save it. The funny part of that story was that when they showed up at my apartment, I wasn't home. They ended up going to my management office, which is in the same building.

TOMMY JAMES

I'm such a homebody—I had just stepped out for a few minutes and don't you know I miss Lennon and McCartney at my door!

I got a chance to meet them later of course. I got to [know] John Lennon a little bit. He was kind of a loner. He went through his own troubles in the 1970's.

You know, when the Beatles broke up, I think we all felt like we were going to a funeral. It was not just another group breaking up. These were people who, no matter what their internal problems were, changed everything about society, Western civilization. These people literally turned the world upside-down. Who else can say that? A few people maybe, but for the baby boomers, the biggest group of people ever to go through American society were totally influenced by these people.

It's unfortunate but what crushed them was that they had so much responsibility, or at least *felt* that they did, laid on their shoulders. Everything that they did, everyone wanted not only to know about but to also *do!*

When they broke up, you saw them fighting with each other and getting nasty, and all the lawyers and accountants. It got so ugly that you just had to turn your head the other way. It was a blowout.

But they had a nice run. I don't know what we expected from these people. I mean they're only human beings, you know? But they really took us on a wonderful trip. They changed everything.

Do you have any favorite Beatles songs?

To tell the truth, I didn't like the Beatles when I first heard them. I thought they were terrible.

I worked in a record store during my high school days, and I remember all the hype and publicity: "The Beatles are coming, the Beatles are coming."

Shortly after President Kennedy was killed—I remember the sequence of events, it was the next month December 1963—we started getting shipments of Beatle records at this little record store in Niles, Michigan. And I hated this stuff. "I Want to Hold Your Hand" and the flip side, "I Saw Her Standing There," I thought were some of the worst songs I ever heard. I said "What's so special about these guys?"

But the next year, *A Hard Day's Night* came out and that was it. That record flipped me out! I realized then that we were dealing with something much much bigger than an appearance on *The Ed Sullivan Show* and much bigger than all the hype.

You know, at one time, the Beatles had the Top Five on five different labels! These guys had been waiting in the wings for their turn at bat. But the ironic thing is that most people in the music business did not care for their music when it first came out. It sounded like a cross between bad Chuck Berry and terrible recordings.

The British studios back then were not state of the art. Of course that all changed quickly because of the Beatles. But all of what they called the British Invasion were, for the most part, very Doo-dah-doo-dah songs and I didn't care for them. But boy, when *A Hard Day's Night* came out, that's when I knew we were dealing with something phenomenal. I knew these guys were going to be around forever!

JULIAN LENNON

JULIAN
LENNON

"I get fan letters now from kids saying, 'I never heard of the Beatles before you sang this song.' It's like 'Whoaaa!' It's incredible. You get these little tiny kids starting to listen to Beatles stuff. It's great."

•

The offspring of John Lennon's first marriage to Cynthia Powell at the height of Beatlemania, Julian Lennon grew up in the shadow of his father's artistic genius. While a daunting prospect for most young men, Julian has established his own successful career as a singer/songwriter, in spite of the inevitable comparisons and criticism.

Julian scored big in 1984 with his first solo album, the highly praised *Vallotte*. His latest LP is the critically acclaimed *Mr. Jordan*.

We talked to Julian during his most recent U.S. concert tour.

What's the difference in touring this time around, as opposed to the first time?

Well, I guess with playing the first tour you feel the pure energy from the stage. It excited me, having that energy. I tried taking that band into the studio and getting that same feeling. And to a certain extent we did, though I feel we could have gone a bit heavier. We just pulled back a little bit.

Could you explain the title [of your second solo album] The Secret Value of Daydreaming? Is daydreaming something you do a lot of?

Yeah, well, there's a lot of spare time so to speak. You know, when you're on the road or whatever you're doing, your mind wanders a lot. It's just another way of thinking—daydreaming. Just relaxing and letting your mind go.

You're working with veteran producer Phil Ramone. What does he contribute to your sound?

Well, what he does is, if I run out of ideas or hit a brick wall, he suggests ideas. I mean, I can like them or not like them.

What I generally do is go into the next room and work out something better. Something better than what he does. There's always that bit of competition going on.

How fast was this album recorded?

Real quickly. It felt very quick. We did the actual writing in the studio, when we came off the last tour. It was about a month later, or something, so time was short to write. A lot of work was done in the studio, which I didn't particularly want to do. We were scheduled to that sort of thing so we had to. Next time around, I'm taking some time.

Were you pressured to follow up the success of the first album?

Well, I felt the second one was real good and I still think there's some great songs on there, but it could have been just a tiny bit better. I'm very proud of it. But I just think if I had more time to spend on it, I could have dealt with it better.

Is the public accepting you more now on your own terms, rather than just being John Lennon's son?

Oh yeah. Absolutely.

Your mother Cynthia is very proud of you. What was her reaction to your live show when she saw it in Los Angeles?

She generally enjoys what I do, keeps happy and in the background, and once in a while says, "Look after yourself." She's great, just like a worrying mother—a mum.

What advice has she given you dealing with fame?

None really. Just basically to look out for myself and the sharks in the business. She's seen that I haven't done too badly, so she's proud of me.

How did growing up around Beatlemania and post-Beatlemania affect your childhood? Do you recall a whole lot about it and would you call it adverse or positive?

I don't know. See, I didn't really recognize what was going on, but I knew. Obviously I had the music around me all my life, so to speak, so with that happening all around me, I tended to look elsewhere for music and influences. I heard the Beatles songs God knows how many times. I didn't need to hear them again. I'd look elsewhere for influences. My mother came up with Steely Dan and I said, "Yeah, I like that for a change." So I started listening to that.

It was great to hear "It Won't Be Long," the Beatles song that you're doing on tour. What went into that decision?

A lot of critics have said, "Well, why bring up the ghost of the Beatles, blah, blah, blah..." The only thing is, if it wasn't me doing it, it would be someone else.

I get fan letters now from kids saying "I never heard of the Beatles before you sang this song." It's like "Whoaaa!" It's incredible. You get these little tiny kids starting to listen to Beatles stuff. It's great.

Your audience is getting younger—

Yeah, that's true, especially for this album.

You're a New Yorker now. You recently moved from England, right? Has it had any influence on you?

Yep, that's true. No, it hasn't really had any influence on me. I've found it to be a good base to work from. The band hangs out there. The band are my best mates, you know. I haven't really had time to settle down or think about what I'm doing. There's still cardboard boxes full of junk around the place. There's no really settling in yet. I have to wait until the tour is finished before I do that.

You were at the Rock 'n' Roll Hall of Fame dinner when the Beatles were inducted, right?

Yeah, it was great. I wasn't actually going to go until someone dragged me along. I didn't actually know I was doing anything for that either. But it was really good.

You brought Sean out onstage in New York.

Yeah, that's true. He was standing in the wings and I thought, "C'mon, c'mon." The audience was wondering what the hell I was doing, you know—"C'mon." He didn't want to come out, but he enjoyed it.

I hear he's into newer English bands like Depeche Mode.

Yeah, he is, but I'll sort him out.

You mentioned in an interview that your father said he would float a feather to let you know that he was looking after you. Have you seen the feather?

I haven't personally, no. But my mother says she has.

ERIC
BURDON

Hamburg was a very hot scene then. The Beatles didn't begin in Liverpool, really. The Beatles were born in the streets of Hamburg. That's where they got a chance to get away from home and get totally crazy. They'd do five shows a night, [taking] pills to keep awake, [drinking] German beer to keep going—the low life, the hard life, the club life, the characters, the input, the output. That's what fuses bands together.

BILL WYMAN OF THE ROLLING
STONES

THE
ROLLING
STONES

*"They told people about us, and we got a
record deal. And then, when we were
looking for that second single, in the
autumn of 1963, they came around and
gave us that, which was a savior at the
time."*
—*Bill Wyman*

•

The first British hit the Rolling Stones ever
had was "I Wanna Be Your Man." The tune
happened to be written by two young men
named John Lennon and Paul McCartney
and it marked the beginning of a long and
curious relationship between the two camps.

The Stones' rough edges and racy compositions were in marked contrast with the
Beatles' matching suits and four-part harmonies. They were the perfect foil for the
Fab Four.

Although it was often rumored that the
two bands were rivals, they were actually
quite good friends. The Beatles printed
"Welcome Rolling Stones" on the cover of
Sgt. Pepper and the Stones repaid the favor
by including a picture of John, Paul, George,
and Ringo on their subsequent album, *Their
Satanic Majesties Request*. They often showed
up in each other's studios and, in one notable

'67 session, Brian Jones played alto saxophone on "You Know My Name (Look Up the Number)." In his recent book of sketches, entitled *The Works*, Ron Wood includes a haunting portrait of John Lennon.

We spoke to Rolling Stones' bassist and band historian Bill Wyman, and guitarist Ron Wood.

BILL WYMAN

The Stones and the Beatles share much history. One of the things I've noticed about the Stones in the recent years is that Mick Jagger and Keith Richards have written more separately than together. This is something we saw happen to the Beatles later in their careers.

Oh, they work much more separately—that's the problem. You know they used to write together. Now Keith writes songs on his own and Mick writes songs on his own. And sometimes one doesn't like the other's song. It's obviously better the way it was, close collaboration, but you do get more extreme and variety in the material.

Whereas some kids are growing up getting to know George Harrison as a solo artist, or Paul McCartney as a former member of Wings, the Stones have experienced the same thing, only from a different perspective.

What's it like for you to run into fans who weren't around for your early albums?

I know two kids outside at one of the shows, outside one of the places, they grabbed hold of me and said, "It's great to meet you. We've been fans of the Stones since way back. Way, way back. We were early Stones fans." And they were only in their early twenties. So I said, "How far back?" And they said, "Ah, all the way back to "Miss You" [from *Some Girls* in 1978.] And thinking about it, that was a long way back.

In their short time together, and especially as live performers, the Beatles went from the cellar that was the Cavern Club to the newly minted Shea Stadium—from five hundred fans to fifty-five thousand. The Stones, by virtue of their longevity, have experienced that and back again. What's your preference when it comes to the size of the shows?

They're all the same. The only problem [is] the indoor ones are nice to play, but they're a real hassle to get in and out of, to keep organized. There are so many problems when you try to get a small gig together. We'd love to do little clubs, but we had to keep canceling them because the word got out before it should have, so we couldn't do it.

Bill, you're the Stones' resident historian and scribe, with a few books in the works. Aren't you working on one that concerns the work of former Beatle and Stones collaborator, Michael Cooper?

Yeah, one is on Michael Cooper, the photographer who did the *Satanic Majesties* cover, the three dimensional cover, and who also did the *Sgt. Pepper* cover for the Beatles, along with many other things. He died in 1974. His son and assistant came to me last year and asked me if I could help them put it together, because I'm in good contact with a lot of businessmen. So we've been working on that, his whole life story in photos, with comments from various people.

When the Rolling Stones met the Beatles for the first time, not only was it a significant meeting of the two most influential bands of the first twenty years of rock 'n' roll, it was a heady meeting of two very talented groups of men. It happened at an early Stones gig, didn't it?

When we were at the Station Hotel, the Beatles came down. We were playing one day, a Sunday, and it was February of '63. They had a couple of hit records and we hadn't even made a record yet.

So we were just playing there, and all of a sudden we looked up. We saw four, sort of dark silhouetted guys standing in front of the stage. They had black leather overcoats and hair that was sort of—actually, we had the longer hair. But they were like four stereotyped guys, you know? They all looked exactly the same. So we kind of casually looked, and the crowd had their shirts off, up on tables—that's the way it was at this place. We said, "Shit, that's the Beatles."

Didn't that meeting directly lead to your first hit, "I Wanna Be Your Man"?

We had a chat with them afterwards; they all hung around. And then they came back to the flat in Chelsea and we stayed up all night rapping. Then they invited us to this show they had to do in London, so we all went there and we all became really good mates. And we were always seeing each other then. They told people about us and we got a record deal. And then when we were looking for that second single, in the autumn of 1963, they came around and gave us that, which was a savior at the time.

RON WOOD

Ronnie, when you were in one of your earlier bands, did you cover Beatle songs and other great songs of the time?

We used to do a lot of Motown stuff, Eddie Holland, Marvin Gaye, as well as a lot of Stones and Beatles covers. We'd also do Howlin' Wolf and Muddy Waters.

Didn't you also work with George Harrison on Dark Horse? *I understand that you were on "Ding Dong" and "Far East Man." Is that right?*

I was very close with George for a period. We spent a long time together at Friar Park in Henley and up at my house in Richmond Hill.

I remember we did thirteen hours solid on those vocals ["Ding Dong" and "Far East Man"] because he was such a perfectionist.

Do you remember hearing the Beatles early in their career?

Yeah, they used to have a radio show every Friday where they played live and spoke and I'd never miss an episode. In fact, whoever has the rights to those radio shows should dig them up. They're incredible.

Woody, can you name any favorite Beatles songs?

I've got so many. Let me try and get one. Apart from the obvious like "Strawberry Fields," "I Want to Hold Your Hand" is one I used to like a lot. And what was the one with the harmonium? "We Can Work It Out!" Ahh, I loved that one.

PAUL AND LINDA McCARTNEY

PAUL
McCARTNEY

*"I thought, 'Oh God, I don't know what's
going to happen here!' But I really got
into it. I must do it for a living
sometime!"*

•

One of the world's most consistent and significant musical talents, Paul McCartney stands alone in his extraordinary achievements and is included in the *Guinness Book of World Records* as the most honored man in music.

A prolific songwriter and crafty instrumentalist, Paul thrived on his tumultuous relationship with John Lennon, creating some of the most enduring and innovative music of our time.

Paul was often referred to as the cute Beatle and the favorite Beatle. His refined manners and sunny personality made him a darling of the press and the heartthrob of millions of frantic teenage girls.

Yet, since the dissolution of the Beatles, Paul has continued to enjoy incredible commercial success and legions of new fans through his work with Wings and as a solo performer.

Paul has also established himself as a devoted family man and has included his wife Linda in most of his post-Beatle musical endeavors.

Scott Muni first met Paul at the height of Beatlemania and has talked with him frequently over the years. The following interview coincided with Paul's 1984 press tour for his movie, *Give My Regards to Broad Street.*

There was something in print, and I can't remember where I read it, that your great idol was Fred Astaire. Is that true?

Oh, I really love him. I mean, I was raised on all those films. He's just incredible, all that dancing! I love his voice too!

Give My Regards? *Is that your way of saying that that's what you want to do, sing and dance?*

It's harking back to "Give My Regards to Broadway." In actual fact, there's a railway station in the movie called Broad Street. So it's actually just a joke. I don't know if it's really me harking back, but I *do* love all that stuff, Cole Porter, Gershwin, and that style of writer. They're very clever writers.

I got to see the movie already and the locations were like going back to London again. I don't know how many locations you used, but you must have been really busy.

Yeah, we got around!

How come you didn't spend more time in that scene on the street? You were a regular street singer playing for whatever money people would put in your case. I wanted to see how much money you'd collect!

Well, I was out there for quite a while, but you know films. You could have an hour's footage and the man says, "We're just going to cut it down to a minute." That's his job. He's the director, and if he feels that works best, you can't just say, "I want the whole fifty minutes in." But I was out there for a while.

What are the street singers called in London?

We call them buskers.

When you actually filmed that, how many people came up and asked for a Paul McCartney autograph?

Nobody actually asked for an autograph but there were one or two people who wandered up and looked a bit funny at me. You know, like "Aren't you—Paul McCartney?" I said, "Are you kidding?—*[Mock sings]* Yesterday, jinga jinga, all my troubles seemed so far away, jing jinga." You know, I was doing this ridiculous version of "Yesterday."

It was great, actually. I really enjoyed doing that. If what you do is play a guitar, then the most basic form of that is to be on the street as a busker. It's real live music and you're actually there, nose to nose with your audience.

It was a bit scary at first. I thought, "Oh God, I don't know what's going to happen here!" But I really got into it. I must do it for a living sometime!

[Laughing.] Did you make any money?

I *did* make money! There were some people out there, like this great old Scottish fellow, out on a binge, who gave me all his change.

But the joke was, I said to the assistant director on the film, "Now what's going to happen here is that I'm going to make some money, so whatever happens, this money has got to go to charity. I know somebody's going to say 'Wouldn't you just know it, he's so stingy, he took the money.'" I said, "I'm going to get nailed for this!"

So it went to charity, and sure enough, on the radio the next day there was a woman saying, "Wouldn't you just know it, he took the money." You can't win.

You were also quoted as saying that the movie contains your favorite song, "Here, There and Everywhere." Is that indeed your favorite?

It's difficult to choose any favorite, you know? It's one of my favorites. You kind of look at your songs and figure which are the ones that are the best constructed. . . .

I think "Yesterday," if it wasn't as successful, would be my favorite. But you get that thing, when something's just *so* successful, people [performers] often just don't want to do THE BIG ONE, the one everyone wants them to do. They shy away from that. So yeah, "Here, There and Everywhere," with "Yesterday" a close second.

Is that the original title, "Yesterday"?

No, it was originally called, as *you* know, "Scrambled Eggs." It fits: [Sings] "Scrambled eggs, oh, my baby, how I love your legs."

You know, if you don't have lyrics yet and you want to play someone a song, you have to kind of say something.

"Michelle" was a similar kind of thing. I used to play it at parties, these really arty, bohemian parties. We used to have them and we'd be hanging out and being very far out. So there'd always be a guy in the corner with a guitar.

So I used to pretend I was French. *[Sings in an exaggerated Maurice Chevalier style]* "Michelle, my belle, jou jou jou—" And nobody knew the difference. But that later got developed into a song.

Now in the movie, Ringo got a pretty good-sized part. He's there most of the time, both as a musician and an actor, along with his wife, Barbara Bach. When you were putting this together, did you think about contacting George?

No, I didn't actually. The truth of the matter was that George was out of the country for that year. He wasn't in England. And anyway, to tell you the truth, I know George wouldn't have wanted to do it. George doesn't really have any aspirations in acting, I don't think. He never did in the old movies. He was the least keen of us to do some acting. Ringo was always the most keen, and I'm not sure whether John and I was second, but George was always the least keen. He just didn't like it. He thought it was daft.

So I'm sure if I asked him, if he would have liked to have been in it, the answer would have been "No thanks." It's not like I excluded him on purpose because I hate him or anything. It's just that I knew he would not have done it and he was out of the country.

I was in London when you were filming. We did a couple of live shows, but I couldn't get a hold of you. But in my attempts to get George, I was told pretty much that he was retired. That was one of the words used. He wasn't doing any interviews, recording, or doing anything involved with music at all.

I got a feeling a little while ago that he was really fed up with the music business. And listen, when that happens, what are you going to do? Pretend that you still love it?

Do you think it had anything to do with John's death?

I think that probably had something to do with it. But George doesn't really like doing interviews. I mean, sometimes it can be a pressure. If you want to be out, playing in the park, and instead you've got to sit and do an interview. . . .

And George was always a little bit more forthright than the rest of us. He'd just say, "I don't want to do it." And there are people who just feel that way.

For instance, Michael Jackson doesn't like doing interviews. [It] doesn't mean he's a recluse. I asked Michael, "Why?" and he said he just wasn't comfortable.

So in truth, I think he has just gotten disenchanted with the whole idea, and I know why it was too. He's kind of fighting to get radio play with some of his stuff and he probably thinks, "Ah, the hell with it, why bother?"

He's not some sort of crazy recluse who lives up in some place and guards himself from the world. He's got a lot of friends and amongst those friends he's very gregarious, gets about and stuff. He likes gardening, I'm told. And you can't help it. If that's what his bag is, then you've got to allow him that. You can't say, "Listen George, you're a musician. You shall not garden."

The Everly Brothers have a new song called "On the Wings of a Night-ingale," and you wrote it for them, didn't you?

Oh yeah, for the Evs. Dave Edmunds rang me up, see we'd worked together on the film. He said, "I've been asked to produce the Everlys." They're his idols, and mine too. You know when we were kids that's what it was, the Everlys' "Dream." Them and Ricky Nelson, and it was just swoon-time!

So I've always loved them and, in fact, a lot of us people who were in groups would do like, well, I'd be Phil and John would be Don.

You know, you just took a character each and we'd do all the

Everly stuff. We did "Bye Bye Love" and "Cathy's Clown," a lot of their stuff. Even some of the B Sides like "So Sad to See Good Love Go Bad," so I really loved them.

A lot of people of our generation really have a soft place in their hearts for them. And it was very sad when they broke up. No one could understand it, you know? It's the brother thing. You don't understand it, but you *understand* it.

So when we heard that they were getting together again, I think everyone was pretty pleased. So Dave rung me up and said, "Can you come up with a song? I've asked a bunch of people." So I said, "Give me a week and I'll see if I can come up with something." I wanted to do it like mad because I love them, but I didn't want to do anything bum. I didn't want to give them anything that didn't work.

So after a few days I came up with the idea to do the "Nightingale" thing. So I made the demo, sang it myself, and I thought, "This sounds like an Everly track."

Did you do two voices like the Everly Brothers had?

Sure, this time I was both! *[Laughing]*

There's another project that you're involved with, that I know comes straight from your heart, and that's the Buddy Holly week you organize every year. Tell us about that.

What happens every year is, a couple of months before the anniversary, we get our heads together and say, "OK, what are we going to do this year?" And we always manage to come up with something.

We had a dance contest a couple of years ago. And one thing that happened through that dance contest was great actually.

Through something like just wanting to keep Buddy's music alive—because I publish it too which is also part of the reason obviously—but one of the kids who entered this dance contest was an unemployed guy and he won. So he got to go to Dallas and ended up marrying the partner he had. So it was a real life romance thing where they've become dancers and they're also in the movie now!

So it's like a real success story. And if you do that sort of thing, while trying to keep Buddy's beautiful music alive, well, that'll do me!

How about Wings? Is there a tour upcoming or anything with the band? Will that ever happen again?

No, I think the Wings lineup is finished. I suppose there's a chance that we might put a new lineup of Wings together. But as far as I'm concerned, we're finished with that period. So in other words, it might not be a Wings tour, but it might be something else.

See, doing the movie, we did a lot of live playing to all the people in the ballroom or all the people on the set and there was often quite a big crowd around. It was almost like a concert and I think I re-discovered that I really like playing to people. Just like that busking thing, I mean, talk about nose to nose.

So I quite fancy doing it but it's really just a question of getting some time.

OK, I have a quickie for you: This date, October 16, fifteen years ago, it was announced that you were no longer dead! You turned up and said, "I am alive, and here I am!"

And I still am! An anniversary of being alive! That's great.

JIMMY PAGE (with Led Zeppelin)

JIMMY PAGE

"If it hadn't been for the Beatles, there wouldn't be anyone like us around . . . the sort of band where there are musician writers."

•

Jimmy Page was already one of England's hottest session guitarists when he joined the Yardbirds in 1966. When that seminal rock act fell apart two years later, Page united Robert Plant, John Paul Jones, and John Bonham to form the perfect replacement, Led Zeppelin.

Led Zeppelin's impact on a generation cannot be measured simply by record sales and sold-out shows. Like the Beatles, Led Zeppelin also spawned countless copycat acts. Even today, MTV and record charts alike are overflowing with bands cast in the image of the maestros of metal mayhem.

But Led Zeppelin also demonstrated a softer, acoustic side seldom seen in hard rock bands. And as with Lennon and McCartney, their wide range of expression is clearly the result of an incredible chemistry that existed between dynamic lead singer, Robert Plant, and the equally commanding presence of guitar wizard, Jimmy Page.

Jimmy Page is a guitar hero of legendary proportion. Now a solo artist, Pagey continues to influence the licks of many an aspiring rock guitarist. Not surprisingly, he counts the Beatles among his own most significant influences.

What were your impressions of the Beatles when they first came out?

I didn't really like the Beatles' first records at all. Because there was this big thing, this unfortunate sort of media hype. And when they came down to London they did this God-awful place called Leyton Baths. They just had "Love Me Do" out, although they did play "Please Please Me." It was weird, the reaction. It didn't really sort of go the way it would have if it was another six months later. Nobody really mentioned them, but they weren't—there was too much of this thing that preceded them.

But by the time their other songs came out— They are the group, as far as I can see it, that actually progressed and matured within their music in that space of time. There is no other that you can really put your finger on apart from them.

The period I liked best is the "Magical Mystery Tour," "Blue Jay Way," and that sort of stuff. They were really going for something in those days. For a band to improve that far, I can't really think of any other [that's done it].

But they opened the door for all of us as singer/songwriters because prior to that it was a different situation. It opened up the door for all the writing groups and it gave them hope. People who thought they could never write a song, they then thought "Oh, I'll have a go."

If it hadn't been for the Beatles, there wouldn't be anyone like us around—the sort of band where there are musician/writers.

If you were in a reasonable band in your part of England, you'd go down to, let's say, EMI or Decca for an audition. And if you happen to pass, the staff producer would take you on. But it was usually his best friend who wrote the songs.

Consequently, even if there had been a brilliant writer in the band, or whatever, it would not have materialized, because the producer's friend was writing the songs. With the advent of the Beatles, plus Dylan, it gave everyone the incentive to try to write something.

Did you ever personally spend time with any of them?

I met Ringo once, sort of, at a party. I met McCartney a few times, and I met George on a few occasions.

I'd like to have met John Lennon. I really would like to have met him. I would have liked to have been in a group of people and just hear him talk. I would have liked just to feel his presence.

They are the only group I can think of in rock 'n' roll history that improved to such heights from their early days. It was incredible the way they kept improving. It was like an avalanche, and it was a short time that they were together.

I don't see how anybody could not have been touched by something that they did, even if they were cynical. From all the songs they did, from their beginnings right up through the end, there's no way that you could not have been touched by that.

W A R R E N
Z E V O N

What I can say about the Beatles, very simply, is that I play rock and roll because of them. . . . The Beatles also did something that parallels the development of classical music, in my mind. Everything was a development of the thing that came before it. Everything was innovative. There was no idea or fear that something was too far out. Everything new they did was supposed to challenge you. . . . The Beatles continued to be new as long as they were the Beatles.

DONOVAN

DONOVAN

*"John was so funny and so direct that to
break the silence he went up to the
Maharishi, who was sitting cross-legged
on the floor, patted him on the head and
said, 'There's a good little guru.' "*

•

Like a modern day minstrel, Scottish-born
singer/songwriter Donovan Leitch took his
cue from Bob Dylan but chose to flavor his
own folk tunes with a decidedly psychedelic
air. As a result, Donovan captured on vinyl
the bohemian, drug-inspired Carnaby Street
scene so prevalent in London in the mid-sixties.

Donovan soon became part of the Beatles' select inner circle, attending their
recording sessions and sharing an interest in
meditation and the teachings of Maharishi
Mahesh Yogi.

When did you first meet the Beatles and what were your impressions?

My first meeting was when Bob Dylan had just got done playing two shows in London. He was staying at the Savoy and I went
to visit him. His roadie brought me in and said that Dylan was in
the back, watching TV.

It was very quiet; nobody was around and we arrived back at
this tiny little room on the end of the suite. It was dark, with just a
television on, and there was ice skating championships on from
Austria.

I sat on the floor, Bobby was on a chair, and we didn't say anything to each other like "Hello," because the best thing for artists to say to one another is nothing—everyone is always asking questions—so we never ask each other anything.

Anyway, as my eyes became acclimated, I realized that there were other people in the room sitting on the sofa. My eyes became accustomed, and there was John, Paul, George, and Ringo. So our first meeting, we never said anything.

I was very impressed because I was about three years younger than they were. Then as they got tired or were taking a break, we all got up and we were formally introduced. Actually, informally introduced.

George said later that I was too impressed by them because I was younger and thought I wasn't as good as the Beatles. He also said that I was, and am, fully a part of their music. And George gave me a lift in his car and that's how I met the Beatles.

You contributed lyrics to the song "Yellow Submarine." Reconstruct that for us.

Paul came around to my apartment and parked his Aston Martin in the middle of the road with the doors open and the radio blaring. And he walked away from the car.

He came up to the apartment and was playing me "Eleanor Rigby" with different lyrics, and he also said he had another song that was missing a verse. It was a very small part, and I just went into the other room and put together "Sky of blue, sea of green."

They had always asked other people for help with a line or two, so I helped with that line. He knew that I was into kids' songs, and he knew I could help. I'm sure he could have written the line himself, but I suppose he wanted someone to add a line, and I added a line.

But more importantly, in India, I introduced John Lennon to a finger-picking style that I had learned with great difficulty. There were only three folk singers in England who played this style at the time, and any time I tried to learn it from them, they refused to play it, which I thought was terrible. But I learned it from this one guy one day and I taught it to John and he taught it to George.

When John learned a new guitar style, he usually wrote a new song. With this style he wrote "Julia" and "Dear Prudence." That finger style that John plays on *The White Album* is the one that I taught him. Just as I learned many things from the Beatles about song formation, George definitely picked up the style that I taught to John. And a finger style that they had not known before led to some new songs.

Didn't George also contribute some lyrics to your song "Hurdy Gurdy Man"?

Yeah, in India, George wrote the verse, "When truth gets buried deep beneath a thousand years of sleep, time demands a turnaround and once again the truth is found."

It was a beautiful verse and George was upset later because I didn't use it. I said that singles used to be three minutes long and by the time that long solo was played, I wanted to add George's verse, but Mickie [producer Mickie Most] said, "That's it."

So we just served the song rather than add the verse. But it was a wonderful verse and it was right in keeping. So George wrote that verse.

There is a recording going around of Paul playing "Blackbird" with you in the background. Could you explain what that is all about?

It was around his house at St. John's Wood or Applewood in one of the back rooms. It was bootlegged. I was hanging around Paul at the time and we were just singing and picking stuff like that. Yeah, that's where that came from. It was just an evening, one night, and we were just playing.

Did you attend any Beatles recording sessions?

Yes—*Sgt. Pepper.* I visited because those sessions were actually huge parties [with] incredible amounts of people. Of course the great orchestra session—I forget the name of the track—but a couple of the other tracks, I visited as well.

What was the environment like at these sessions?

Well, it was like a Stones session, except not quite so much of a party. It was like a concert really. Everybody was there, there were five or six cameras, all the orchestra had suits and tails. It was a huge party and an amazing session.

What was the whole India experience like?

It was great to be there, because we were all touring at the time, but we had these few weeks together. The press were outside, but inside the compound it was great. I got a chance to learn and play and hang out with musicians that I was very impressed by.

We all were able to lay back and relax. Paul Horn, the great flute player, was there. We played music and George experimented with Indian instruments that were brought in. We sat around and played and picked and learned meditation.

But for me it was a chance to meet the Beatles on a level far away from pop music and what we were all involved in. It was quite a unique experience to be able to shut ourselves off from everything that was going on. It was fun.

Isn't there a funny story about John and the Maharishi?

Yeah, that is a funny story. You see, Maharishi was quite a relaxed guy, but there was an embarrassed silence in the room. It was the four Beatles, Mia Farrow, and myself, or was it Mike Love? We'd all just arrived, and nobody was saying anything—we were all wondering what to say.

John was so funny and so direct, that to break the silence, he went up to the Maharishi, who was sitting cross-legged on the floor, patted him on the head and said, "There's a good little guru."

We all laughed. It was funny. John was very funny, and he always said exactly what he felt.

CYNTHIA
LENNON

*"I spent a lot of time married, being not
supposed to be married."*

•

Cynthia Powell met John Lennon at the Liverpool College of Art in 1957. After a tumultuous courtship, they were married in 1962
and their only child, John Charles Julian,
was born just eight months later. However,
with John soon swept up in the delirium of
Beatlemania, his family was quickly rele-
gated to the back burner. God forbid that a
Beatle should have a wife—and a child, too!

After years of strain and prolonged separation, not to mention the significant presence of Yoko Ono, the Lennons divorced in
1968. Cynthia took responsibility for Julian's
upbringing and has twice remarried.

In recent years, Cynthia Lennon has become more accessible to the press. No longer
the shy and withdrawn Beatle wife, Cynthia
is now actively sharing her side of the story.
In 1978 she published an autobiography, *A
Twist of Lennon*, a candid account of those
early years with John and how she came to
terms with the dissolution of their relationship.

Elegant and soft-spoken, Cynthia talked
with us in 1986 while she was on a press tour
to promote the Ray Coleman biography,
Lennon.

Was it frustrating to see someone as talented as John never really satisfied? It seems like no matter how great his work was, his inner drive made him uncomfortable with his success.

Yes, I think he loved the success. He loved the fact that they worked so hard, but he was always a restless spirit. He couldn't resist the change. His frustration, I think, had a lot to do with the bull in life, all the dishonesty from other people towards him.

I think it was all too overwhelming to him. He didn't believe what other people said about him. The adulation and being called brilliant and a genius was all very hard for him to live with. Because underneath it all, he was very modest.

He was modest in himself, yet very outspoken. He couldn't resist the honesty. He didn't believe what others were saying about him, because he knew himself better than anyone. He knew his own faults and misgivings, and I think that's what frustrated him so much.

Could you explain how being Liverpudlian was so critical to understanding John?

They say to live in Liverpool you must have a sense of humor —it's born in you. You have to, to exist and survive there, because it's a very tough place to live.

A lot of it has to do with the time in which he grew up, also. We didn't have the fear of nuclear war; we didn't see that much outside of Great Britain. We were coming out of a war at that time; things were fantastic. Money had more value; there was freedom; we could see beyond the British Isles and listen to music from abroad. The world was broadening out then, and the world was their oyster.

Tell us a little bit about Julian. You must be awfully proud.

Can I tell you a lot about Julian? *[Laughs]* I try to be modest, but I'm very proud of him. He's worked very hard. He hasn't had it easy. His life has been highly emotional—ups and downs and lots of sadness and tragedy.

There was a certain stage in his life, when he was about seventeen, when I thought "That's it, he's had it—he's not going anywhere." I sound like [John's aunt] Mimi, don't I? Although I didn't drag Julian along, like Mimi dragged John to art college.

(STAR FILE/JANET MACOSKA)

CYNTHIA LENNON

But I did send him away from home. I sent him to London to a friend of mine who was a musician, Ray Cooper. He's a really lovely person, and the right sort of person for Julian at that time. He was also a pianist, and Julian was very interested in the piano. I was hoping to guide him even further into the music business.

He went to stay with Ray, and Ray educated him and gave him a different outlook. We'd come from a small market town in North Wales and not a lot was happening. No work, no prospects, no qualifications on his part.

So the moment he went to London, his eyes were opened a bit. And Julian became his own man. He began working on his own, with his mate Justin [Clayton]. And for two solid years, they worked on getting their act together, writing their music, getting their sounds together. And they drove everybody potty who lived within the area.

So you saw rock and roll as Julian's ticket just as it was John's?

Absolutely. Although it's different nowadays than it was in John's day. You see, Julian had an artistic talent, so it was either art or music. But the music was his dream, and he worked at it. It was the only thing he worked at all his life.

Would you say that John was a bit of a paradox in that he was so outwardly brash, yet inside a little insecure?

I would say that John was in constant need of proof of love and security, and he was constantly testing people for that proof. That's why he never really got the true feeling or response from people. People would say, "You're wonderful." But he knew in his heart the ones who were honest and the ones who weren't honest. The ones who weren't really got a mouthful, didn't they?

It seems that John sometimes took that posture with Brian Epstein. Brian handled the affairs but John never let him forget that it was the four Beatles who were the attraction.

Again, that was John's way of testing him. He was testing how Brian could stand up to John's attack. That's why they loved each other so much. John loved anyone who would stand up to him. Most people just withered and died, but anyone who could stand up to that, they were OK.

Like the Beatles, Brian had no role model because no one had done anything like this before.

That's the brilliance of it all. He had no experience. He had been working in a record store and his family's furniture business. He had absolutely no experience at all. For him to go through it and cope with it all, I thought was absolutely fantastic. We all had such complete faith in him, we never gave any thought to the fact that he had never done it before. He masterminded the whole thing—it was incredible.

Brian was a frustrated performer, a failed writer. He wanted to be onstage and he fulfilled that dream in a very unusual way.

It's been a long time and an unreal story, Cynthia, but we want to ask the most basic question of all: Relate your first impression of John Lennon.

He came into my life when I met him in art college. I became totally enamored with him and fell madly in love with him within six months of seeing him. I knew that he was a bit of a dangerous character. My upbringing was totally different to the way he was behaving. I saw something in him that everyone else saw in him later on. My feelings were a bit different—female. But my first impression was the talent, the honesty, the aggression, and fascination—total fascination.

It's interesting that you end your book, A Twist of Lennon, *with the words "No blame."*

I wrote that as a message to John. I had no contact with him after the divorce, and I had lovely memories of my time with him. The most important thing that I wanted to get across to him, because I knew he'd read it, was that I wanted to applaud all of them. We had all been through it. It was hard and we are only human. So I was trying to say to him, "Please don't feel any guilt about it. No blame. I understand."

That was my main reason for writing the book.

Tell us a little bit about John and the Beatles in the Hamburg days.

The atmosphere in Hamburg was electric, and it was pretty rough. The Reeperbahn was a very rough area of Hamburg. The people that John and the Beatles had to play to were mostly drunks. There were a lot of fights. There was tremendous atmosphere.

But they learned their trade and their skills there. They learned how to project themselves and get themselves across. They didn't have time to be smart. They just had to get in there. It was raw rock 'n' roll. They got years of good experience there.

That was the time with Stu Sutcliffe. Could you shed a little light on the Beatles' first bassist? He's an enigmatic figure in Beatle history.

I think that Stuart was John's closest and dearest friend. Not acquaintance, but a dear friend. They were on the same wavelength, but they were opposites.

Stuart was a sensitive artist and he was not a rebel, as John was. He wasn't rowdy or rough. But they complemented each other beautifully.

John taught Stuart how to play bass. He wasn't a musician, but John wanted Stuart to be with him. And that's how Stuart went to Hamburg with them.

Most of their touring years found you at home, with Julian. You didn't get to travel too much with them on the road, did you?

I went on one tour, and that was the first tour of America. That was tremendous. But that was enough for me. It was incredible. The security. The fans. We didn't have any freedom at all. I think we saw a little bit of Miami. But to get away from the hotel, we were put in meat trucks because of the tremendous response from the fans.

On The Ed Sullivan Show *they showed a picture of John and flashed: SORRY GIRLS, HE'S MARRIED underneath him. How did that make you feel?*

Well, I spent a lot of time married, but being not supposed to be married.

How have the books that have been written affected you? Many books now come out that do not paint such a rosy picture. What are some of the things you'd like to clear up?

Well, just the extremes and the sensationalism of his so-called past. I was there. Certain people have written things like they were living with us day-to-day. A lot of these people were employees. People who saw very little of the inside lives, our lives at the time.

I'm so annoyed because John's memory is precious, as is my memory and Julian's memory of John. I feel extremely frustrated and angry that other people should make a fortune out of our lives' memories. And they don't have it accurately anyway.

What inaccuracies are the most irritating?

Inaccuracies about wife-beating, woman beating, total drug abuse, and homosexuality. And for Julian and Sean to grow up with that—they're John's heritage. That's John's life. And it's got to be honest.

Talk a little bit about your first experimentation with LSD.

Well, John was always looking for something new. But this particular time, he didn't go out looking for it. It was criminal as far as I'm concerned. It's amazing that we got home alive that night. The strange thing was, at that point in his life and in all their lives, they needed an escape. And this was handed to them, in the form of LSD.

John took a lot of LSD, but he handled it. There were a lot of people who couldn't handle it, who committed suicide, and other terrible tragedies. I knew that the stuff was poison, mentally poisoning for me. I knew what I went through with it, and I did not take it again.

When you and John split, was it a hard decision or did you have a feeling that things were changing?

Well obviously, John fell in love with Yoko. I think it all built up from the death of Brian. [In 1967, Brian Epstein died from an accidental drug overdose. He was thirty-two.] I think it built up from the change in the Beatles' role.

They stopped performing, and all they were doing was recording. Their lives were becoming very insular and not exciting enough. They weren't individuals anymore. They were grouped together and weren't allowed their freedom. And I think it all mounted up to that situation.

Yoko arrived, and they were on the same wavelength mentally. And she was just the right woman for him at the time.

You seem philosophical about it. Were you bitter at the time?

I've always been philosophical in life. I think that's what kept me sane.

John spent his time searching for something more out of life. Do you think that by 1980, he was satisfied?

No, I think he was still searching. He would have gone searching for the rest of his life. He would have never been the stay-at-home family man forever.

What is your life like now—now that the Beatles and John are a part of your past? What's your career like now?

I have got a career of my own [as an artist and writer], a life of my own. Even if it's twenty years later. I was quite content to be what I was at the time, to exist as I did.

Was being John Lennon's wife your role back then?

Yes, it was, because I loved the man. I met him as a student, and I had a son by him. And I was as fascinated and in love with the Beatles as everybody else was and obviously is. It was a tremendous experience. And I'm privileged that I had the experience of going through that. Even though it ended tragically, on quite a few occasions. There was a lot of sacrifice along the way. We lost a lot of dear friends.

When I married John, I was not necessarily career-minded. I was quite happy to be a wife and a mother. Now, after the years of experience of being in the shadows to a certain extent and being pressured by newspapers for this story and that story, I now feel that I'm entitled to my own career. And that's what I'm doing. The opportunity is wonderful.

It's also very important, now that I'm old enough and wise enough, it's very important to get across the truth about those years.

Is there anything you look back on and wish you could do over again?

I wouldn't have changed a lot. But I would have been a little more aggressive with the hangers-on, the drug pushers, who were there purely for what they could gain from being close to the situation. I felt they divided a lot of us, split us up in many, many ways. Those kinds of things are present in every area of life, but perhaps if I'd have been a little older or more aggressive, things might have been a little different.

John established that he was willing to devote his talent to the betterment of the world. It's pretty easy to see him involved in USA for Africa or Live Aid.

Oh yes, I'm sure he would have been—it probably would have been his idea. There's always someone with great ideas like that.

Have you ever met Sean?

No, I've never met Sean. But Julian has and they have a good relationship when they see each other.

Would you like to see a film version of John's life?

I think that would be the most difficult film to produce. It would be very difficult to get the right actors to portray the part. But it would be fascinating. What a story!

Actually, there was a film about the Beatles that I saw a few months ago. It's been out a few years but I couldn't watch it at the time it came out, because it was too upsetting. I watched it quite recently. And it's horrendous to watch yourself being portrayed on film, with somebody else saying lines that you would never say in a million years.

This is the difficulty of films. It's more than writing a book or having an interview. It's very difficult to portray the feeling of that time. I should think it would be an immense film to make.

What goes through your mind when you hear Beatles songs on the radio? It must happen to you all the time.

Well, there are certain records or tapes that are very evocative of the past. They are special messages from special times. It's a history of my life. It's somewhat sad and somewhat fantastic. I'm very lucky actually. It's beautiful.

If you had this one chance to tell people what's most important when it comes to remembering John Lennon, what would you tell them?

John Lennon was a human being. He was vulnerable. He was humorous. He was compassionate. He was a dreamer. He was a wonderful musician. He was a poet. I could go on forever.

I have a wonderful memory of John. Hopefully, his children and their children will always be proud of his memory.

WALTER SHENSON

"I'm delighted that they [the films] are so good, because they represent the Beatles at the height of their careers."

•

In short, Walter Shenson brought the Beatles to the big screen. An independent producer formerly with Columbia Pictures, Shenson tackled the formidable task of creating film comedies with four musicians who had no prior acting experience. And as we all know, he succeeded brilliantly.

Both *A Hard Day's Night* and *Help!* have stood the test of time and are as refreshing and entertaining today as they were at the time of release. Shenson had enough foresight and confidence in his product to protect his rights to those films, and in recent years, he has personally overseen the release of *A Hard Day's Night* and *Help!* to the home video market.

How did you first get involved with the two films, Help! *and* A Hard Day's Night?

At the time I made *A Hard Day's Night*, I was living in London, having been sent there from Hollywood by Columbia Pictures. I was an executive for advertising and publicity for all of their European productions.

I left that job to become an independent producer, and I produced a few low budget comedies in England which enjoyed some success in the U.S.

Then United Artists asked me to produce a low-budget comedy for them starring the Beatles. At that time, they were very well known in England, but not so in the U.S. They had not done the famous Sullivan show as of yet. Perhaps their records were beginning to sell in the States but not nearly as well as in England.

Anyway, UA had a record company, UA Records, and the reason they wanted this movie made is that they would wind up with a soundtrack album. Nobody at that time, at least none of the company executives, knew if the Beatles would last. Therefore, they didn't want me, as the producer, to spend too much money, and to get it out quickly so that they had a soundtrack album while the Beatles were still hot.

They left it up to me to produce whatever I wanted, and we came up with *A Hard Day's Night.*

You've just put A Hard Day's Night *out again. How, after fifteen years, did you get the rights to it?*

Since no one knew if the Beatles would become famous—more famous than they were—or last or not, it wasn't very difficult for me to negotiate a deal with UA to merely license this movie I was going to produce for a limited period of time. We agreed on fifteen years. So fifteen years after *A Hard Day's Night* went into general release around the world, the copyright reverted back to me. That was in December of 1979.

So we are now preparing to reissue *A Hard Day's Night* with a new soundtrack, stereophonic sound this time and the Dolby system, so that younger movie audiences will be able to see this movie and hear it with the same sound fidelity that they are accustomed to today.

How did you get involved with Help!*?*

When we made the deal for *A Hard Day's Night*, we decided on a three-picture deal, so that if we all got along and if we could come up with the right material, the Beatles would make three pictures for me.

While we were working on *A Hard Day's Night*, we were thinking of ideas for a second picture. The Beatles loved the idea of moviemaking. They were very young at the time, Paul and

George being about twenty-one at the time, and John and Ringo were about twenty-three. They loved the whole process of making movies. They were very bright young men. They learned the technique of moviemaking very quickly and I think they liked the whole setup.

I brought in a brilliant young director by the name of Richard Lester, whose career began with this movie, and had an extremely bright script by a writer from Liverpool named Alun Owen. With this brilliant script by Owen and Dick Lester's genius, I think we made a terrific movie and the Beatles loved every part of the moviemaking. So they were most eager to get back to do a second movie a year later, because they had commitments to travel around the world to play concerts and cut record albums.

So about exactly a year later, we embarked on *Help!* It was a totally different type of movie than *A Hard Day's Night*. *A Hard Day's Night* was in black and white and had a feeling of actuality to it; it *seemed* like an exaggerated day in the life of the Beatles.

Help!, on the other hand, was more like a "movie" movie. It was like a live cartoon. It was a bigger picture; we went to the Bahamas and the Austrian Alps for locations, it was in color, [we had a] long shooting schedule, and a bigger cast of actors besides the Beatles. Things that add up to make a more expensive movie.

Both, I'm happy to say, are excellent. Both, directed by Lester I might add, are landmark movies in my opinion. I'm delighted

(COURTESY OF MPI VIDEO)

PUBLICITY PHOTO FROM THE MOVIE "HELP!," PRODUCED BY WALTER SHENSON

that they are so good, because they represent the Beatles at the height of their careers. There are no other movies around; there never will be any more unfortunately, and at least future generations will have something to see to know why the Beatles were as famous as they were.

You mentioned earlier that the contract was for three movies. Why didn't you ever make the third film?

I think the reason that a third picture was never made is two-fold.

One, I never was able to come up with a script or story line that everyone was able to agree on. We didn't want to do another exaggerated day in the life of the Beatles, and the Beatles didn't want to perform as "the Beatles" in another picture. They wanted to perform as four other characters. I found this rather difficult, because it was very hard to separate these four young men from the image they had created as the Beatles.

I mentioned this to John Lennon and he agreed with me, but he still thought we should not have a movie with the Beatles doing something as "the Beatles."

Of course there was always the suggestion that they could play the Three Musketeers—there were four of them—but that was a rather corny idea, and thankfully, nobody wanted to do anything like that.

The other reason is that, by the time we had come up with an idea that was any good, I think the Beatles were beginning to split up. They are, as you know, extremely progressive and they wanted to move on to other things. Even the music was beginning to change. If one saw *Let It Be*—the filming of their album—I think one could detect a certain kind of breaking up was taking place at that time. So a third picture just never did take place.

It's very sad. I would have loved to produce a third picture with the Beatles but we just couldn't find anything to do and we just drifted apart.

You mentioned earlier that Help! *was a more expensive picture than* A Hard Day's Night. *What was the difference in the two budgets?*

The budget on *A Hard Day's Night* was very low. It was about five hundred thousand dollars, which, even in those days, was very reasonable. *Help!* was about three times that, which is still pretty inexpensive for a movie of that scope. One doesn't have to spend money to get quality. I've never equated the spending of money with good craftsmanship anyway, so the budget isn't really important if the material is there.

So you're saying that United Artists finally had confidence in the Beatles as moviemakers, which is why they increased the budget for Help!*?*

That's it exactly. The reason nobody balked at spending more money for *Help!* was, number one, the Beatles were so successful as entertainers, with concerts and records. Number two, *A Hard Day's Night* was such a successful movie that it was agreed to spend more on a second picture. Even that amount of money, with stars the magnitude of the Beatles, was a very low amount to spend.

Explain the changes in the films over the fifteen years of your copyright agreement. You mentioned that A Hard Day's Night's *soundtrack was being reissued.*

As I mentioned before, the soundtrack is being rerecorded on stereophonic soundtrack and using the Dolby system which is really marvelous because it is the sound that young people who buy records expect to get in movies today. It is brilliant, very well done.

We had the best film sound engineers working on it. The crew had just received an Oscar for doing *The Empire Strikes Back* and were preparing *Raiders of the Lost Ark*, and we managed to sneak *A Hard Day's Night* in there for them to do the Dolby track.

I also added a two-minute prologue to *A Hard Day's Night*. We didn't change the body of the movie—that hasn't been cut—but I recalled that one of the songs that was written by Lennon and McCartney for the movie, called "I'll Cry Instead," wasn't used. We just never found room to put it in anywhere.

Since those rights, what we call synchronization rights, were part of the movie, I decided to put that song in as an overture to this new Dolby version. Then we photographed stills of the Beatles from *A Hard Day's Night*, with certain graphics and optical effects, and edited that to the beat of the song. It's a delightful little piece that acts as a prologue to the picture.

Are there any plans for changes with Help!*?*

As of now, I haven't addressed the problem of what we want to do with *Help!* I want to keep it off the market for at least another year. It's been a year since John was tragically killed. I think the last thing I want to do is put out a picture which anyone could say was an exploitation of this tragedy. So I think I'll keep that picture off the market as long as I possibly can.

A Hard Day's Night has been off two years now, a year since John died, so I think it's time. The mourning period is over. And it will be good for people to see him as he was in *A Hard Day's Night*, and I think we'll wait another year before we do anything with *Help!*

What do you feel personally is unique about each film?

I think the good thing about *A Hard Day's Night* is that with the script by Alun Owen and this fine direction by Richard Lester, we were really able—forever, for posterity—to capture the real essence of the Beatles. Their personalities are honest and true. There is a contagion that takes place from the screen to the audience so that there is warmth, there is fun, and there is music. One even sees the love that they had for each other in this movie. I think it's a great movie mainly for the historical reasons, and of course, for the entertainment as well. That's *A Hard Day's Night*.

Anything you want to say about Help!*?*

I haven't seen *Help!* in a long time. I remember it has some very sophisticated comedy in it, very funny stuff. It's a very good-looking picture, a first-rate crew, a beautifully designed movie, the costumes are good.

It's really first-rate moviemaking, and I think it holds up fifteen years later. It does not look like a picture made in 1965. Of course, it has a half dozen super songs by the Beatles written by Lennon and McCartney, and again it's a fun picture. It's good comedy and we all know there's a shortage of those these days. I think it will be a pleasure for people to see it.

Do you think the Beatles projected as well on film as they did on stage?

I think that the Beatles' performances in these two films are incredibly good, in that they were not trained as actors. Any trained actor will tell you that the hardest thing to do is to be yourself, to stand there and let your own personality come through. This is what the Beatles have, and do, better than anybody I know.

It's very difficult not to perform as someone else when you're standing in front of a camera. There was never a time in either movie when we got the feeling that the Beatles were trying to be something that they weren't. And I think this comes across.

Do you have a favorite song or scene that comes to mind?

My favorite song and sequence takes place during the song "And I Love Her." It's a tender sequence. The boys are arguing with Ringo, they have to perform for a television rehearsal, and by the time the song is over, you realize that the kidding was just that—kidding. And everything is OK among them.

Is that also your favorite song?

Yeah, I think so. It's very difficult, when the Beatles have written so many great songs, to pick out one favorite, but that one sticks out for me because it was performed so nicely on screen.

What do you think of some of the other rock movies that have been made?

I'm not a fan of rock movies. I think I've been spoiled by the two pictures that I've produced. I feel that nobody can come up to the Beatles. As a moviemaker, I think that I should see these other movies just for the techniques. But rock movies are not my favorite kind of movies.

What makes the Beatles' films popular even to people who are not necessarily fans of rock music, or the Beatles' music for that matter?

I don't consider *A Hard Day's Night* or *Help!* rock films as such. I think they are comedies starring four young men who happen to be rock musicians. They're not only musicians, they're composers and singers and very, very talented.

And their talent comes through in these comedies. I think they are very special. I don't know of any other movies that star rock musicians that have the quality of being so true to the personalities themselves.

I think that the lasting popularity of these pictures is mainly because of the incredible popularity of the Beatles. But the Beatles were in other things that won't last as long, mainly because these pictures entertain in addition to showing the Beatles as they were at that time.

The Beatles are on film in live rock concerts, which are very good. But unlike *A Hard Day's Night* or *Help!*, they're not movies with stories and they don't have a beginning, a middle, and an end.

So the audience has a double interest: the interest in seeing their favorite rock stars as well as following the story. And that combination is certainly one of the reasons that the films are popular and also will continue to be popular with new audiences that have heard about the Beatles but never got a chance to see them.

Older fans will continue to look at these films for nostalgia reasons, and the young people will come along to see them because they've heard so much about them.

I feel very good about that fact that, when *A Hard Day's Night* first came out in 1965, a lot of older people really didn't understand what the Beatles were all about until they saw it. Most of the people of my generation, who had children who were buying the records, were being driven out of their living rooms with this music.

So I'm very very pleased that our movie, *A Hard Day's Night*, converted a lot of older people, a lot of nonbelievers. They realized that the Beatles were more than just four boys with long hair, making a lot of noise.

Do you think that John's death will affect the attention the films will get in the future?

I don't think that the tragedy of John Lennon's death will affect the attention folks give to the reissue of *A Hard Day's Night*. I think Beatles fans are Beatles fans whether John is here with us or not. I also feel that enough time has gone by, so that terrible hurt has also gone by. When I see *A Hard Day's Night*, I feel good about it. I see John as a happy person and that makes me feel good. And I think that people who love John for what he stood for, his music and everything else, will enjoy this picture. It's a bit sad, but it's a happy sadness, not a sad sadness.

I don't think the one-year anniversary of John's death will have any affect on the distribution of *A Hard Day's Night*. Certainly, there's no conscious effort to time this reissue with the anniversary. I think Beatles fans will come when they come, when the picture plays, whether there's an anniversary of John's death or not.

Could you please evaluate each of the Beatles as an individual performer?

You have to remember that this was a long time ago, and people change over the years. But at that time, they were probably the most honest actors that one could ever work with.

Don't forget that they were not a four-headed monster, they were four people. [They] all had the same natural quality. Maybe it had something to do with their background, their traditions, and their culture. Maybe it had something to do with the way they were brought up. But they never tried to be anything they weren't. This was very, very hard to believe, considering that there were four of them and they were all perfect to work with, just being themselves.

We tried to make the script so that the characters were not interchangeable. We wanted to give John his own lines, and same for George, Paul, and Ringo—something more akin to what we thought they were like.

As we got to know them more, we changed lines and we changed roles a little bit. We didn't know them well when we got started. But halfway into the movie, we all became close friends, and we accommodated each personality with a character.

The script was written by Alun Owen after he spent a weekend with them up in Dublin, Ireland, when they were on a concert tour. And by being with them for a weekend, he got to know them a little bit, and wrote the story he wanted to write and gave each Beatle the character he thought they should have.

But spending such a short time with them, he didn't get to know them that well. Dick Lester and I got to spend more and more time with them. During the filming, we began to see other characteristics that one had which another didn't. But not very much. Basically Alun's script is the one that we used.

We did add sequences to fit the specific personality. They looked like they were ad-libbed, but they were scripted.

My association with them was limited to the filming of the two movies, but as anyone who works in films will tell you, you become a big family and everybody gets to know everybody very well.

Everybody works on the set, the technicians as well as the artists. So we all got to know each other. They probably got to know some things about me that they didn't know when they first met me. And I found out things about them.

Ringo is much brighter than he appears. I think George is rather quiet, but has a lot of depth. John, I felt from the very beginning, was a real genius.

I had never met anybody that young, at twenty-three, who was a musician, a composer, a songwriter, an artist, an actor, and a poet, all rolled into one. He was a very rare person and just developing.

He was extremely curious. We came from totally different backgrounds. I was an American, a generation older, having been born and raised in California, and working in the movie business. I was like no one he'd ever met before. Not that I'm that unusual, but I wasn't of his world.

So he became curious about me. And I found that very typical of John. He wanted to know about people with different backgrounds.

One weekend, I had the pleasure of going to the Riviera with John and his then-wife Cynthia to attend a film festival in Cannes. And it was a very pleasant four days.

John had never been to the Riviera. He'd been to Paris to perform, but never to the Riviera. He was a pure delight to be with. He was soaking up a tremendous amount of new experience. He was one who appreciated that. A lot of people are very blasé about those things.

At that time, John was unsophisticated. Not naïve, by any stretch, but certainly unsophisticated. He acquired that sophistication soon enough.

John was my favorite because of all these things I mentioned. He also kept one on one's toes. You did not want to say stupid things around John, because he would catch you at it and think less of you. And in those days he was outspoken enough to tell you you were a fool if you were acting like one.

Paul McCartney was charming. A nice young man, attractive to be with, and extremely witty and good to be with socially. He was a well-mannered twenty-one-year old, with a sophisticated sense of humor. He was also silly enough to be a twenty-one-year old, too.

All of them were indeed favorites.

Do you have any plans for putting A Hard Day's Night, *or* Help! *on TV?*

Eventually, after the rerelease of *A Hard Day's Night* and *Help!* what will happen to those pictures will be the same sequence of events. There will be cable television, videocassettes and discs, and, perhaps, another network sale. And, like any good picture, any picture that has "legs" as we say, we hope it will be in front of the public at all times in all mediums.

DAVID
CROSBY

Our first tour in England was a disaster, a raging, Grade A, number one disaster. The promoter had billed us [The Byrds] as being better than the Beatles. Now the Beatles were kind fellows. They came down, and they knew that we weren't better than them, so they were nice to us. They said, "It's all right, lad. I know your amp broke and you broke a bass string, but it's all right. Don't cry." So one of the first gigs we did, we looked down into the audience and there's about half of the Rolling Stones and three quarters of the Beatles. We were about three years older and had just come from California and we're looking at our idols and we were so scared, man, we couldn't even open our teeth.

BILLY PRESTON

BILLY
PRESTON

*"They said, " 'Sit in. You want to stay
and help us finish the album? Take a solo.'
They just made me a member of the
band."*

•

No other professional musician played with
the Beatles more often than Billy Preston. In
fact, he was the first non-Beatle to ever re-
ceive credit on a Beatles record. Seemingly at
every important stage of their career, Billy
was there in one capacity or another.

Billy was playing keyboards with Little
Richard when he first met the Beatles in
Hamburg. And he forged a lifelong friend-
ship with the band during those rough-and-
tumble early days.

Eventually signed to Apple Records,
Billy sat in on the legendary *White Album*
and *Abbey Road* recording sessions, and later,
jammed with the band for their last live appearance on the rooftop of the Apple Building in 1969.

*Billy, you first met the Beatles in Europe when you were touring with
Little Richard's band as a part of a caravan of stars. As an American
abroad, what were your initial impressions and memories?*

When I first saw them, out of all the English acts that were on
the show, I liked them best. It was because of their harmonies and

they had a look that was kind of odd. They were nice guys, so I'd always stand in the wings and watch them. They used to dedicate "A Taste of Honey" to me.

So we became friends. They were curious about Little Richard and about America. They'd come to me and ask questions, you know? So we'd hang out, and I remember getting them free steaks and free cokes at the Star-Club in Hamburg, Germany.

When you were with them in Hamburg, did you have any reason to anticipate the kind of splash they'd make, the kind of mark they'd leave?

No, I didn't. But I remember when I came back to America from that tour, I brought back "P.S. I Love You" and "A Taste of Honey." I never thought they'd be as big as they were. I kept hearing, "The Beatles are coming, the Beatles are coming." I was amazed. And when I saw them again, they were like the same little act. They were unaffected by everything that happened.

One of the highlights of the Beatles' early career was meeting their idol, Little Richard. What do you remember about that meeting? I re-member seeing a picture with all of them together.

I was in the room when that picture was taken. They were excited.

Every night it was like five or six bands on the show, and Richard would close the show. Oh, it was great! Everybody hung out and it was good rock 'n' roll.

What was it like to be one of only a handful of Americans who knew the Beatles before February of 1964? And what did you feel like when you saw them on The Ed Sullivan Show?

Oh, I was really proud. I said, "I know those guys!" I had some pictures from Hamburg, and I was showing everybody. On their first tour [of America], I was in San Francisco, and I went over to see them.

I went to the Cow Palace and was in the dressing room before they went out. It was exciting, and I was very happy for them. And they were happy to see me! We went out and partied.

I thought they were great on stage, but you couldn't hear a thing because the roar was fantastic. They were kind of surprised and amazed at all the excitement. In the dressing room they were saying, "Hey what's going on? Everybody's going mad, Beatle people!" *[Laughs].* They were making a joke.

Tell me how you came to drop by the studio when they were recording Abbey Road *and* Let It Be.

I was on tour with Ray Charles, and we were in London. George Harrison was at the concert and thought, "Hey, that looks like Billy Preston!" So he called around and found out that it *was* me. He called me at the hotel and invited me over to see the guys.

When I got there, they were filming *Let It Be* and recording and all. We started reminiscing and playing old rock 'n' roll songs. They said, "Sit in. You want to stay and help us finish the album? Take a solo." They just made me a member of the band.

I was in the Beatle office every day, had breakfast with them, and lunch. It was exciting, you know? Fabulous!

I saw Let It Be *and was torn between how sad it was to watch the disintegration, and knowing that those four guys had given us so much. You were there. What was it like for you?*

Before I got there, Mal Evans had told me that they had been going through a lot of depression and that he was glad that I came around, because it gave them a lot of life. It made them happy a little bit.

And there was Billy Preston, on the rooftop of the Apple Building, playing with the Beatles on their last performance.

Oh, that was exciting. See, we were trying to figure out where we could have a concert where everybody could come. So John came up with the brilliant idea to just play on the roof and play for everybody. And it was great because we knew the police were going to come. But we got to do all of the songs we wanted to do. It was planned perfectly!

I haven't seen it in a while, but I remember it like it was yesterday.

I don't have any official statistics or anything, but I'd venture to say that you played more with the Beatles as a band, and as individuals, than any other nonmember.

Yeah, I played on other albums as well. I played on "Something," and *The White Album*, and a bit of *Abbey Road*. So over that period of time, while they were doing *Let It Be*, they were working on other projects as well. I lived over there about six months out of the year.

You were on Abbey Road? *We wouldn't know that for sure because they weren't too heavily into credits on those albums.*

I played certain pieces on "Something." *[Sings]* "I don't know, I don't knooooow Da Da Dum Dum Dum Dum Dum." I also played on "I Want You (She's so heavy)."

Was there less tension during the Abbey Road *sessions than on* The White Album?

Yeah, there was less tension. They were out of Apple studios, and Apple had become a real headache to them, trying to get equipment that they wanted. So they were back in Abbey Road, and it was more comfortable for them.

Seeing them from Hamburg through Apple makes you a rare, start-to-finish collaborator. How did you like the music at the end compared to the material you saw at first? What were your views of individual Beatles as players? Let's start with John Lennon.

John was a good rhythm guitar player. He used to tickle me because he would make funny faces. He was a funny guy. He was very witty and would keep you laughing. Man, he was a sweet guy, and I miss him everyday. Wow, what can you say?

Paul McCartney, especially his bass playing.

He would play the tonic! He would give you the basic root and chord structure of the tune. It was really solid playing.

George Harrison?

Oh, George had some unique licks. His solos are like a singer would sing. He had a style, kind of like a crying technique. He was a really good player. He's a very emotional guy; he's very spiritual and sensitive. He's a very kind-hearted person.

I spent most of the time with George. In fact, when I first joined Apple, everybody was going to cut a couple of tracks of me. And at the time, John had Yoko, and Paul was getting leery about the office, so me and George hung out, and he helped me with my projects for Apple. We spent most of the time together.

Was George's spirituality evident?

It was great. He brought an organ to his house for me. And I remember one day, when the Hare Krishna people were staying there for a while, I was on the organ when one of the Hare Krishna people comes in. And he started chanting "Hare Krishna." And I was singing, "My Sweet Lord." I sing, "Oh, My Lord," and he'd go, "Hare Krishna." Yeah, we would have service there together.

In his house he had pictures of Buddha, Krishna, and Jesus. It was a very spiritual and warm place.

You two got pretty close, didn't you?

Oh yeah. We feel like we're together all the time, just through spirit. I haven't seen him in a while, but every time I'm there, I have my bedroom in Friar Park, my organ is there, and my picture is up over his studio. That's really great.

His studio and his place, Henley on Thames, is fabulous. There's an eighty-five-room castle and two ten-room cottages on it, lakes, caves. Oh, it's fabulous.

I'd like you to comment on some of the Beatle songs you played on, starting with the solo on "Get Back."

"Get Back" was like a funk tune to me. It was a soulful song. And they said, "Hey, take a solo." So I just played. I played my heart out.

"Let It Be?"

"Let It Be" was a great song. That song inspired [my song] "That's the Way God Planned It." I had another solo on that one.

You also played on "I Dig a Pony" on the rooftop.

188 · *Ticket to Ride*

"I Dig A Pony." They used to write some funny songs. Some of the ideas they came up with were amazing. Because John would come up with a line, then Paul would come up with other things.

John's writing was really unique, because he would play on words. Paul's was really melodic. It was great music and it was great to see them put it together.

I love "I've Got a Feeling." That was a soulful song, too. And like I was saying, the way they counterwrote each other happened there. John had his thing, and Paul had his, and there were two different things all together. But they fit.

Besides doing studio work on George's All Things Must Pass, Extra Texture, *and* Dark Horse, *you also played on the* Dark Horse *tour. That tour was plagued by some negative press. Do you remember much about that?*

It was kind of frightening for George, because that was the first time he was headlining. And he worked so hard. He worked hard getting the album together and getting the band together and with rehearsals. By the time the tour started, his voice was gone. And he was also a bit nervous, you know.

So I was trying to give him all the support I could. His idea about the Indian musicians, I thought was fantastic. With the [different] cultures, we lived great together. We had the Indian food and they had ours! Yeah, we exchanged ideas, and that was great.

You mentioned your album That's the Way God Planned It. *George produced that record. What was that like?*

I remember when we went into the studio, he said that he was going to have a few friends come over and play on it. And he got Ginger Baker on drums, Keith Richards played the bass, and Eric Clapton played guitar. It came out great, and everyone enjoyed themselves.

As I recall, you also played onstage at the concert for Bangladesh.

Oh, that was a great night. We did two shows. And during the first show I didn't dance! But during the second show, the spirit was so high, I couldn't sit any longer.

The idea of the show was great, because all of the musicians got a chance to play together. And plus, we were doing something good for other people.

You've done work on the Plastic Ono Band LP, as well as two Ringo Starr solo records. And, if memory serves, John, George, and Ringo were all present on one of those sessions, right? Any highlights come to mind?

I remember one night, when we were in between takes, and there was John, George, and Ringo along with some other musicians. We were all saying, "This is great! We should go out and get another band together, get everybody together, have other musicians."

And then John Lennon said, "Yeah, that would be great, but it would be like starting over." I remember him saying that and then, years later, he comes out with the title "Starting Over" on his own album.

You've covered Beatle songs like "Blackbird," "Here, There and Every-where," and "A Hard Day's Night"—

And one of these days I'm going to do an album of my arrangements of Beatles songs.

JUSTIN HAYWARD AND JOHN
LODGE OF THE MOODY BLUES

THE MOODY
BLUES
(JUSTIN
HAYWARD
AND JOHN
LODGE)

*"I think there was a kind of a calm,
waiting for this storm to happen. There
was a period when we were waiting for
something to explode, and the Beatles
supplied that explosion. BANG!"*
—*John Lodge*

•

Originally formed in Birmingham, England,
in 1964, the Moody Blues are still in the
business of music-making, and quite successfully at that. Their trademark brand of lush,
orchestral, poetic rock 'n' roll is as riveting
now as it was back in 1965 when they released their first hit single, the timeless classic "Go Now."

Justin Hayward and John Lodge joined
the Moodies in 1967 and are now, admit-
tedly, the creative core of the band. And like
so many rock veterans, both their songwrit-
ing and performance styles were greatly influenced by the Beatles.

You were also starting out not long after the Beatles were up and running. Tell us a little bit about the atmosphere of the British rock scene, prior to and after the Beatles hit.

John Lodge: I think there was kind of a calm, waiting for this storm to happen. There was a period of time when we were waiting for something to explode, and the Beatles supplied that explosion. BANG!

Justin Hayward: I can remember "Love Me Do," and I can remember exactly where I was when I first heard it. That was the first one to hit me.

I was aware of the name "Beatles," but it was just one of those things where I couldn't place them. I was at a friend's house, and we were in a band together.

And you just knew straightaway with that record that this was something different, and the world was going to be different after that. It was a new sound. I know that is sort of the classic thing to say, but it *was* a *new* sound.

John: The first recollection I had was when we were in a band called Al Right and the Rebels, along with Ray [Thomas] of the Moodies.

I remember we were doing a show at a place called Tenbury Wells in a farming area south of Birmingham. Ray and I had been working in the band for about four years, and we'd heard about this music coming from the Beatles. Birmingham rock 'n' roll was a lot different from any other kind of rock 'n' roll in England, probably a bit more melodious.

So we were doing this show and somebody said "Oh, the Beatles are here today. They're top of the bill and they've just released their record called 'Love Me Do.'"

So we went on first, all dressed up in our Mexican outfits doing our bit. And then they came on and played this rhythm and blues via Hamburg.

Justin: You could see it coming, it was like a tidal wave. It was unstoppable once that whole Liverpool thing got started, and I guess it was mid 1963. Everything seemed to happen so fast back then, without you noticing it. Things happened, moved on, and changed every week.

John: I think the other thing that changed is that British rock music was founded on American rock music; it just was. The Gene Vincents, the Buddy Hollys, Little Richard, going back to Bill Haley, Eddie Cochran—it was all just built on that.

And English bands were trying to emulate that, and it was taking a lot of time. There was a period of time where we had to find out how we could do that.

And what was happening in England at the very turn of the sixties was like—bubble gum music, very whitewash, very calculated. And it was really uninteresting from English people's point of view.

Justin: The British always made the cover versions of the American rock 'n' roll. And after a few years, the British took the classic rock 'n' roll image and turned it into a cabaret kind of thing, where they were onstage Sunday nights at the London Palladium. It became very square, really. And the Beatles just burst through that. They made it possible for everyone to just pick up a guitar.

The big difference for musicians was that before the Beatles, you always had to have three guitars, a drummer, and a singer out front. And the Beatles just changed that. They proved that you could do it all at the same time.

The album I always really loved, and it was when they started experimenting with chord structures, was *A Hard Day's Night*. They began to move away from the standard three chord thing and just went into more interesting structures.

A Hard Day's Night was the album for me and "If I Fell" was the song. It started off in a different key to how it ended up, and it's a beautifully worked out song. There are some songs on that album that were very emotional and evocative. And for everybody just starting to write songs, as I was, it was a real turn-on and eye-opener.

The Moody Blues and the Beach Boys did a Fourth of July concert together in Washington, D.C., a few years back. As I recall, Ringo was on drums for that show. Tell us a little about that.

John: I think Ringo's image in America was slightly different than in England. In England, he is, was, and will be, this solid rock drummer.

But going back to the Beach Boys concert, I remember when Ringo got onstage, as soon as he started hitting the snare, I went, "Oh yeah, that's it!"

And it was great because Justin and I didn't know what we were going to do on the Beach Boys show. So when Ringo was belting away, the back beat was there, and you really couldn't go wrong. And then of course we all flew down to Miami and did the show on the beach on the same day, and it was fabulous.

Here's a question we ask a lot of folks, and with mixed results sometimes. Can you pick any favorite Beatle songs? Do any of them stand out?

John: There are sort of two phases. You know—the sort of "Please Please Me" Beatles at the very beginning and, I think as a record, "Strawberry Fields." I just couldn't follow that one—it was great.

Justin: I always liked *The White Album*, because it was so rough and loose and I loved all the things that were going on. But there's a Beatles album that's got some great stuff on it, but has always been very neglected. That's the other side of the *Yellow Submarine* album. Do you remember that? It was all George Martin stuff, with the Beatles doing five songs on the other side. And every one of those tracks was a classic.

It was between *Sgt. Pepper,* and *The White Album,* and "Bulldog," which is one of my favorite all-time John Lennon numbers.

John, didn't you play a little bit with George Harrison?

We did a concert in Birmingham in March of this year [1986] for the children's hospital. Electric Light Orchestra, the Moodies, Robert Plant as well, put a concert on to raise money for the hospital. And on the encore, obviously we were all onstage, George joined us. The whole show was videoed. In natural fact, a two-hour special went out in England, and hopefully it'll make it's way over here 'cause it was a great show.

DICK CAVETT

*". . . when we came back from
commercial, he [John Lennon] looked over
at the band and thanked them for playing
all of Paul's songs."*

•

Dick Cavett has forged a most successful career by simply being himself. And his considerable wit and wisdom, which were
showcased so well in the early seventies on
The Dick Cavett Show, permitted him access to
some of the world's most inaccessible celebri-
ties.

In 1971 and again in 1972, Cavett invited
John Lennon and Yoko Ono to appear on the
program. The pair eagerly accepted and used
their air-time as a forum for world peace,
their particular passion at the time. Cavett
would later appear as a character witness in
John's U.S. Immigration hearings.

Cavett further broke with talk-show tradition in 1971 when he taped an entire show
with George Harrison and Ravi Shankar.

Tell us about the time John and Yoko appeared on The Dick Cavett
Show. *When did you first hook up with them, and how did it come
about?*

I met them in the St. Regis hotel in their room on a rainy day.
He was immediately personable and felt like someone I had known
for a long time and perfectly easy to talk to. He was a decent guy.

Yoko, although she didn't talk much, seemed pleasant enough. One thing that did happen was that John pulled out a 16 mm film camera and said, "Could I take a little thing of you?" It later ended up in a movie of his, which then became a video. I had completely forgotten about it.

He did the same thing a few days before with Fred Astaire, having him dance into the room in Yoko's dream or something.

I remember them saying that they would do the show and saying that I was the only one remotely interested in some of the things they were. I think that's how he put it, although I wasn't sure how remote or immediate my interest was.

Does anything stand out in your memory about their appearance on the show?

He did an odd thing on the show. As he walked out, I remember he held his cigarette out and said, "See Janov, it didn't work!" And this sort of half-registered.

Afterwards, somebody said to me, "Did you notice that?" I said, "Yeah, what was that all about?" Turns out that whoever wrote the primal scream book, [Dr. Arthur] Janov, assured him his smoking would be stopped as a result of his therapy or whatever.

But they didn't seem nervous. [They were] easy, personable, and unremarkable in the sense that they were not intimidating; not a guy who was aware of how gigantic, how revered, or how rich he was, or how powerful, if he wanted to be.

Is their appearance one on which you look back fondly?

I think I did two ninety-minute shows with them, and maybe one other brief appearance. And yeah, I look back on them fondly, although I haven't actually looked back on them. I saw excerpts of one and realized that I'd love to get it out and look at the rest of it.

My secretary recently saw the [Jimi] Hendrix show, and the Lennon shows, and something is being done with the Lennon show, although I don't know what, so I shouldn't talk about it. But they ought to be seen, because so many people ask me about it. And since the Tom Snyder/Lennon show is on the market, I might as well get mine in—not for money of course!

One of the songs John and Yoko wanted to do on the Cavett show was the controversial "Woman Is the Nigger of the World." The network censors had a few problems with that, didn't they?

I don't remember when I found out that there was a problem with the song, but I was told that "Woman Is the Nigger of the World" had to come out.

[Imitating himself] "Why?"

[Imitating censor] "'Cause it will be offensive to blacks."

[Imitating himself again] "Oh yeah."

So I asked a lot of smart-ass questions that let people know I went to college and probably studied debate. But I really wanted to know why it had to come out. Because even if I knew why *they* thought it had to come out, it's not within my nature to acquiesce.

So I just said, "Well, I refuse." And we went to a higher authority. I probably attended a couple of meetings, said some impertinent things. Like they said that they asked four black employees if they would be offended. And I said, "Oh, did you ask *the* four black employees?" The lawyer started to kick me saying, "Save the jokes for later."

So the upshot of it was that they said it absolutely had to come out; there was no argument. And I really didn't know if I had anything to say about it or not.

So we compromised. I taped an insert that said, "The song you're about to hear has caused some controversy here at the network. There is a feeling that some people might be offended by it, but we feel that you should be able to make your own decision. Now here's the song."

DICK CAVETT

So the show went on with that insert and I don't think, to this day, anyone's complained about the song. Although there was a torrent of complaints about the mealymouthed insert that "Mr. Cavett" felt was necessary to put into the show!

Did you discuss the Beatles or anything about their music on the show?

On the show, we'd always go out to commercial with music, and then come back in [to the show] with it. And Bob Rosengarden could play anything at the drop of a hat with a signal and a downbeat. So maybe the last three words Lennon said would contain some reference and Rosengarden would play the appropriate Beatles song.

So once, when we came back from commercial, he [Lennon] looked over at the band and thanked them for playing all of Paul's songs.

When John was embattled in his fight with U.S. Immigration, you appeared on his behalf as a character witness, correct?

Yeah, I was, but I can't imagine what I said, although I know it was in *The New Yorker.* I remember thinking that I didn't prepare for it that well, that I was better at doing my show. I didn't know what would be the most effective thing to say.

The New Yorker's "Talk of the Town" covered that, and I didn't know they were there. I was stunned to read about it later.

The other day I ran into the lawyer who spoke just ahead of me. [At the time,] he said the Lennons were really a square couple, that they don't go out and seek the bright lights and the action and the jazzy parties.

Has it come out that the [Nixon] "Administration," as it was euphemistically called, "the Regime" wanted them out of the country? No doubt about it.

So I remember getting up and thinking, "God, I'm just sort of rambling here." But I was trying to say that the Lennons were not dangerous, and that there were plenty of things that they'd be better off giving their attention to.

Did you keep in contact with John and Yoko after that?

Not too much, although I did find a couple of letters from him that I probably didn't answer, in my awful way. I think one was written before they came on, and then one after. And then they came on again and they were friendly.

When I was going down to the court thing, I remember him coming up and saying, "Hi, Dick." I thought, "Why does he wear round glasses? They aren't becoming to anyone." I wondered what Lennon would look like in any other shaped glasses. I have a feeling that those glasses had something to do with his image. [They] made him look less threatening.

What were your feelings when John was killed?

I didn't think that Lennon was that—revered. I had no idea, and I doubt if he did. He couldn't have.

I knew people would be sorry, you know, as opposed to glad. But the numbers were overwhelming; like a world figure, like Gandhi, had been assassinated at an earlier time in history. Astounding.

I doubt if anybody knew. Even the people themselves didn't know how much they had invested in Lennon. I'm sure he'd have been embarrassed by it.

Has anybody ever straightened out the Jesus Christ quote? I remember at the time, it hit the fan something fierce. I don't remember what the wording was, but he was right. They were certainly more popular than Christ. You can tell by church attendance and the lack of Christianity demonstrated in the lives of most people. Everybody seemed to get the idea that he'd said, "We're better." It was an interesting flap.

We're interested in your assessment of the impact that the Beatles had on society, entertainment, music, etc.

The Beatles meant almost nothing to me at that time. I liked their music. I felt I could identify it. I knew it was a great booking coup to get Lennon.

I'd had [George] Harrison on, and I liked him very much as a person. But rock music in general has never meant much to me, but I like a lot of it.

I don't mean that I didn't like them at all. Since then I've realized that. And after Leonard Bernstein began telling us that it would not be amiss to compare Schumann with Lennon and McCartney's work, I began to realize that I liked it. It was good.

Then I really did realize, and my ear tells me, that they're superior.

Do you have a favorite Beatle song?

I can play "Eleanor Rigby" on the clarinet in B-flat, so maybe that's it! Oh yes, yes I do, and it's quite an obvious one. The one I really like the most—*[Hurriedly hums]* "Yesterday!" Is that McCartney?

Yeah, that's Paul. Did you ever meet or work with him?

I never met him. I did ninety minutes with George Harrison and Ravi Shankar. That was a good one. I'd like to see it again. I met Ringo at the airport once in London.

I think Paul's been asked to do the show. And then the last time he was around, doing everything in sight when the movie came out, I wasn't taping. Yeah, I'd like to do him, and maybe Ringo one day.

I remember when I was writing for Jerry Lewis, living in a little apartment in Bel Air, I saw a newscast in black and white saying, "There's a musical group taking England by storm. They have funny haircuts that resemble mops, and they're called, let me see here—the Beatles, and here's what they look like."

I remember thinking, "Hmmmm, looks like an act. Probably never hear of them again."

TOM PETTY

Elvis was before my time, but I was just kind of a weirdo kid and, at the age of eleven, started collecting all these records from the fifties. That was a strange cross to bear when you're in the fifth grade. But, when the Beatles came, I was old enough to kind of take part in that. That was my music. That was the era of music that really got me excited the most.

THE MONKEES

THE
MONKEES

"I distinctly remember driving down the
main drag where I used to live saying,
'God, I'd like to be one of the Beatles!'
And you have to be careful what you wish
for!"
—Mickey Dolenz

•

The Monkees were, very simply, America's
answer to the Beatles. A true product of
Beatlemania, they were conceived initially to
star in a television comedy series as an exten-
sion of the Beatles' film personalities—four
lovable musician chaps who romp through "a
day in the life" and wrap it all up with a
song.

However, the success of the Monkees ex-
ceeded all expectations. And for a time, their
popularity seemed to rival even that of the
Beatles themselves.

Davy Jones, Mickey Dolenz, Mike Nes-
mith, and Peter Tork dominated the Top Ten
record charts and TV screens alike. And although not really a band at the start, their
light pop songs and stage antics did the trick
for millions.

Although the two bands were pitted
against each other for a time, the Monkees
never ceased to be major fans of their so-
called competitors.

We spoke to Jones, Dolenz, and Tork on
their 1987 reunion tour.

DAVY JONES

How do you think the Beatles and the Monkees will be perceived years from now?

I don't know if they'll recognize individuals in years to come. I mean, [people may not know] the Monkees: Mickey, Mike, Peter, and Davy—and the Beatles: John, Paul, George, and Ringo, but you always seem to remember the groups.

Did you feel like there was a competition between the Monkees and the Beatles?

There is never any competition between bands. The Beatles were never in competition with the Monkees. We had a lot of respect for each other.

Didn't you sing backing vocals on a Ringo Starr Japanese TV commercial for leisure suits?

Yeah, I happened to be in the studio at the time with Harry Nilsson. We were hanging out. [They were] crazy days, you know, just getting about from party to party. We had been having a bottle of liquor all night, playing music, writing tunes, and we went into Ringo's session.

[Sings] "My suit, my suit, I really love my suit." I just happened to be there at the time, and it was just one of those crazy things.

I shared a lot of time in LA with Ringo and George Harrison, but not so much with Paul McCartney and John Lennon.

It was a case of time. It wasn't like we didn't want to spend company with each other. It was just that our schedules didn't gel.

If you had to pick a favorite Beatle song, what one would you choose?

"Penny Lane."

PETER TORK

Where were you and what were you doing when you first heard the Beatles?

Well, as you know, the Beatles were an enormous impact. I was a folk singer until the Beatles came along. There was no particular virtue to, or we didn't know from, commercial music in those days. Elvis Presley was waning in those days, and he was just another schlock musician. He was scary when he first came out, but six or seven years down the road, he was just Old El doing his thing.

And all the commercial musicians were to be despised, so all that was left was Pete Seeger and the folk music world. That was the only thing that had any integrity.

So we were on the Village streets; me, Steve Stills, John Hopkins, John Sebastian, Richie Havens, even Richard Pryor, who was doing comedy at one of the downstairs clubs—then along came the Beatles!

They were scary too, although not in the same way that Elvis was. The Beatles would do these sweet little harmonies and then throw in a blues lick on the guitar. You know, original music ideas with lots of thought and creativity. God, it was so good.

So when somebody told me that this [the Monkees] was going to be like a Beatles thing, with singing and music and comedy, I took to it like a duck to water.

Do you have any favorite Beatles songs?

I have a couple of them. "Penny Lane," "Eleanor Rigby," and "Strawberry Fields." Those three are just monster songs. And then there's the whole *Sgt. Pepper* album, with "Fixing a Hole" in particular. But then how can you dispute a magnum opus like "A Day in the Life"?

But that era of Beatles songs marks the peak of the Beatle world for me. Especially those three that I mentioned first. "Penny Lane" just rips me up every time I hear it.

MICKEY DOLENZ

How did the Beatles affect you?

I was a fan like everybody else. I remember as early as '64, living in the Valley in California, going to high school when the Beatles broke. And me and all my friends were tremendous fans.

I distinctly remember driving down the main drag where I used to live saying, "God, I'd like to be one of the Beatles!" And you have to be careful what you wish for!

What did you think of the comparisons between the Monkees and the Beatles?

I don't think the Monkees were anything like the Beatles. I don't think there's any comparison at all. A lot of people did make comparisons, but it was chalk and cheese.

They had nothing to do with each other, except for music. But the sensibilities behind the Beatles and the Monkees were very, very different. We were much closer to the Marx Brothers: "The Marx Brothers of Music," if you will.

But I was just a big fan [of the Beatles] and remain so to this day.

Did you get a chance to meet them, to know them?

Yeah, we met them and got to spend quite a bit of time with them.

I went to England, on my first trip there, and the publicity people set up a Monkees-meets-Beatles thing. And little did they know, all I wanted was an autograph. I met Paul McCartney, and I couldn't even speak. I was dumbfounded, but we got along real well.

Then I went to some of their sessions. "Strawberry Fields" was one, and you'd be surprised, it was very tame. Everybody sat around, played a little bit, and then had tea. Four o'clock, everybody breaks "We must have tea!"

Can you settle on one or a few favorite Beatle songs?

Oh God, there are millions! "Drive My Car," "Rock 'n' Roll Music," although it wasn't one that they wrote—ahhhh! The list is endless—"Girl." Oh, I mean, you could name *any* song!

ROGER McGUINN

ROGER
MCGUINN
(OF THE
BYRDS)

"It is a very strange business, where in a couple of years I could be in a position where they'd be listening to what I was doing."

•

In just a few years, Roger McGuinn went from imitating the Beatles, as a struggling folk singer, to influencing the Beatles, as a member of the seminal California folk-rock band, the Byrds.

McGuinn formed the Byrds in 1965 along with David Crosby, Chris Hillman, Gene Clark, and Mike Clarke. They made an immediate sensation with their soaring, ambitious harmonies and McGuinn's stylized twelve-string Rickenbacker guitar.

The Byrds were eventually called America's answer to the Beatles, and they even enlisted the skills of Beatles publicist Derek Taylor for a time.

The two bands crossed paths frequently during the salad days of the sixties and Roger McGuinn recalled several of their more memorable encounters for us.

Roger, your twelve-string electric guitar has been your most identifiable sound which, considering your singing, is saying something. Tell us how George Harrison played a role in getting you to try it in the first place?

I had been playing a Gibson acoustic twelve-string that Bobby Darin had given me after he'd broke my other twelve-string. I was interested in making electric music because we now had electric drums and bass to contend with and ride over. So I had a pickup for my Gibson guitar.

At the time, I don't remember there being an electric twelve-string on the market prior to Rickenbacker, but I guess there was. We didn't have a lot of money prior to our cutting "Mr. Tambourine Man" and we went to see *A Hard Day's Night*. Saw it a couple of times.

The second time through, I noticed that the guitar George Harrison was playing was not a six-string, even though it looked like one. You see, the head stock of the Rickenbacker twelve was kind of sneaky; it hid the six octave strings behind the six regular strings, instead of having them in consecutive order like most twelve-string guitars.

When George turned it to a certain angle I could see that there were pegs sticking out the back of it. And I went, "Aw, it's a twelve-string!"

So I went to the music store and checked it out, and they had one. There were only about sixty of them made in the world at that time—and I got one of them.

There's an interesting story that goes with your song "Eight Miles High." For many folks, the song was perceived as a drug song—or as referring to drugs. But it had nothing to do with drugs. In fact, the title was derived from a Beatles song, wasn't it?

"Eight Miles High" was never a drug song. We were into drugs when we wrote it, and I was part of the drug culture, although I'm not anymore.

The fact that we were talking about "eight miles high" was misconstrued as a drug song, but the song was actually written about an airplane ride over to England, about our culture shock when we got there, and our treatment from the British press.

I was originally going to call the song "Six Miles High." The reason for the six miles high was because airplanes usually travel at around thirty-nine thousand feet, which would translate into six miles. I am sort of scientific and would prefer to be more accurate.

But Gene Clark and I talked about it and he thought that six miles high, although scientifically accurate, didn't have a poetic ring to it that [the Beatles'] "Eight Days a Week" had. I agreed with him and we changed it to "Eight Miles High."

What was your first impression of Beatle music?

I loved it! The first time I heard the Beatles I was living in the Earl Hotel on Washington Square Park [in New York City]. I was scuffling. I had just stopped working for Bobby Darin's publishing company and started working in little coffee houses for a living.

I saw a clip of the Beatles on television, the one Brian Epstein had sent over, with the screaming girls going after them and everything. I guess this was just as "I Want To Hold Your Hand" and "She Loves You" were released. I loved that stuff, and I went out and bought the album, took it back to my apartment, and learned all the songs.

So I started playing them at the coffee houses. In fact, one of the coffee houses I was working at put a sign out front: BEATLE IMITATIONS, which was really embarrassing for me. But people came in and threw money in the hat, which is how you made your money.

And within a few short years, Roger McGuinn was influencing the Beatles.

It is a very strange business, where in a couple of years I could be in a position where they'd be listening to what I was doing. The most rewarding thing, aside from making money and getting a number one hit—meeting the Beatles and having them respect what I was doing was very rewarding.

They came down to see us in London. Derek Taylor was with us and he introduced us, and we rented a little hotel room right upstairs. We all went up there and hung out. It was kind of awkward and we were just sort of standing around looking at each other.

Then John said, "I want to see your little glasses." So I gave him my glasses which I used for vision, and since he was near-sighted himself, he was very curious about that. He always had to take off his glasses because he didn't want to appear with them on stage. So I had given him a way to wear glasses and still be cool. He thought that was neat.

Then George and David [Crosby] started talking about guitars and stuff. Still it wasn't a very long meeting, maybe about twenty minutes, and then we all went home.

There's a song on Rubber Soul, *written by George Harrison, called "If I Needed Someone." The prevailing riff from the song sounds a lot like a riff you had in "The Bells of Rhymney." In fact, didn't George write to Derek Taylor and tell him that?*

Derek delivered the message and said, "George wants you to know that the song 'If I Needed Someone' was inspired by the lick in "The Bells of Rhymney." In fact, George later told me himself. And even if he hadn't told me, I would have known it anyway, because it was the same lick. But I was very honored to see that.

In a way, we had sort of an international secret code going back and forth through records. You know, like those movies from the Second World War where the BBC would play a certain song and the agents out in Germany would get the message. So that was fun. And "If I Needed Someone" is one of my favorite songs by them!

Roger McGuinn and the Byrds are also responsible for turning George Harrison and the Beatles on to Indian music. It's a fact not widely known.

I feel like I'm bragging if I say that to someone, but yeah, that's true.

We were up in their house in Bel Air, and we were sitting on the bathroom floor. Because of all the security guards, and all the people surrounding the house, that was the only place we could have any privacy.

Crosby and I had our twelve-strings with us, and John and George were in there listening to David tell them about Ravi Shankar. So we told George and John about Indian music. We showed them the licks and they were blown away. They loved it.

I guess I also helped them get into Eastern religion, which was strange too. I remember asking George if he believed in God, and he said, "Well, we don't know about that yet." I thought that was very fascinating, because he didn't answer in the first person. He answered in the plural, like the Beatles were a gestalt or something. It was like they had combined minds. They couldn't think in terms of their own personal choices. I thought that was really interesting.

And the positive side of that was something that I really admired a lot. That was the fact that they stood up for each other as a really strong team. If you attacked one of them, the other three would come down on you in a second. It was really a tight unit.

Anyway, I'm sorry about the Eastern religion, but they got out of that later.

You were also present at a party with John Lennon and Peter Fonda. And, after some partying, Peter went on a verbal binge about being dead and coming back. Lennon was startled, but came out of it with a song, "She Said She Said."

He kept telling John about his scar and how he'd been dead for a while. He had some sort of operation and had technically died and came back to life.

We were all on acid, and John couldn't take it. It was too much, and he didn't want to hear it. He said, "Get this guy out of here!" It was morbid and bizarre.

We had just finished watching *Cat Ballou* with Jane Fonda in it. So John didn't want to have anything to do with any of the Fondas *[laughing]*. He was holding the movie against Peter, and then what he said was on top of that.

I had heard that the Beatles came to see the Byrds at the Whiskey A Go-Go in LA. Do you remember that at all?

I don't remember them coming to the Whiskey, but I do remember them being in the studio when we were cutting songs like "She Don't Care About Time." I remember George and Paul being in the studio for that.

A Byrd's song, "Artificial Energy," contains the line, "She's got a ticket to ride." Was that an intentional reference?

I guess we just used it. It was the line, "She's got a ticket to ride," and I guess we used it because once lines are out there, they sort of become public domain or building blocks for other songs. I've heard that a lot in different songs, where they take a line from one song and use it in a totally different context.

Can you think of any favorite Beatle songs?

There are so many wonderful songs. I think my favorites, and maybe they're the bubble gum ones, but "She Loves You" and "I Want to Hold Your Hand." I really love those songs. And more for their musical value. Their words weren't so meaningful, but the chord changes really had magic in them.

They had all those changes that I'd loved in folk music. The way they went through those chords is still something that gave me goose bumps. I love those songs.

Of the older stuff, I like "Rain" and "The Long and Winding Road."

DEREK
TAYLOR

"There's a song, 'Penny Lane,' that says,
'You think you're in a play, and you are
anyway.' And I think that's how all of us
have gotten the trip; seeing life as being a
bit of a play or a great novel."

•

Derek Taylor was the Beatles' press agent
and, later, the press officer for Apple Corps.
Ltd. In fact he was a veritable Jack-of-all-
trades, using his best streetwise promotional
skills to parlay his experience in the newspaper business into a serviceable position as the
band's liaison, peacemaker, and spokesman.

An author as well, Taylor helped Brian
Epstein with his autobiography, *A Cellarful of
Noise*, and handled the text for George Harri-
son's *I Me Mine*. His own published works
include *As Time Goes By* and *It Was Twenty
Years Ago Today*, the latter a tribute to 1967
when he was the publicity director for the
Monterey Pop Festival.

Another of Taylor's pet projects was *All
You Need Is Cash*, a British film spoof on the
Beatles featuring the satirical group, the
Rutles.

There's probably one question you've been fielding more than any other;
a question which is foremost on the minds of rock fans everywhere, and
here it comes. When are the Rutles getting back together?

It's a definite problem now. The Rutles have a very busy schedule. Dirk [McQuickly] is busy with Gilbert and Sullivan these days. Stig [O'Hara] went to Australia where, if you remember, Leggy [Mountbatten] went to live. Leggy and Dirk have a difficult relationship. So I think we're going to have to wait for that.

And of course, there is also the problem of royalties, and Normal songs looking for half of the Rutles royalties. It may be some years before that bottle of litigation has been drained.

Thanks for clearing that up. Now to your latest book, It Was Twenty Years Ago Today. *It's your third book, but you've helped some other folks with theirs.*

Yeah, I mentioned *Fifty Years Adrift* on the cover flap, along with *As Time Goes By*, but not the book I did with Michelle Phillips, or the one with Brian Epstein [*A Cellarful of Noise*].

What prompted you to do this latest one?

It's a companion to a film which we made in England, San Francisco, and New York, based on the year 1967. It used *Sgt. Pepper* as a thread, a springboard to show what kind of a year it was. The film is a two-hour documentary, already screened in Canada, New Zealand, and London to massive audiences, and going out in America on public television. It should be seen, not only for the Beatles, but [because it's] very American as well. A lot of the counterculture were Americans.

Can you recall your first exposure to Sgt. Pepper?

I have to be inexact in this, if I can make that clear. I heard it at John's house in Weybridge. I heard some of it, if not all, with him sort of chattering. That would have been in May, when we went over for Brian Epstein's housewarming.

But hindsight tells me that I must have heard it in LA, before that. I have a clear memory of playing it for everybody in the Monterey Pop Festival offices, around lunch time. Al Kooper, Michelle [Phillips], and all those people were there. They were all knocked out by it, because it was so breathtakingly better than anything else around.

But by the time John got to play it for me, they had gotten

DEREK TAYLOR

used to it, and he was more interested in "Baby You're A Rich Man." As I tried to explain in the book, it was so familiar to him that it was old hat.

I'm not trying to say that they weren't excited about it, because they knew it would be a big hit. They hadn't made any mistakes up until then.

Twenty years later, it's still the album by which all others are judged.

Everyone's opinion is subjective, but I still find it a very fresh album. I've heard it a lot today.

According to Paul, the idea stemmed from the Beach Boys' Pet Sounds *LP.*

I've never discussed that with him, but I do know that they were very keen on the Beach Boys. They were excited by the Byrds as friends, because the Byrds were much more exotic. They came in after the Beatles had hit, with a brand new sound.

The Beach Boys were around when the Beatles began and were therefore looked upon as fair competition.

So when the Beatles were top of the heap, America had surrendered to the British invasion. Not to put the Beach Boys down, but even Freddie and the Dreamers were hotter than them then. So was Herman's Hermits and so on.

But when the Byrds came, it was then an answering cry from America to what the Beatles had begun. So that became rather an exotic relationship. They were stealing bits from each other, and giving bits to each other.

George wrote a letter to me, when I was living in LA: "Tell Jim [Byrds leader Roger McGuinn] that something from 'If I Needed Someone' is derived from something in 'The Bells of Rhymney' and something from 'She Don't Care About Time.'" These people could give one listen to something and pick up a trick or two, absorb it, and know that they weren't going to be sued by each other. Nobody sued each other then; it was all "love and peace."

The international movement in rock music began in that cross-fertilization.

You visited the Haight-Ashbury district with George Harrison back in the years before that movement. Was George disillusioned by it?

Yes, he was, although I was not. I had been through the area before, when we were planning the Monterey Pop Festival. I had seen it at a time in the correctly called Summer of Love, as early as February or March.

I had to go there and convince Ralph Gleason that we were not all nasty people from Hollywood. So I was there, and I had a sense of the place, the Victorian buildings, and the hippies just running around having a wonderful time. Apparently there was no work being done; people were just hanging out, although we had work to do.

So I had no preconceived ideas when I went with George, because I had been there. It had definitely changed by August, but I don't actually buy George's view entirely, because it didn't seem to me to be as bad as he found it.

He says it was like the Bowery. But he had had a little LSD at the time as he was seeing people with faces like Hoovers, fish heads jumping out of doorways, etc.

But there were actually very many nice people following us down the street, in rather a Pied-Piper sort of way.

Somebody gave George a guitar and asked him to play, and he was reluctant, thought it a bit corny, almost like a movie we were creating there: Here is the "Beat" in Haight-Ashbury, with his beautiful wife, Patti, her beautiful sister Jenny, his friend Derek, his old friend Neil [Aspinall], a strange Greek fellow called Magic Alex. We were an exotic bunch of English loonies.

For one of the hippies to suddenly give George a guitar seemed too scripted. However, if George said no, it would have been brutal, callous, and silly. So reluctantly, he played a few bars of something, sitting on the grass on Hippy Hill.

I thought to myself, being very straight at the time, "This really is some kind of a dream." Were I young and susceptible, I would have thought I was in heaven. And that's what I saw the whole thing as being about. It really was a time of dreaming. You have enough bad dreams and bad vibes that we can create a few little plays within a play. So we did.

I took them to Haight-Ashbury with the best of intentions. That it didn't work out for George is unfortunate. A lot of people enjoyed the day.

Is it true that George Harrison wrote "Blue Jay Way" while waiting for you to arrive at his house in Los Angeles?

Yes. It was incidental that he was waiting for us. But I've never liked that thing that it was about me. It's an awful and vain thing to say.

But in fact, the basis of the song was fundamentally simple. Whenever he [George Harrison] or any of them came to town, they would give us a ring, because we were the friends in town.

They'd ring and say, "We're here."

"Where are you?"

"Blue Jay Way."

"Where's that?"

"I don't know, up in the hills."

"Never mind, we'll ask a policeman. There's plenty of them around."

So we set out. And while he was waiting, with jet lag, and Patti, he sat down at an organ in the hall and started, "Please don't be long. . . . My friends have lost their way. . . . There's a fog upon LA. They'll ask a policeman on the beat; there's so many there to meet."

So by the time we got there, it was virtually intact. Of course, at the time I felt very bad. Here were these wretchedly jet-lagged people, and we were about two hours late. But here, indeed, was a song which turned up in *Magical Mystery Tour* [the film] through a prism with about eight images, with him in a red jacket, sitting and playing piano on the floor.

So there you are.

One other little thing that gives you the picture of the interpretation of Beatle lyrics. In one of the great books, called *Twilight of the Gods*, the author says, "This song is about the lost young of our time. 'My friends have lost their way.'"

And then there was another interpretation that said the line, "Please don't be long," was actually giving instructions to the young: "Don't belong." As in "Don't belong to society as we know it. Drop out."

So it's just a simple little song!

George Harrison also says that you had a hand in another Beatle song, "Savoy Truffle." Did you actually write some of it?

A bit of it. It's funny. We always say, "If I had a bit of that song, I could have cleaned up! This is the big one, Derek; we could have cleaned up!" In fact he said that about this book, before I left. "This could be the big one!"

We know, in fact, that there's never *a* big one. They're all a little part of the big one.

But the song was "Savoy Truffle," and George said "We need a bit here—Da da da da da da, da da." So I thought again of Alan Pariser, my good friend, who'd done a film called *You Are What You Eat*, which was a very pippy thing: "Don't eat meat, man, or you'll be filled with the adrenaline of frightened animals."

So I said, "You know that what you eat, you are." So that was the bit from "Savoy Truffle."

Then one night, John and I were sitting with Neil Aspinall. He'd written the first bit of a song called "Happiness is a Warm Gun," which he'd gotten from an advertisement. And he needed a middle bit. So he said, "Neil, take some notes, we'll get some stuff down. Think of phrases."

[We came up with] "lizards on a windowpane," which is a very LA image. There are always lizards jumping up and down windowpanes.

Then there was, "There's a man in the crowd with a mirror on his boots." That was a naughty man who went around football matches looking up girls' skirts. He actually slotted a mirror in the toe cap of his shoe, which seems to be a complicated way of getting a thrill, but there you are. So that became, "The man with the multicolor mirror on his hobnail boot," which is beautiful meter, isn't it?

Then there was the line about the bar of soap, "A soap impression of his wife which he ate, and donated to the National Trust." Well, the National Trust is a body in England which looks after the common land, the open air, out in the country.

So that was a rather crude reference to a man who eats a bar of soap and then goes behind a bush and evacuates, donating this curious thing to the National Trust.

There is all sorts of stuff like that in that song. And when you put it all together, it's a series of layers of images. It's like a whole mess of color.

I'll tell you, I listened to *Sgt. Pepper*, and I don't know how they could have been so inspired. When Ringo goes to that high note at the end of "With a Little Help from My Friends," and they all come in underneath, there's such cooperative skill there. And isn't that the thing?

I don't know how those men knew such things at such a young age. Because they were only boys. George Martin was older, but that doesn't account for what was real genius.

Yours was a special relationship with the boys. You seemed to be able to click with them on a wit level, thereby solidifying your place in their entourage.

I could tell jokes. I mean, I know all that old Liverpool stuff. Those awful jokes, like the one about the encyclopedia salesman knocking on the door of a very promising-looking house in Liverpool. A little, ignorant-looking boy answers the door, and the guy says, "Is your mother at home?"

"No, she's in prison; she's a prostitute."

"Well, is your father in?"

"No, he's in jail; He's a burglar. They're both doing time."

"Well, what about your sister?"

"I haven't got a sister. She's dead."

"Well, what about your brother?"

He says, "Well, my brother is at the university."

So the encyclopedia salesman brightens up and says, "Oh, well, maybe he'd be interested in buying a book?"

And the boy says, "Oh no, he's in a bottle. He's got two heads!"

So that kind of thing, said well, amused them. The only advantage I had over them was that I was ten years older, and knew all the jokes first.

But I was amiable and eager to learn, and I did know about [the] newspaper [business]. But I knew nothing about publicity, and I still don't. I'm just an enthusiast with winning ways.

Weren't you with the Beatles in Paris when they first got the news that "I Want to Hold Your Hand" went to number one in America?

Yes. That moment was the big one, without being facetious. You have no idea, as an American—you can't see from outside what America means to the other worlds. America is the big one. It's the big power, the country everybody knows.

Let's put this in perspective. The Beatles were top of the heap. Europe was wiped out. France was not really falling, although I'd formed the impression that they'd got as close to success in France as any English band could. The French don't like the British a lot, and the feeling is mutual, though I do [like them].

But could America be won over? This was the one. And as I say, as an American, you can't see how this country seems abroad.

Success here was something to aspire to. Nobody had done it, except for the movie stars.

So when the telegram came through: CASHBOX, NUMBER ONE —IT'S HAPPENED, it really took a lot of reading. It's like winning the big lottery. [You think,] "It can't be true," and you read it over and over.

But yes, it was true, and the phone calls followed it up. And they were really hopping around with delight. They were coming to America anyway, they'd been booked on *Ed Sullivan* for two or three shows at a good rate. Epstein had got fares paid, as well as hotels. So that was a very nice coup. The Sullivan show was a perfect setting. It wouldn't seem so now, but it was.

And bang! They got a number one.

So I was on the phone home, ringing [my wife] Joan to say that I was OK. George said, "Let me talk to her." And he said to her, "Mrs. Taylor, we're number one in *Cashbox* magazine in America. Isn't it great?"

It was a good, innocent, sincere moment. It showed that these were people that were not blasé then, and never did become that way. I say, as an honest man, that George is as delighted today with his own small success as he was thirty years ago.

There is an innocence and decency about these people which transcends the enormous fame, which damn near got them.

Were you on the plane when they first came to America?

No, I was not, and I was very angry. I was still a newspaper man. That's when I decided I would have to join them. If I wanted to get on this adventure—and I did—then I would have to get involved.

I then made sure I didn't miss out on anything else. I decided that I didn't want to participate in anything else.

I can't think of a single television performance ever that had a greater impact on more kids than the Beatles on Ed Sullivan. *More people saw that, and were affected by that, than is countable.*

The Beatles were right on, weren't they? There was no deception. There was never a question at a press conference where they would bluff their way through an answer. If they didn't know, they'd say they didn't know.

They had a healthy ignorance that made them very accessible. They also had the discipline from playing in Hamburg and [from] Epstein's management to do those nice bows at the end.

So they weren't horrifying to parents. They may have looked a bit weird, though they don't now. They're neat now. And yet the music was so alert and progressive that even heavy musicians thought "Hey, these guys are good." I mean, America took some impressing.

Almost everything that happened to them, except for the ending, was so incredibly well scripted that you can't believe it actually happened. How could you write a better story? So they would do two Hollywood Bowls, two Sheas, a Dodger, a Candlestick, and then bye-bye!

And then the final words spoken on the film would be "I hope we passed the audition!" And there would never be a reunion.

Tell us a little bit about doing Brian Epstein's biography, A Cellarful of Noise.

Well, we should have taken more time, and I should have written it better. I notice that [Beatle biographer] Hunter Davies has a poor view of the writing style. I'd say it was the writing of a *Daily Express* journalist, done on the run.

It's the sort of thing you do by numbers. You get the salient facts, then you need a crucial little link at the beginning. "Raymond Jones, a leather-jacketed boy wanders into the store looking for a record called 'My Bonnie' by the Beatles." Then you just bang the book out as fast as you can. I never wrote anything so long, so fast.

Journalists in those days could knock out three thousand words on the phone immediately after seeing an event. It wouldn't be well written, but it would be printable.

And that's what *A Cellarful of Noise* was. We wanted to tell an incredible story, and a lot of it stands up. They were, and are, the biggest thing since Elvis. And in some ways [they] are bigger than Elvis; and in some ways, not as big. Elvis is king, but they were the Beatles. And Bob Dylan was their hero.

I know you weren't there, but what did you hear about the summit meeting between the Beatles and Elvis?

It was the big summit. There was a carefully arranged photograph in which the print was squeezed to make it look like they were shaking hands. I think it's published in *Photoplay*. But in reality, I'm not sure if a good photograph was ever taken of those five people together.

But whatever it was that you would photograph could never be like the moment. Like, "What's going on here? Can this all be in one room?"

I talked to them and I talked to Neil about it. It may have been an anticlimax, although I doubt it. It may have been one of those moments that was so heavy, or weird, that you can't really take it in. You don't know how you felt.

George, however, remembers meeting Elvis backstage some years later, when Elvis' clothing had become so bloody enormous: capes, huge collars, looking like the Boss from the Flash Gordon series. So George said, "I felt so small. There I am in sneakers and jeans, and here's this giant."

Although in the seventies, the Beatles and Elvis, you couldn't have put a wafer between them in terms of power. It was still possible for them to see each other as strangers in a strange land. They occupied different worlds, didn't they?

I think that poor Elvis, for one reason or another, lost the handle on reality. Whereas the Fab Four never really left the real world.

I remember Brian saying at the very beginning, "God, Colonel Parker doesn't know how lucky he has it to just have one of them. It's such hard work taking care of four."

But Elvis could have done with three equal chums. The Beatles at least had each other. There were four equals having a load of laughs together. It's important not to have illusions about yourself, and it's important to have friends who can criticize each other, cut through the bullshit, and pull the rug away from somebody who's getting a bit beyond themselves.

Tell us a little bit about the Australia trip. It seemed to be even more frenzied than the America trips.

When the Beatles arrived in Adelaide, it was like a healing tour. There was a big open car; with no threat of danger, the boys could sit on the back of it. I think I was in one of the open cars, as a matter of fact.

226 · *Ticket to Ride*

And the entire population of the great city turned out. It was what I call the peak of the black and white period, before color. And here were images out of the air, before *A Hard Day's Night*, so they hadn't been seen on any screen. And here they were in their midst.

The Australians were also the first people to provide the Beatles with balconies from which to wave. And there's something about a balcony appearance which reminded people of royalty, or the darker side, of Hitler.

America was always much more frenzied than it seemed because there was never any peace outside the hotel. And the noise of screaming all night, thousands of fans with no home to go to, so you really got claustrophobia.

I once went to Atlantic City's steel pier for a four-second walk. I got so panic-stricken I said, "Where are my friends? Where are the road managers? Where am I?" So I turned around and walked straight back into the hotel and felt safety at last.

From Atlantic City, they went to Philadelphia. Do you have any recollections of that show?

I have physical memories. I can remember where I was standing. I think they were in the middle [of Convention Hall], and I think there was a row of VIPs, including Dick Clark, who'd been successful there and then moved on. But he came back for that show. There was a very strong DJ presence at the Philadelphia concert. And I seem to remember them being surrounded by people at one end of the hall, although I don't know if I'm right.

It was a very urban concert, although Philadelphia is surrounded by a lot of greenery. There were a lot of police, all the men in suits. It was an extremely good feeling because it is a rock 'n' roll town. People were always anxious to tell us that, and it did show.

There is something about all the concerts, but this one I remember, especially with Dick Clark there—and that fellow's famous. And Fabian's from there and [Frankie] Avalon, names that were only legends to us.

In The Longest Cocktail Party *by Richard Di Lello, he talks about the chaotic days of Apple. How accurate was that book?*

They were chaotic days if seen from the outside. The book was extremely accurate. It's as good as you'll get on any subject. We never made a note. Rolled joints all day for our guests and ourselves. We manipulated our guests, not so we could control them, but so we could get a handle on who wanted what. And we had hundreds of people through our room, everyone with a different need, whether it was a Krishna or a Hell's Angel.

Ken Kesey wanted to recite. Or a Joe Smith or Mo Ostin from Warner Brothers wanted to say hi. "Put them in the back room, Ringo, roll them a joint." "Lauren Bacall's downstairs, wants to meet them. I can only find two of them." It was crowd-pleasing on the grand scale.

In Fifty Years Adrift, *you said that the best part of 1977–78 was the Rutles. How wryly accurate was that spoof?*

It was a great show. The best documentary we'll ever see on the Beatles.

So the concept was to get all the footage you can and watch it, replicate where you can with twists of irony. And if you're going to get George [Harrison] involved, then he must not be a protected person.

You can make fun of the Maharishi, so he becomes Arthur Soltzen the Surrey mystic. George becomes "Stig," a silly name. Paul must be impersonated in a merciless way—at the royal show, doing that trick where he points to his watch saying, "We've got to go," as if they'd been on stage for three hours. And they'd only done four songs.

And of course, John and Yoko are shown being a bit silly—in the shower for peace.

But my information is that they all took it very well. George, of course, gave full support. He played the reporter with the white wig on.

In a way, the Rutles removed the responsibility of making a documentary from the Beatles, by being a once-removed parody. It's the same way *Sgt. Pepper* took away the heat from being Beatles. It's a nice thing to be able to watch yourself watching yourself.

George loves the Rutles. He speaks highly of the Rutles in *I Me Mine*. His dream would be that if he could live his life again, they would all be in one big band, the Bonzo Dog Band. So that they, the Beatles, wouldn't perhaps be so heavy and important.

It is important for me to say that there is more to life than the Beatles. There is nothing more tedious than a one-note, obsessive maniac approach to this thing.

Dig it, enjoy it, relive it if you like, but there is a big Rutle world out there that is worth looking at as well. The Beatles were wonderful, but there are other things in life too.

In your opinion, did John finally come to reconcile his role as a Beatle? Did he ever get comfortable with the entire thing?

There are letters in the book that show it became a fairly comfortable thing. 1971 and '72 were the bad years, '73 and '74 were the mad years when he was out on a limb. I started to see him a lot then, because I was drinking a lot then too, having a lot of laughs.

By then, he could see it safely from a distance, and by '76, when he was sober, he was quite fascinated by where they'd been and how well they'd done. He was a multi-level kind of genius, wasn't he?

He was a historian, he was a trivia collector, a concerned man, but also very flippant as well. Cruel and generous. George would say he'd give you anything off the walls. So would George.

He'd go to the window and say, "It's like a great big garden out there, only I don't have to do it or pay the gardeners. Isn't it great?" And that's a wonderful way of looking at Central Park. It shows a good, uncluttered way of looking at life. So you don't own Central Park—although he was busy acquiring apartments apparently.

But you can take a cheerful view of that too. It was nobody's business if he wanted to own all the apartments in the Dakota. Secondly, it could have been just a big joke. He could have easily said, "Wouldn't it be marvelous to own all the apartments in this building," and then give them all away. I don't know whether he said that, or whether he didn't. But he was quite nimble enough to have crazy dreams and realize them.

I remember him saying during 1964, when we were in Sweden, "Funny thing. What would you rather be known for, making a hundred thousand tables or smacking up the world like Hitler?"

Life is a matter of choices, isn't it? You can be terrible, or wonderful, and sometimes there's hardly any difference between the two. Because it's all mad, anyway.

There's a song, "Penny Lane," that says "You think you're in a play, and you are anyway." And I think that's how all of us have gotten the trip; seeing life as being a bit of a play or a great novel.

Tell us about George's relationship with John after the Beatles. In the early days, he was a follower and always looked up to John. But afterwards there was a bit of tension. I remember that John was a little upset with I Me Mine.

John said, "He mentioned every two-bit guitarist on the way up, and I'm hardly in it. I was his friend and sort of father figure."

Actually, there were several references to John. John was never that accurate. He used to talk about "millions of things" when he meant "three."

So having helped George [with *I Me Mine*]—I didn't ghostwrite it, I interviewed him—I would say that it wasn't intended to be a Beatles tribute by George. And had a few weeks or months passed before the horrors of December [1980], that too could have been dissipated.

I'm not entitled to take an inside view of John and George's relationship, but it's always been my impression that it's an over-simplification to say that George was always a follower. Intellectually, and in terms of shared vision, George and John had a lot in common. They were people who really enjoyed hanging out together in the dreaming, acid days, in '66, '67.

George is pretty remarkable. He is a self-educated powerhouse of understanding and knowledge. He's a man who couldn't take his O levels [basic exams] at school because he didn't work hard enough, yet he knows a lot of Latin.

So I've always seen them [John and George] as intellectual equals. It's not just John and Paul, there were other factors.

MICHAEL HUTCHENCE (OF INXS)

I remember the Beatles at a very young age. One of the first albums I bought was *Sgt. Pepper*. Even though I was quite young, I remember being real caught up in all the mysticism and finding all those clues and the whole trip of the Beatles . . . the mystique behind them. It still lives with you; it really doesn't disappear.

RINGO STARR AND WIFE
BARBARA BACH

RINGO STARR

*"I made a decision in my life that I was a
musician. . . . And I left the factory. I
didn't know, nobody could have known,
that it would turn into this. It was just
in my own soul."*

•

Ringo Starr once called himself the Mr.
Show Business of the Beatles. And time has
proven him right. The most quirky and col-
orful member of the band, Mr. Richard Star-
key still commands our attention.

Scott Muni's first encounter with Ringo
Starr was a wild one. Scott helped Ringo re-
cover his cherished Saint Christopher's
medal, which had been torn off the hapless
Beatle as he ran through a crowd of rabid
fans outside a New York City hotel. The
next time they met, Ringo fainted as Scott
was setting up their interview.

Ringo was a happy-go-lucky kid with a
hard-luck streak. He got a set of drums at the
age of fourteen, left school a year later.

His role as "Beatle Ringo" was perfectly
suited. He charmed the press with candor
and cunning. The plots of *A Hard Day's Night*
and *Help!* revolved around him—and he
kept it all balanced as a steady, creative
drummer.

Ringo scored his first hit single, the aptly
titled "It Don't Come Easy," in 1971 and
went on to land numerous songs on the top

of the charts, including "Back Off Booga-loo," "Photograph," and "You're Sixteen."

Ringo has dabbled in acting, directing, and commercial appearances. And he currently hosts the brand new PBS series for children, *Shining Time Station*.

In 1987 he lent his charming presence to help promote a British restaurant chain. *Ticket to Ride* caught up with Ringo at the grand opening of one of these ventures, The London Brassiere in Atlanta, Georgia, where he was working the room along with such luminaries as Willie Nelson and Bill Wyman.

Ringo showed us to our table.

Ringo, what made you get involved in a restaurant in Atlanta, Georgia?

Well, see, it's not like we opened the restaurant. Bill, Willie, and I are just the show-business faces. I mean, we really are.

Alan Rubin is in charge of the restaurant, as he's opened them in England, in Europe, and hotels. He knows the business. So it'd be silly if, say, Bill and I opened a restaurant. We know nothing about it. So we got involved with these people who opened restaurants in England and they asked us if we would be involved in this.

They chose Atlanta, we *all* chose Atlanta, because of the involvement with the Peachtree Center. They gave us this fine room, and we turned it into magic! And I believe the same company is going to open more in several counties across America— several counties?—in several *towns* across America.

OK, Ringo, why don't you play maître d' and show us the menu?

OK. "Cream of Broccoli." I never eat broccoli anyway.

"English Country-Style Pâté." That means it's French, but we throw in a couple of chips and things like that.

"Melon." That's exciting.

"Supreme Chicken." I don't know, I've never seen a "Supreme Chicken" farm in my life!

"Fricassee." I love that word, "Fricassee of vegetables." Work that out for yourself. And the first hundred phone calls we get that can explain fricassee of chicken will get a free record. Whose record should we give them?—Eric Clapton's. He likes chicken and he's a personal friend of mine.

Why do you think people will come to this restaurant?

I think people will come to this restaurant because of the menu. It's good food, it's a beautiful location, and they'll get to know about it because Bill and I and Willie are involved in it. See, the problem with a restaurant is that no one ever wants to go and kiss the chef.

Since we're on the subject, what's Ringo Starr's favorite meal?

Quail's eggs. That's my dream meal. And they will be available every Thursday and every Saturday. Quail's Eggs!

This is yet another role for you. How would you describe it? Drumming up business?

Our active role in the restaurant is when it opens we're here, and that causes some kind of commotion. Then everyone will know about it. That's our active part.

See, no one wants to talk to the manager. You wouldn't have come all the way here to talk to the manager of a restaurant. But you'd rather talk to me.

What kind of people do you think will be drawn to this establishment?

Oh, I think anyone who enjoys fine dining and a pleasant atmosphere will enjoy it here. And it's only one thousand dollars a head! *[Laughing]* It's not really, folks!

If you could invite any group of people to dine with you, who would be in that party?

Well, always, there would be Barbara [wife Barbara Bach]. I think John Hurt; he's always interesting. Jack Nicholson, because Barbara likes him. I never liked him! Only kidding, Jack! And Eric Clapton; he's always fun. David English, a most charming man. You could go on forever. I mean if you could pick your table, it'd be like picking your ten best records. Out of the millions of records I have, ten is real hard. But just for interesting conversation, Alan Pariser, another interesting human being.

By the way, I'm introducing "Back Off Boogaloo Burgers" tomorrow night. Don't forget to order your "Back Off Boogaloo Burger!" *[Snickers]*.

Speaking of music, we recently saw your appearance on the Prince's Trust show from London. Did it feel good to be playing with some old friends?

It was great. Wasn't I fabulous? George was brilliant.

The feeling was so great, especially for George and I. See, we hadn't done anything live for years. I mean we were on each other's albums and things like that. But we hadn't appeared live, so we were probably the most nervous at the show.

All the other people, like Level 42 and Mark King, they've all done it lately. If we'd have been doing it in the sixties, we'd have been used to it too. It was exciting to get up there and do it again.

You recently did some recording, didn't you?

I recently did an album in Memphis, with [producer] Chips Moman who did Elvis, Willie Nelson, and everyone you can name. We did a fine album, fifteen tracks. But we put it on hold for the summer.

After this restaurant opens, we'll go back to England and sort ourselves out. Then we'll figure out what we're doing and pull it together. We were going to do more tracks with Elton, but he got a film offer he couldn't refuse and just let me down! *[Sings]* Ain't that a shuu—ame.

You also worked on George's Cloud Nine, *something he said he enjoyed doing very much.*

Oh yeah, I think it's the best album George has done in a year! It's up and it's good, and he has some great songs, like "Fish on the Sand." Let's see, what else does he do? Ah, "When We Was Fab," which is the one I think should be the single. But it'll be left up to the powers that be, who'll do whatever they want.

He did it with Jeff Lynne. Jim Keltner was on it, I was on it,

Gary Wright, Eric's on it, Elton's on it. You know, all us people who are out of work, we get together.

Have you heard the Beatle compact discs yet?

Yes, I've heard the CDs. I personally prefer the vinyl. They [the songs] weren't made for CDs, and it's very clean. If you want to make a real CD, you make it with a digital studio.

But when they just CD stuff you've done, like the stereo stuff we did in mono, which didn't work—I just feel it's a bit clean. But I'm sure all our listeners will love it, and they'll go out and buy it, just so I could open another restaurant!

You were the first ex-Beatle with a number one hit. How did you feel about that?

Oh, I was amazed. I was the biggest Beatle for two weeks.

You appeared with George, Eric, and a bunch of other folks on the Carl Perkins cable TV special. What made you decide to do that?

Everyone came out for Carl, because Carl is a brilliant artist and a great writer. You know, he, along with Elvis and Chuck Berry, really turned our heads around, in Britain especially. See in America everyone was fighting for rock 'n' roll. And we were just crazed for rock 'n' roll. So I can't refuse anything to do [with Carl]. He's such a wonderful human being. And I did record three of his tracks.

He invited George and Eric, and it's so great because it's the only time you'll ever play with those people in that situation. So it was a great time.

What would you call your best-ever drumming performance on record?

It's called "Rain." I still think to this day "Rain" is the best drumming I've ever done.

Weren't you responsible for part of Eric and George's song "Badge"?

Was this in the paper today or something? Every interview I've done, they ask about "Badge."

I only contributed one line and the title had nothing to do with me. I stumbled into George and Eric, and they were writing this song were and stuck for one line. And I wrote "The swans that live in the park."

And every time that record is played I only want to hear that one line because I wrote it. There are fifty other lines they wrote and I don't care. I just want to hear my line!

It's been many years since you were "Beatle Ringo." How do you look back on that, after all these years?

I made a decision in my life that I was a musician. I was an engineer, working in a factory. I was an apprentice, going to school, learning how to do blueprints, bend metal, hammer, and chisel. And I made a conscious decision, "I am a musician." And I left the factory.

I didn't know, nobody could have known, that it would turn into this. It was just in my own soul.

I said, "I play drums, and that's what I do." I still could have been playing in some nightclub behind strippers, like in Hamburg.

How about the Nike sneaker use of "Revolution"?

Well, I can't talk about that, because there's a little trouble. There's a little trouble, because no one asked me. And *they* said we did it for publicity!

You just wrote a song with Joe Walsh that Joe released as a single. It's called "In My Car."

And it's gone Top Forty! Good ol' Joe Walsh. Well, nobody wanted that album, and I don't know why. It was released in Canada and Germany, because the English company wouldn't release it. And the American company wouldn't release it either. And I don't know why because it has some fine tracks.

Do you have any acting projects in the works?

No. But acting has always come naturally to me. Can't you tell?

Is there any new music out there that interests you?

Yeah, there's a new group called Black, from Liverpool, that I feel are really good. I thought Boy George was really fabulous at the beginning, but, of course, he failed.

But there are very few new bands that I'm really into. If I ever went to the library to pick an album, it'd probably be twenty years old.

With Live Aid and Amnesty International, cause concerts have come into vogue. You did the concert for Bangladesh with George which was one of the first of that order. What are your recollections about that?

Fabulous. There were two shows, one we did in bright daylight. And all the tunes Bob Dylan did, he turned into a waltz and forgot to tell us. And the second show was in complete darkness, and I couldn't read the words, so if you listen to the record, I sing the same verse three times.

BEN E. KING

BEN E. KING

*"As we were being told that we were
finished here, the Beatles and people like
that started bringing our music back
over."*

•

Ben E. King had his first hit single back in
1960 when, as lead singer for the Drifters, he
turned in the classic ballad "Save the Last
Dance for Me." As a solo artist, King has
since topped the charts with such standards
as "Spanish Harlem" and "Stand by Me."

It was "Stand by Me" which recently enjoyed success once again as a reissue, that has
the unique distinction of being reworked by
both John and Julian Lennon.

Like other musical greats of the early sixties, King had a strong influence on the Beatles. He toured Britain prior to their arrival
in America and befriended the boys during
their formative stages.

*Being a veteran of music long before the Beatles made their American
splash, you probably had a different slant on them initially. Did you?*

When they first came out, I really couldn't get into what they
were doing. In between the screams and all that, you have to wait
until some of the hype wears down, and that's what I did. They
took America by complete storm, as we all know, and everybody
was so tuned into Beatles.

See, I had met them before they even got to the States, before they were ever known. I knew Brian Epstein very well and he brought them by the theater. So I met them when they were just little kids, just forming together. He brought them by a lot of the shows that I was doing. So I chatted with them.

So I was familiar with their sound before they were a hit in the States. I could get into them more in England more than here, because it was so hyped.

It was a couple of years later when I started actually reading through some of the publicity bits that were going on and listening. And I said, "Wow, there are some fantastic songs here!" And then I started putting them in my act.

Did you get a chance to see them perform?

Yeah, but again, in England. It was unbelievable, like seeing Elvis live. It was that kind of madness, also like when I saw the Rolling Stones live. *That* kind of madness. You wouldn't have believed it. From the time they said the name, you couldn't hear the first five songs. You'd hear the beginning of them and that was it.

On your album Rough Edges *you covered some Beatles songs, including "Come Together." How did you arrive at that decision?*

I was working with [producer] Bob Crewe, and we wanted to come up with songs we knew were great songs. And when he presented "Come Together" I said, "Yeah, that's a great song."

You also did a version of "Don't Let Me Down," another song predominantly written by John Lennon. Did you set out to do a Lennon song?

That was done from a lyrical point of view. I didn't do it because I liked Lennon—which I did. I didn't do it because of anything else.

Once Bob and I sat down and started playing songs, I just said, "Yeah, I love that." It wasn't until later that I realized what I had selected.

The same attitude about lyrics applied towards "Imagine." I happen to be a big fan of John's when it comes to people who write great songs. I think he wrote brilliant songs and I'm one of his biggest fans. He tends to say things that just don't leave you easily. They stay with you.

Did you ever hear from any of the Beatles regarding your versions of their songs?

Oh yeah. I got messages from John [saying] that he loved my versions of his things. As a matter of fact, someone just told me that when he recorded "Stand by Me" he was looking for me to come in and do it with him. But I happened to be on tour at that time and he wasn't able to grab me. But I am very thankful that he appreciated the things that I wrote. And I'm sure that he knew that I loved his stuff too.

I got the chance to meet Julian and I passed those words on to him. I said, "Your father was not only a fabulous artist within the industry but he was also a marvelous and well-respected songwriter. And I want you to know that."

You mentioned Julian. He also covered "Stand by Me," making that song one that's covered by John and Julian. What do you think Julian's reasons for covering "Stand by Me" were?

I imagine he did it for two reasons. One being that it was a way for him to thank his dad for all the good years and memories. And two, because the lyrics of the song connect with his father very well. It was one of the ones that his dad didn't write that felt like he might have written it. And that's great because he did a great performance on that.

As a songwriter, I love to hear someone do a song that I've written that sounds like something they may have written. I love that.

You've recently appeared at the Prince's Trust benefit concert with Ringo Starr and George Harrison. Were you having as much fun as it looked like?

They were crazy. The thing I was more impressed with than anything else, with all those stars and big names there, was that there were no egos.

I'm not good with people with egos. I'm not good with people who do the whole show-bizzy-bizzy bit; you know, all that "Meet me for lunch, dear." I'm terrible with those kinds of people.

So that was great. We were all sitting around eating ham sand-wiches, drinking beer and sodas, and laughing about the good old days. And fortunately for me, I was in a crowd of people that were not one-day wonders. These guys were going back ten, fif-teen, and twenty years. I'm talking about guys like Eric Clapton, Elton John, Ringo, George, guys who have been out there for a long time. And all the little pretty bits about whatever life is in show business were long past.

We were able to sit down and laugh and joke. Ringo was in-sane. I hadn't seen him for quite a few years. I told him that the last time I saw him, we were at a party in LA and he says, "Oh yeah, I remember that. You were on the balcony and you were drunk."

I said, "You're lying, 'cause I don't drink like that!" *[Laughing]*. So we were laughing and joking about that whole thing.

George Harrison is a very serious person and a very nice per-son. He's very quiet, very businesslike. And he's always nervous. That's what I like about him most. I can't believe that he's still nervous.

He'd always say, "I'm so nervous about this." And I'd say, "Nervous about what? They're going to love you." And sure enough they did. He floored the place.

Over the years, the British audience stayed very loyal to you and your music. Why do you think that is?

Well, it's a combination of the foreign thing, but they don't have as many distractions as we have here [in America].

We tend to throw away things much quicker than they do there. They have a history of preserving things and that's one of the reasons I respect them. They love their queen as much today as they did a hundred years ago. They love their buildings; they love the pubs; they love holding onto things.

And when they find music that they all like, they do the very same thing. They hold it; they cherish it; they treat [it] as some-thing that shouldn't just be thrown away.

And fortunately for R and B music and artists such as myself, we found a people, a place, and an outlet for our music with that kind of feeling about what we were doing, or we wouldn't have survived.

This country wouldn't have allowed us to survive. But as we were being told that we were finished here, the Beatles and people like that started bringing our music back over.

They let them know, "No, they're not finished. Are you kidding? Do you realize what they've given you here?" And that's what's happened to us over the years.

BILL HARRY

BILL HARRY

*"And [the idea was] John could aim to
make Liverpool famous by his music.
Stuart could aim to make Liverpool
famous with his paintings. And I could
try to make Liverpool famous with my
writing."*

•

When one talks about being in the right place
at the right time, consider the story of Bill
Harry. An aspiring journalist and music fan
in the late fifties, Bill met John Lennon and
Stu Sutcliffe while a fellow student at the
Liverpool College of Art.

Bill Harry saw the need for a music and
entertainment paper in Liverpool and, while
still in art school, he started the now legendary *Mersey Beat*. Single-handedly, Bill produced and distributed that vanguard music
sheet and proudly featured record reviews
by Brian Epstein and John Lennon's "Beat
Column."

Very simply, most of what the world
knew about the Beatles prior to their arrival
in America came courtesy of Bill Harry and
his hot-off-the-press reports in the *Mersey
Beat*.

Bill recently launched a new music magazine, *Idols, 20th Century Legends*. And he
continues to author a seemingly endless
series of books on his most favorite of sub-
jects—the Beatles.

Bill, you met and befriended John Lennon and Stu Sutcliffe while they were at art school. Tell us about how you met them.

I started at the junior art school at Gambier Terrace. When I started there, among the various students was little Cynthia Powell, who later went to the Liverpool art college itself.

So when John started at the college, I'd been sort of looking for Stuart Sutcliffe, actually. There had been rumors that there was this guy who was brilliant at his art work. And I was keen to see somebody like that. I was into creative people.

I got to know Stuart and like him. I saw that he was very sensitive and intense. He was looking for the same sort of thing I was looking for. The usual questions: "Why are we here?" "What are we going to do in life?" And all the rest of them. We had long talks.

Then John started at the art college. I was looking around the canteen, and I noticed that all the students who were supposed to be unconventional were really conventional. Everyone wore duffle coats and art college scarves, and they all looked more or less the same. Typical art students.

But I noticed this guy stalking around with a DA haircut and a Teddy-Boy jacket. Quite peculiar.

Then I got to know John and I found that he had a sensitivity about him and an intensely creative energy within him. Most of the other people at the art college didn't have [that]. I thought they were all dilettantes; they were all just dabbling. They didn't have the intensity.

So John and I would get together at a little pub called Ye Cracke, on Rice Street. There had been some rumors that John had been writing poetry, so I asked him if I could have a look at it.

He seemed a bit embarrassed at first. And then he grabbed from his pocket these little scraps of paper. He had written this wacky poem about a farmer. It was a comic verse, which I really liked.

Meanwhile, Stuart was working all of his holidays on his paintings and his drawings. His mother had given him money for a flat and helped support him.

Whereas I was skint. So every holiday I had to work at various building sites and things like that. And with my first pay I bought this blue jacket and Stu really admired it.

He said, "I wish I could have a jacket like that." And I said, "I wish I could have a painting of yours, but I can't afford it. So you can have the jacket for a painting." So Stu did an oil painting of me, and he did it in the style of Van Gogh, which I really liked.

So you and John and Stu would go to the pub, Ye Cracke, during your off-time at school? What were some of the things you talked about?

When we used to gather at Ye Cracke, we'd have John, Stuart, myself, and this other guy called Rod Murray. So I said the whole of our creative thing seems to be dominated by the Beat poets, but Liverpool has such vitality of its own. Stuart and I had already talked about writing a book on Liverpool with me doing the writing and him, the drawings.

I said, "We should really try to express our own environment. Liverpool is such an exciting place, but nobody outside Liverpool knows it. We've got character here; we've got places—Let's actually do something."

And [the idea was] John could aim to make Liverpool famous by his music. Stuart could aim to make Liverpool famous with his paintings. And I could try to make Liverpool famous with my writing.

Where were Paul and George at this time? Weren't they in school too?

Right next door. The buildings were attached. It was one building at one time, and they just put up these barriers in the doors between. But they were actually in the same building.

Paul and George would come over at the intervals or breaks, and go to the life rooms in the art college. I remember them at one point, rehearsing at one end of the room, while I was in another corner with Rod Murray playing skiffle, playing a kazoo. At that time, in the late fifties, Britain had been swamped by this skiffle movement.

We also ran the art college dances. Stuart and I were appointed on the committee for the student union. So we ran the dances. We had them playing at a lot of the dances, along with the local jazz band, the Mersey Zippy Jazz Band.

Of course, they [the Quarry Men] didn't have any money themselves, so they couldn't get a PA [public address]. So Stuart and I proposed that the student union pay for a PA system that we could lend to them, and in exchange, they would play at the art college dances. But of course they took the equipment off to Germany.

A couple of years later, I went to Manchester to see their first radio show at the Playhouse Theater. We had coachloads of fans traveling together. So one of the people at the art school on the student union had been appointed to try to get the equipment back off the Beatles.

This guy approached John and said that he wanted this equipment back. And John told him, "Hard luck, mate. We sold it in Hamburg!" And there was nothing they could do about it.

I remember at the time we all came out of the playhouse, we all got in the coach, but Pete Best couldn't reach it. He was swamped by all the kids. Everybody was going berserk over Pete Best. So the rest of us had to leave in the coach and drive around and leave him behind a bit.

Was he the most popular Beatle at that time?

Pete, at the time, seemed to be the most popular Beatle in Liverpool. I remember doing stories in *Mersey Beat* about how girls used to sleep overnight in his garden, just to be near him.

At one time, [Cavern DJ] Bob Wooler said that Pete was so popular that they should have brought him to the forefront. The standard thing was that the drummer was always at the back. This Liverpool lineup had been developed with most of the bands, which was three guitars and drums. And that was what people used to call the Liverpool Sound; lead, rhythm, bass, and drums, with the three lead vocalists doing harmonies.

So what they tried to do was bring Pete to the forefront of the stage with his drums, and the others to the side of him. But when they did, the girls mobbed the stage so he had to go behind again.

You also introduced Brian Epstein to the Beatles, didn't you?

That's right. When I started *Mersey Beat*, I was still at the art college. So I had to run down every lunchtime and do copy, get the adverts.

I also did all the distribution myself. I had three main distributors in town and I personally took it around to them. I went down to the Cavern and all the music stores and record shops in Liverpool.

So I went into NEMS [North End Music Store] in Whitechapel and asked to see the manager and it was Brian Epstein. I showed him *Mersey Beat* and he said, "Oh, this is interesting. I'll take a dozen copies." He phoned me that afternoon and said, "I can't understand this; every one of the dozen went. I've had papers on my counters which have laid there for weeks and these were gone in a half an hour."

So he ordered one-hundred-forty-four copies of the next issue and that was the one where the cover story was about them recording in Hamburg. That was in July, 1961.

Brian phoned me up again and said, "This is remarkable; the whole shop is crowded, and the lot went!" Actually, the Beatles themselves were hanging around there. They always used to go to NEMS.

So Brian had me down to his office and said, "This is remarkable. Is all this happening in Liverpool? Can I write for the paper?" So we had him doing the record reviews.

Didn't John and Paul also contribute to Mersey Beat?

We had the column by John which was a beat column filled with all his writings. Then we printed all the letters Paul would write me when they traveled.

So the next stage in that was Brian started advertising in *Mersey Beat*. Then he phoned me up one day and said that he'd like to go down to the Cavern and see the Beatles, and could I arrange it? So I arranged it, and that was the day he went down to the Cavern and saw them for the first time.

You coined the term "Mersey Beat" and started that magazine. How did it get going?

That's correct. What happened was I really thought of doing the paper and I was always interested in magazines. And, as I said, I was still at the art college.

I was originally going to do a jazz magazine called *Storyville and 52nd Street*. One side would be modern jazz and you flipped it over and the other side would be trad [traditional] jazz.

But I was also hanging around the music scene with the lads at the Jacaranda, the coffee bars and things. At this time we were still skint, so at the Jacaranda we'd see if we could afford a piece of toast for four pence. If we had five pence, we could get jam on it. But we used to sit around and talk all the time.

I began to make all these notes. And talking to all the different members of bands, I began to amass this huge list. Then I checked with Bob Wooler, the DJ, and he got a list of over two hundred odd groups, and I found out all these venues.

I thought, "Surely nobody knows what's going on in Liverpool. I've never heard or read about it, but there's literally hundreds and hundreds of groups playing everything from swimming baths to ice rinks. This is incredible!"

So I borrowed fifty pounds from some civil servant and started *Mersey Beat*. We got an office for five pounds a week and some second-hand furniture. I got my girlfriend to be my only member of staff.

So I had it started, but I had to think of a name for it. And I was sitting quite late at night in the office and I thought, "Well, I've got to cover the whole area of Merseyside." And I had the visualization in my mind of a policeman's beat, a policeman covering this area. So I thought I'd call it *Mersey Beat*. I was covering the Merseyside area and it was a pun on the music as well.

The Beat music, like the "Beat" in Beatles.

Right. Up until this point, all the groups had been calling themselves rock 'n' roll groups. So, after *Mersey Beat* started to get established, Liverpool became the center of the whole scene. There were posters everywhere about all the gigs. All the local shops had the tailor's dummy with guitars in their hands. There was a tremendous feeling in the city.

So the groups started calling themselves Beat groups. And it went on, you know?

You're a man who's written many books on the Beatles. Describe how you go about deciding what angle to approach each time you set out to write one.

Basically I get letters from all over the world: Russia, Poland, Australia, Greece, and all over the States. People are interested in so many fascinating aspects.

I just received a big package from Poland the other day which contained all rare Russian articles on the Beatles. The Russians loved the Beatles.

So I get input. And I put them all together and make notes. And for over twenty years I've been making notes—and I have files.

The books seem to write themselves. For instance, when I looked at the Beatles museums, I found out all of the museums and all the college courses [offered]. I was getting information on all the new shops that opened. I was getting postcards and hand-outs.

I thought that all this information has to be put together in one book. So anybody who needs to buy anything about the Beatles, whether it's at an auction house or if they wanted to buy a table-cloth, they'd know where to get it. And that's when I put the *Beatles for Sale* book together. And all of them fall into place like that.

You were with them from the very beginning. Why, in your opinion, are the Beatles still so popular?

They changed so many things. They had an effect not only with the music, but on the complete lifestyle of the people, speech, dress. There was great revolution. The establishment had always controlled everything and the Beatles broke that establishment.

They were Northern people who finally made it in the South, then internationally. They broke so many barriers. Every little thing they did in their career seemed to break a new barrier.

The photographs they had on the first albums were completely different from anything that had been on covers of albums before.

Every stage they went through they created something different, something new. Breaking records all the time. When they made the films, it was completely different than what had been done before.

People growing up, the teenagers, really came about in the fifties in America with rock 'n' roll. And the next big stage was the Beatles. All the people grew up with that music and they became such a big part of the life.

It wasn't just the music, it was the whole lifestyle. When people think of something that happened with the Beatles, they remember what they were doing at the time.

Now it's transcended that. The young people, who weren't around at the time of the Beatles, have this nostalgia for the sixties, the feeling and the excitement.

So you have second generation Beatles fans. And it builds up because there are so many aspects to them that are so interesting.

The records still seem to evoke this freshness and aggression. And they're still valid today, twenty-five years later.

JOE WALSH

I remember being in high school, watching television, when I saw the Beatles on *Ed Sullivan*. I was shaking my head yes and my parents were shaking their heads no, and I announced that that was what I wanted to do.

RICHIE HAVENS

RICHIE HAVENS

*"That was my basic statement to myself:
'Everything's changed now! Something
has happened.' And it was 'I Want to
Hold Your Hand.'"*

•

Richie Havens' passionate vocals and fiery
brand of acoustic guitar have served him well
throughout a long and critically acclaimed
career.

A Greenwich Village folk singer when
the Beatles arrived in America, they forever
changed Havens' musical direction and interpretation. And while he has achieved great
success with his own compositions, he is well
known for his numerous remakes of Beatle
standards. It is no coincidence that Richie
Havens' latest recording is a compact disc
featuring a sampling of songs written by the
Beatles.

*Richie, on your latest album, you do a cover of Paul McCartney's
"Arrow Through Me." It's another in a long line of Beatle-related
covers for you. Why "Arrow Through Me"?*

I love that song. "Arrow Through Me" is one of Paul McCartney's best-written songs. Basically, the subject matter is not new,
but spoken about in a new way. It's sort of the sympathetic, non-
spoken pain that men can feel and usually are not supposed to talk
about.

There are lots of songs that come out now that actually give a man's point of view in the compassionate way that men feel, as well as the passionate way they feel. And they're very new in the sense of projection of what men feel. I think that was a little bit true in the fifties, but it's more sophisticated now. Men can cry in songs now. So that song, to me, was a very deeply moved and hurt person.

Can you remember your initial reaction upon hearing the Beatles?

Absolutely. I'll never forget it as long as I live. I was alone actually, at home on the Lower East Side of Manhattan. Third Street and Avenue B—East Village they called it.

I lived in a five-story walk-up, which I loved. You knew who your friends were because they would walk up those stairs only if they wanted to see you [*Laughs*]. So I had a nice, low-key existence going on.

At the time, I was passing the basket, just at the point where I had an inkling that I might be recording something, finally.

What happened was, I was in the living room and my radio was on the refrigerator in the kitchen. And I heard this music coming into the room and I went "Uh-oh. Everything's changed now!" That was my basic statement to myself: "Everything's changed now! Something has happened." And it was "I Want to Hold Your Hand."

And I realized, having listened to "I Want to Hold Your Hand" and having played music all through the fifties, that this was not only the new teenage music, but it had actually advanced from what we were doing in the fifties to a real clarity of sorts.

And even at that, they were using parts of things that I had sang in the fifties in the structure of some of the things. But I realized right then that the Beatles had started something different.

And the thing that it was, technically, was that they started off with the chorus. That was the basic difference between our music and their music.

Did you ever get a chance to meet any of the Beatles?

It was very interesting. It's also strange because it didn't have anything to do with the music of the Beatles at the time. It had to do with the consciousness that my partner and I perceived they must have had.

I had already done *Mixed Bag* and it was popular in Europe. They had heard [my version of] "Eleanor Rigby" and they liked it very much. They hadn't told me that, but someone who knew Paul and John told me that they really liked the song. I said, "That's great; I love it too!"

Me and my partner had come from Woodstock realizing that there was never going to be another one. And the problem with it was that there weren't any politicians there. If they knew that was going to happen—they knew *that* was going to happen—they would have been there. And since they didn't get the chance, they clamped down on the possibility of missing out on any future ones so they [Woodstocks] were not going to happen anymore.

Likewise, new laws came up about mass gatherings and we thought "There's got to be a way to do this without having that problem of 'mass gathering.'" So we actually conjured up a way to have mass concerts in a far-off controlled environment. It [the show] wasn't advertised until a certain time. And when you do advertise it, you advertise it in every theatre across the States and put up a big screen and do it live in the theaters. You could control millions. And that was our idea.

So we thought that if there were two, maybe three, people who would think this is worth anything, it's got to be the Beatles. They were the guys who had the mind to think that this could be something. And that was our fantasy.

So we were playing a kind of a dare game with each other for a while. I said to my partner Mark, "You know, we could really get to meet them if we wanted to. All we'd have to do is say it out loud three times and we'll meet them." And he smiled at that and said "Well, let's say it."

So we both said it out loud, three times: "We want to meet the Beatles!" We felt kind of silly doing it at the time.

The next day we were at Mark's house and the telephone rings. It was this ex-editor who was asking him to take some pictures for *Fortune* magazine of these new businessmen from England. Seems they had just opened this new boutique and a record company named Apple! *[Laughing]*.

And Mark's mouth fell on the floor. He said, "You're not going to believe this, but I'm going to see the Beatles on Friday!" We did it. We said it and it happened.

So I had decided that I was not going to be able to go, since it was a business shoot. But Mark would get the chance to see if they were interested [in our idea]. So he said that if he got the chance to talk to them, he would.

The next day, I left Mark's house, was crossing town, and passed by a place called The Salvation. I was actually going home and was going to keep walking. But I decided to go down to The Salvation to see who was there. It happened to be Hendrix and the Chambers Brothers, who I knew for years. So I just went down to check it out.

When I got downstairs to the door, one of the guys who was on the door said, "Hey, Richie," like he knew me for a long time. But I didn't recognize him. He says, "Hey, my brother will be down in a little while, why don't you hang out and say hello to him. I'm sure he'd like to say hello to you." I didn't know who his brother was. I had no clue. I thought, "Who is this guy? And who is his brother?"

So I waited there to see who this guy's brother was. Turned out to be a chauffeur that I had driven with a couple of times who was driving around John Lennon and Paul McCartney. And he comes walking in the door with both of them!

I can't believe this. I'm going to meet the Beatles before my partner does tomorrow!

Of course, I never mentioned anything [to them] about what we had talked about because I never mentioned anything at all. My mouth was on the floor. They had the conversation with me because I was just in awe. And I couldn't wait to call Mark and tell him I met them before he did! *[Laughs loud and long].*

What were they talking to you about?

Well, they really liked the record *[Mixed Bag]* and they were talking to me more than I was talking to them. But I was talking to them about "Eleanor Rigby." And they really loved it and went on about that.

And I learned something. And I thought at the time: "This is why I got to meet them, so I could learn something just now that I can live with and know is so."

A young girl got up and walked over to the table and says to Paul, "I hear you wrote 'Lady Madonna' about America." And he said *[imitating]*, "Oh no, I was looking through this African magazine, and I saw this African lady with a baby. And underneath the picture it said 'Mountain Madonna.' But I said 'Oh no, "Lady Madonna,"' and I wrote the song."

And I thought, "Ah ha! They're human! They're not people from Mars. They're not very conscious, intense revolutionaries. They're none of those things. They're just human guys who play music and write songs." That was a good release for me.

Your cover of "Here Comes the Sun" is a classic by itself. Why'd you choose that one? And have you ever heard any reaction from George Harrison about it?

Yeah, I did get a reaction from George. Actually, I got to know George a lot better than the other guys because I was in more places with George. We hung out together a lot and I actually went to his house a few times, which he later gave to the Hare Krishna organization.

But George and I have had conversations, real conversations about music and things like that. He's like me. I think he's a guy who has his own basic feelings about life and philosophy, and only wants to share that. He doesn't want to interfere or interject or impose anything of his own personal ideas that might not be real.

But I heard "Here Comes the Sun" on the radio and I thought to myself that the songs I was singing were so heavy, and so thought provoking, and so laden with conscience and decision making, that I need a lighter song. But I didn't want to sing anything that didn't have any meaning.

So I had been listening to the album *[Abbey Road]* for a long time and I thought "You know, this is a very happy song but it also is a very real song. It talks about the same thing I'm talking about but in a lighter form." And I thought that it might be a way for me to do myself some good by lightening up my own involvement with my own life and maybe put a little lightness in what I'm doing. And I actually *liked* the song.

There was a time that I'd never thought I'd sing that song because it was light. And even though it said what it said, I never thought I'd end up singing it just by hearing it. But I heard it enough times and got to know it, and I said, "This is the right song because it is a real song. And there are lots of us who don't understand an issue-oriented consciousness, so this is definitely useful to get its meaning across through my interpretation."

Let's run a couple Beatles songs by you, and get your reaction to them: "In My Life."

Oh boy! One of the most beautiful songs in the world. To me, it's a way teenagers, young people, could hear a song, relate it to them without actually having had a real long life yet. And then having something to consider opposite of that, like "What am I going to do in my life from this point on, knowing this?" It's a beautiful song.

"Strawberry Fields Forever"

At the time that I did it, "Strawberry Fields Forever" was a song that was the ideal imagery for this Utopian place where we could all escape to and get out of the mess that the world was in. It was like a movie on a record, a fantasy that we could actually visit through music. So in effect, it was a fantasy world we could escape to, to get out of what we were into.

YOKO ONO

"With his kind of mind, he might have known that an outspoken person like him might have had a fate like that."

•

Any way you look at it, Yoko Ono played a pivotal role in Beatles history. Much maligned as the "woman who broke up the Beatles," Yoko shared a remarkable chemistry with John Lennon—one that would not be denied.

The night Yoko met John Lennon for the first time, at London's Indica Gallery in 1966, forever changed the course of John's life. From that point on, it would be a life with Yoko.

Yoko has carved a niche for herself as an avant-garde poet, conceptual artist, filmmaker, and musician, often collaborating with John in these various pursuits. One of their most successful joint projects included the formation of the Plastic Ono Band and their banner song at the time, "Give Peace a Chance."

Today, Yoko Ono is the curator of John Lennon's memory. From the Dakota apartment they called home on New York's Central Park West, site of Lennon's tragic assassination, Yoko raises their son, Sean Ono Lennon, and works to maintain John's artistic legacy.

Ticket to Ride has been a frequent guest in the Lennon home over the years. In fact,

Yoko makes sure that Scott Muni and the staff are invited over for a chat whenever she has the occasion to unveil another Ono-Lennon creation.

From our wealth of interview material, we have selected highlights from our talks with Yoko following the release of the albums *Starpeace*, in 1985, and *Menlove Avenue*, in 1986.

Yoko, there's a concept involved with Starpeace. *Could you bring us up-to-date on this and tell us about some of the tracks on the album?*

What happened was this: At the beginning of this year [1985], I already had a whole lot of songs for the next album. And I thought, "It's time for me to go into the studio."

The motive was a one-parent family, mother and son. I wonder where I got that idea from, right? Anyway, [it was based on] the dialogue between mother and son. And I think it was pretty general. Although it is personal, there are so many one-parent families these days. Mother and son, trying to live together, trying to make it work.

So I had all those songs, and then one day we were in a restaurant with some friends. There were all grown-ups, except for Sean. We were just discussing world affairs and all the things we can't do anything about. And then Sean said to me, "Oh, this is terrible; the world is terrible, Mommy. Life is so sad, it's not worth living."

And I'm saying, "Sean, it's not that bad; life is beautiful. The world is beautiful, and life can be beautiful." You know, the kind of spiel you give when you see somebody trying to jump off a cliff—

And I was thinking, "This sounds so corny." But we are leaving a horrible earth to our children, to the future generation. We messed it up. It's polluted; it's dangerous; I mean, give me a list, right?

So for the past four years, I've been saying, "I'm a mother now. Mother first. So I'm not really going to be saying anything. I've done enough." You know, all those excuses. But because I am a mother, that's why I have to do it. I just had to open up. So I just decided not to do this mother-and-child dialogue. It hit me. I said, "I just have to own up."

And just before that time, "Hell in Paradise," that first song, came and it made me feel like, "Ding! Is it going to be that mother-and-child dialogue really? Because this doesn't fit in."

The next thing that came was "I Love All of Me," "Remember Raven," and then finally "Starpeace." All four big songs just came like that. And "Sky People" I had before, so I thought that this was going to be a different album. It's not going to be mother and child, it's going to be about all of us. So I owned up around February.

I was mastering the album the very same day Live Aid was going on. That very same day! It seems like that was very appropriate. And I waited to the end of the summer to bring it out.

Usually I just say, "Words and music by Yoko Ono." But then I thought, "I want to say something about my connection with John this time." Because we were doing a peace effort for how many years? Twenty years or whatever. So I'm saying, "Conceived by Yoko Ono Lennon." That's the only time I've used the Lennon name, because it seems like it was conceived as part of that history.

(COURTESY OF SCOTT MUNI)

YOKO ONO, SEAN LENNON, AND "SANTA," SCOTT MUNI, CHRISTMAS 1984.

So, "Hell in Paradise" says to speak out but, if I'm going to say that, I'd better speak out too. I'm speaking out to the future generations, including Sean, so that generation doesn't take any double-dutch.

"I Love All of Me," is what it is. "I Love All of Me," in the sense that we are part of the whole world, that you are me and I am you. We are all together.

"Children Power." I did not know that this was children's year. Somebody asked me to make a children's song about a year or two ago. So at the time, I thought of "Children Power," and thought it was appropriate. So I wrote the song, put it on the [album's] list. And then found out that this was children's year. The connection is very interesting.

"Rainbow Revelation." I don't know how to put this, but the first line is, "If you change the anger into love." Someone said, "How can you change anger into love? That's a very difficult thing to do. When I'm angry, I don't feel like loving." To those who say that, I understand. It is a very difficult thing, but I had to go through it.

When John died, I was very angry. And then all the books came out and I was even angrier! But what do you do about it? It just makes you sick and it's not good for your body, even. So somehow you have to transform that into something positive, so you can save yourself.

So I thought "Oh, I see. I'm angry and I'm in that rut of being angry. You can't do that. You have to love something." So the medicine that I had to take, that's what I did. If it gives some kind of idea or energy to somebody, then I'm happy.

And then, there's "The King of the Zoo." "King of the Zoo" is, of course, about John. People kept telling me, "I don't want to hear another song about John, thank you." So I figured I'm not going to keep singing about John. But this is a nice way of slipping it in. We are all the "King of the Zoo," as well.

I thought of the song in 1981 when I was still in a daze. And to keep myself from going totally insane, I was just walking. Walking, every day, through the park. That was my exercise.

So on my way back, I passed the zoo. And each time I did that, I thought about the king of the zoo. So I had a flash of this whole song, though I didn't have the words and I didn't have the music—just the title and the concept. And I kept saying to whoever I was walking with, "Please remember 'King of the Zoo.' I have to write that one." And finally I wrote it.

Next is "Remember Raven." This just kept coming to me, and I kept saying, "I am not going to write this down. It's too strong, and I can't put it out." That's how I looked at it at the time. But it kept coming to me.

So when I finally sang it in the studio, I felt so good. I felt like maybe there were a whole lot of people out there who went through the same pain and anger that I have—all the hurt that happened in the past four years. And I thought that maybe they might feel good too. So I put it in.

"Keep Clear" is about Kyoko. She was the one who lost the teddy bear. I was just sort of trying to sing about her. And then it turns out that it was about me.

"Sky People." Need I say anything? We are Sky People. Sky People ride the subway, by the way.

"You and I." That is about me and Sean. Early one morning, I saw Sean looking out the window. And looking a bit sad. But it was a beautiful, beautiful morning. The sky was almost pink, and you knew that there was going to be a beautiful, clear day. So I was just trying to say, "It's just you and I, and it's not that bad."

"It's Going to Rain" is a song that I kept laughing [through] when I sang it. "Living on tiptoe, aren't you?" Well, we're all living on tiptoes and one day it is going to rain. But it's going to be fine.

"Starpeace" is a song that came to me when Sean took me to this tennis match. I'm thinking about the tennis match, and my head's just going left, right, left, right. And suddenly this song just came to me. I borrowed this pencil and paper from a couple behind me and I started writing "Starpeace."

And I was thinking later, "Why a tennis match?" Of course, my head was going like clockwork, and it was the right time. My intellect wasn't bothering [me], and it slipped in. But also, the ball. The way I looked at it was: One day, a long time ago, in our memory bank maybe, we were gods and goddesses in the universe, arranging all the balls like the spheres and the globes. So we had this small little bird's-eye view, like a tennis court. And we just went left, right, left, right, and played the ball, remembering the days that we were gods and goddesses. So while I was watching that, this universal thing just came to me. It just all fits in in a way, I thought.

Next is "I Love You Earth." This was the only song that I intentionally set out to write. I never said "I love you" to the earth and this is ridiculous. This is where we live and our whole life depends on it. And we never said "I love you" to the earth.

It was almost like a macho guy, who never says "I love you" to the wife, and finds out she has cancer. He wants to say it to her for the first time, "I know I never said it to you, but I love you, baby." I had that flash of a macho guy. And I started to write it as this macho guy saying, "I love you." Then after I wrote it, and I sung it, I suddenly realized that it was me! I was the macho woman, who never said enough to John.

Though I did, and we said "I love you" to each other, but it's never enough. So it's me again and I'm saying "I love you."

There's another thing that is pertinent, that I wanted you to explain. There's a TV movie, produced by Carson Productions, entitled John and Yoko—A Love Story. *What do you know about it and what was your role in it?*

It's almost like I was blackmailed into it, in the sense that my back was up against the wall. Somebody was going to do it, and unless I authorized it, it would have been done in a way that would have depicted John very differently from what John was like.

The reason was, and think of this, John died and all those books came out to destroy his image. And the next thing is it's a very conservative climate.

So John's ideas, John's spirit, seems to be something that was destroyed in the course of it.

Now on one hand, it's a very conservative climate. But, on the other hand, they're talking about sixties revival, the Live Aid, Farm Aid, and everything's coming back. So it's an ideal time to talk about John's spirit in his music.

So I wanted to make sure that it's John's spirit in the music that they are talking about rather than the drug-filled, spooky, hippy who was talking nonsense. Because that is not what he was.

Even with drugs, he was writing "Cold Turkey" to say, "Listen, it ain't that good." Even at that time, in the seventies. So I wanted to make sure of all that.

But at the same time I'm not a professional in the TV medium. So they're not going to take my word on anything like that. All the networks wanted my authorization, and that includes American TV, Japanese TV, British TV, etc.

So with all that, I decided, "Look, in the end, John wanted us to become a family in New York City. We are like the second wave immigrants. We are Americans who came here believing in the American dream." And when I say the American dream, it's not about materialism. It's about human rights, and the freedom of speech, the whole shebang that we believed in. We came here for that—to build a home together in New York City. And that was his last intent.

So in view of that, I thought American TV should do it. Not Japanese TV, not British TV. The Japanese woman and the British man transcended all that and met in this middle land called America.

So the next thing was to find a production company that has very successful credits so that the network would say yes to it right away. I interviewed a few people from a few production companies and Carson Productions was the right one. So I've got the top production and I left it to their professional hands. And that's the best I can do.

I think that it's a very nice opportunity to expose a whole new audience to John's spirit and music. The old fans don't remember the fact that there are some young kids who don't really know about John and Yoko.

One of my friends was saying that she had a sister who was fifteen and [that she] had to explain to her about John and Yoko and what they stood for.

When we did the bed-in the fifteen-year-olds were just about to be born. So it would be beautiful to expose them to John's spirit in music. There's a whole new audience out there.

This is one thing that I added to the various hats that I am wearing. And I know that a lot of people would say, "Oh really?" But I dare to say it, and I'm going to keep John's spirit and music alive.

You've recently realized a dream. Strawberry Fields is now erected in New York's Central Park and it's a living, breathing international tribute to the spirit of John and Yoko.

Every time I walk through it, I get a very strong vibe when I'm there. I don't know why.

It's a mixture of John's vibe, and of the one-hundred-twenty-three countries, and the people who brought the one-hundred-twenty-three countries there, as well as the park people who cared and made sure it happened. And of course, the fans, and the family of the world. I don't know what the vibe is but it's so magical that there are days when I miss walking through it.

There are days when I say that I just have to take a walk, and I always pass through there. Don't you feel that way when you go through it? I really think that something bigger than all of us is happening there.

Peace and tranquility

Yes, it's almost symbolic of the future world. And that's what I like about it.

Yoko, we'd like to change gears here and ask you about some happy history. In a few weeks it'll be Thanksgiving and we want to hear your recollections of Thanksgiving, 1974. That was the night you and John met backstage, after his Madison Square Garden appearance with Elton John. That triggered your getting back together with John, right?

We didn't know what was happening, but in hindsight that was it! It was a very strange happening in a way.

When I heard about the concert, the first thing I was going to do was *not* go there, but just send flowers. That's why I sent one gardenia to John and one gardenia to Elton.

I was doing a gallery show here and the owner of the gallery asked me if I could get a ticket. I told him that I'd try. I thought "I owe him one, so maybe..." So we went and I had an incredibly emotional experience. I was crying like crazy.

After the concert, I was going to leave. Then the gallery owner said, "Can you introduce me to the stars? Can we go to backstage?" I didn't want to do that but I thought, "Maybe I should do him the favor." And so we went backstage. John was so delighted, I was surprised. We just looked at each other. And there was something going on.

When John walked out onstage, the ovation was legendary.

It was like the whole house was going to be wrecked. The floors were shaking. Everybody was so overjoyed and excited, but I saw a different John there.

I saw him bowing and I thought "He never did that with me." He was just a very macho guy, very cocky. We'd go on the stage and do a number and he wouldn't bow or anything. And he bowed once too often and I thought, "Maybe he must be feeling insecure." I felt terrible about that, kind of a guilty feeling.

Much has been said and written about John's post-Beatle relationship with Paul McCartney. Would you describe his relationship with George Harrison in the years after the Beatles?

Just like old brothers, and they were like brothers or maybe even closer than brothers. But there are always ups and downs, you know.

When Paul pulled some tricks on us, when we were still with Allen Klein, our relationship with George was always very good. He used to joke, "Why don't we form a group, and can you play the bass, Yoko?" It was that kind of atmosphere. It was very good.

Just before that though, when Ringo wanted to quit, before the Beatles broke up, I don't think George liked us at all. He was a bit bothered by the fact that I was there. He used to just go to the studio and sit there with John. He was quite nice to us.

There were many different periods. Around 1974, at the time of the Beatles' settlement, George and John did not get along. It was just to do with the settlement.

George admired John a lot and he was always following John and Cynthia. That's history. And John always cared for George. George's song, "Something," went into the record only because of John. John always wanted to make sure that George had a little place there somewhere.

It was stifling for George, because it was always "Lennon/ McCartney." Each time that they have a fight, it's blown up into a proportion that's not real.

I think the only thing that hurt John was that, right before his death, George brought out a book and didn't mention John. If John was alive, and George would have done something nice again, it would have been corrected. So it shouldn't be thought of as a stamp on the book; it's not like that at all. They obviously got along very well, with all the music and all.

[We spoke again in 1986.]

Were you happy with the success of [the album and video] Live in New York City*?*

Oh yes! What John and I were always trying to do was communicate to the people our thoughts on human rights and whatnot.

So in the eighties, just like in *Skywriting by Word of Mouth*, he's coming back again saying, "Peace. Give peace a chance." It was very good, I thought.

The new album is called Menlove Avenue. *Explain the title for those who don't know what that is.*

Menlove Avenue is the street that John was brought up on. That's where his Aunt Mimi and Uncle George had a house. I thought that this might be the last studio-recorded kind of record. Maybe there'll be other things that come out like cassette takes of his songs, or maybe somebody else singing his songs, maybe a documentary album. Those things are possible.

But this is the last of the studio tracks. So I felt that in that sense, I wanted to put his roots in there. Menlove Avenue, that's where he was born and raised, you know?

You took a trip to Liverpool with Sean not long ago. Did you go through the old neighborhood?

Yes. Sean was just ecstatic. We went to Strawberry Fields as well. Strawberry Fields is right in back of his house. It was like his backyard, and he used to play there. And he often spoke about it.

The house is still intact; somebody lives there still. It's not low class, like everybody thinks. It's not like they came from the gutter. It's a middle-class district, and it's a nice detached, independent house.

You say in the liner notes on Menlove Avenue *that when John heard Elvis Presley, it changed his life. Did he talk to you about that?*

Oh yes, they all were just right into it. John didn't read music and I don't even know if there were any music sheets at that time anyway. So they would just get the record from the shops, listen to it, and try to figure out the chords. He was always telling me the excitement of trying to figure out the chords.

He did "Blue Suede Shoes" on the Live Peace in Toronto *album. Why didn't he ever record any other of Elvis' hits?*

That's like the fact that very few people record John Lennon songs. John used to complain about that. He'd say, "They like to cover Paul's song, but why not mine?"

But one of the most important reasons is that people have so much respect for John's songs, and he sings them so well, in his own unique style, that it's kind of difficult to top it, you know? So that's one of the reasons.

So in his case, it was the same thing. Doing somebody else like Elvis, that was too much. Elvis did it so perfectly, why try to top it? It's like history.

Something else I say in the liner notes is that some of the takes on *Menlove Avenue* are the kind of takes that probably wouldn't have come out, unless they were posthumous.

And I'm glad that they did, only because [normally] the record companies would say that these are not the way they should be. But it gives a certain atmosphere and it's very precious I think.

Most artists would love to put out that sort of take as a commercial product. Like Bruce Springsteen went through with *Nebraska*. It was a big gamble, and the record companies were saying that they didn't know about it and everything.

So I don't know if John and I could have gone through that. I'm glad that this could come out, showing his English roots and all that.

He can do Elvis; he can do the Beach Boys; he's a very versatile guy. He can do any of that and still be Lennon. And I think that the tracks on Side Two really show his English roots, and it comes out in his voice. It's quite fascinating.

Were there some tracks that got left off? I heard that there was a take of "Be My Baby" around.

Well, yes, "Be My Baby" is one of a few tracks that I didn't put in because they weren't as good as the tracks on the album, quality-wise. I still wanted to maintain some level of quality, you know? And if I put "Be My Baby" in there, you would have seen a big difference.

Are there any plans to do a tribute album, where other stars do John's songs? Something similar to what John did for you with the Every Man Has a Woman Who Loves Him *project, where various people recorded your songs?*

That's what I'm thinking. So many projects are just on the make. For instance, the Lennon Scholarship was an idea I got from people writing to me saying, "My school would like to have a Lennon scholarship."

And I was thinking that there are so many colleges and universities, that if they had a Lennon Scholarship, how much that would mean to the students. Just think of a student who got a Lennon Scholarship; it would give them such an incentive. It has a certain meaning to it, you know? So I'm trying to do a World Lennon Scholarship, and fundraising for it.

The time frame is not there, but as soon as possible would be great. I think that the first thing I'd want to do would be a fundraising concert. So this has been in the air since the Strawberry Fields time.

There's also plans for a Lennon Center. I initially was going to call it the Lennon Museum, but "museum" sounds a bit hoity-toity, so it will be the Center. It'll be more than just a library of John's stuff. It'll be a center where people can learn how to make music. So I want to organize that too.

These are very big things, you see. And of course, I'll need help. But it takes some time. Strawberry Fields took four years. So this will take until John's tenth [anniversary] maybe. But I'm determined to do them.

And between that, I want to make sure that I put out something of John's every year, so that his spirit won't be forgotten.

Then I get around to wondering when I'm going to do my stuff. But I really don't mind that.

This is a funny situation that I'm in. When John and I were together, of course he could take care of himself. So I was more eager to push my stuff. We cooperated with each other and supported each other.

But aside from that, I was making a point of keeping my independence. So now that he's gone, I feel some guilt feeling or something of "Why him, and not me?" and all those conflicts of emotion.

And of course, I remember him always pushing my stuff. When *Grapefruit* came out, he was right there with me, signing the books.

Now it's my turn. I don't mind pushing *Skywriting by Word of Mouth* or *Menlove Avenue*.

Tell us about Skywriting by Word of Mouth.

It's a beautiful book. If you look around in the eighties, no-body's writing like that. He has an incredible mastering of the English language. It sounds strange for me to say that; I mean he's English, so why not!

But it's not that at all. On a literary level, and I'm not talking about the MTV crowd, it's on a Joycean level, but with a sense of humor. I don't think James Joyce had that kind of sense of humor. So it's very "Lennon" and very working class as well. There's all of that in there.

It's a very refreshing book, just from the style of writing. And with what he's saying—well, who can do that? I can't do that.

I used to be one who was hard to intimidate, but now I think about being a mother for Sean, and I don't try to rock the boat. But John, he just went all out, out there. With his kind of mind, he might have known that an outspoken person like him might have had a fate like that.

I didn't mind being daring. Being daring was like breathing to me. But I had to change my mind on that because Sean needs one parent.

So in a way, when you read *Skywriting by Word of Mouth*, it speaks for all of us who cannot say it the way John says it.

Was this material missing at one point and then recovered?

Right. When John wrote *Skywriting by Word of Mouth*, he was so excited about every page he typed out. That's another story—a Scandinavian feminist taught him how to type, and he was very proud of that.

So he would type one page, and read it to me or ask me to read it back to him. We were having a great old time. Finally he said, "This is so phonetically interesting, sound-wise as well, that I'm going to tape it." He wanted that to come out simultaneously with the book. You know, here's the book and a record of him reciting it.

But that tape hasn't come back yet. It's out there somewhere.

If you get it back, will you do something with it?

Oh yes. See that's another thing. The fact that *Skywriting by Word of Mouth* came back to me was so good. Not just for me, but for the world. Because we can all appreciate it. So maybe some-body is thinking about bootlegging the tape, but when you do that, the quality is not good. Or even if the quality is OK, it doesn't reach a lot of people. And that's very sad. If it's something that all of us can share naturally, it's better.

You and John started a tradition of giving a yearly Christmas message. Do you have an overall thought for everyone at this point?

I think that now we're all standing together at a threshold of a new age. And it's an age of wisdom. We're forced to be wise for our survival. Therefore, we are.

And we're going to enter, together, a century of peace. And I love you all very much.

You know, when we made "Happy Christmas," John was saying that it should replace "White Christmas" for our generation. Then we were so excited about the song, we had forgotten that we missed the Christmas market. By the time we recorded it, it was too late for that year.

But as the years go by, I think it's starting to become our Christmas song, and I'm very happy about that. But isn't that typical of us. John says it's going to replace "White Christmas," and we can't even get it out! It's so funny!

GEORGE
MARTIN

*"The general routine was that they would
sing the song to me, first of all, so I could
learn it. Then we would talk about it
and see what was required."*

•

For every marvelous musical innovation the
Beatles dreamed up, it was George Martin
who helped execute the idea on vinyl.

Already a successful producer of British
comedy recordings, Martin was head of the
British Parlophone label in 1962 when manager Brian Epstein came to him with a
recording of the four lads from Liverpool. As
a result of Martin's interest in Epstein's discovery, the Beatles were granted a recording
audition that eventually led to their signing
with the label.

From then on, Martin's novel production
techniques and trickery, including the use of
complex string arrangements and unusual instrumentation, played an intricate role in
what we know as Beatle songs.

Although Martin has spent the past
twenty years producing a wide variety of artists, including several albums with Paul
McCartney, his work with the Beatles will
stand as his finest hour.

We spoke to him at the legendary Abbey
Road studios following a most auspicious occasion—the star-studded *Sgt. Pepper* twentieth anniversary party.

George, it's a pleasure to see you, especially on such a special day. It really was twenty years ago today, wasn't it?

As a matter of fact, not only is today the twentieth anniversary of *Sgt. Pepper* but it's almost, within five days, the twenty-fifth anniversary of the very first recording we ever made. So it's rather a significant week altogether.

Let's start with 1962. I was very much involved with music and so were you. When Brian Epstein arrived with an acetate, your job was multi-faceted. It was a disc that Brian came with at first, right?

Yes, the first thing Brian played me was a lacquer disc of some of the songs they had recorded in a bad little studio. And it was awful, dreadful. I can quite understand why other people turned it down, poor fellows.

So what did you decide to do?

(COURTESY OF CAPITOL RECORDS)

THE BEATLES WITH GEORGE
MARTIN

I thought it was interesting enough to listen to, and I was looking for something anyway. So I told Brian to bring the boys down from Liverpool so I could have a look at them and work with them in the studio.

I booked some time here at Abbey Road, and spent three or four hours with them. And fell in love with them! That was it.

As a group, and to a man, they exhibited an outgoing style, and obvious wit.

They were cheeky; they had a great sense of humor. I had been making a lot of comedy records and I liked them. I knew they had a great charisma. And by the way, they showed no signs of being able to write songs. The songs they offered were pretty awful. But they had that great charisma, and I thought they were worthwhile taking a gamble on.

Twenty-five years ago, you were a producer, engineer, and musician, and comfortably doing your many jobs here at EMI. Then the Beatles entered your life, and I guess those four young men changed things somewhat!

Immensely. I had already been through different phases in my life. I was known as the comedians' producer before they came along. And after that, I became known as the Beatles' producer. So they certainly changed the direction quite a bit.

Let's talk about EMI/Capitol's release of the Beatle compact discs. Did they approach you at the outset or did you get involved later?

EMI had already decided what they were going to do, on the first four anyway, when they asked me to listen to them.

They were going to put out the Ping-Pong stereo, that fake stereo of the first records. So when I heard them, I was appalled. I thought it was dreadful. Those records should have never been issued in the first place.

[*At this point, the interview is interrupted by two wayward brothers, and George Martin says:*] Oh, there's Paul McCartney and Mike McCartney. Hello, folks.

Mike: Hello there!

Paul: Hi, folks. I'll let you get on with this, lads. I'm just popping in to pick up my things—I'm with the group! See ya, Scott. All the best! See ya, Georgie.

George [*Continuing*] So Capitol asked me what I thought of the CDs and I did tell them that I didn't like them.

I said, "If you want to put this thing out authentically, at least the first two at any rate, they should be issued only in mono. That was the way they were recorded."

They were not recorded in stereo. I know there are a lot of people in America who got used to listening to those awful, primitive stereos where we had the band on one side and voice on the other.

But in truth, these were twin-track recordings [that] we used for a mono mix, originally. And they were issued in the States like that. They should have never been issued in that form.

Anyway, EMI agreed, and listened to what I said and put them out in mono. And I believe there was quite a bit of controversy as a result of that.

In the second phase of the CD releases, you were back overseeing the project.

They asked me if I would then take an interest in it, which I did.

I read a quote from Paul to the effect that he was very glad that you were involved with the CD production and release. He was relieved that they'd be in your capable hands.

I think the important thing to do was to make sure that the sound was authentic and what we had intended all those years ago. We couldn't just leave it alone, because if we had, it wouldn't have sounded the same way.

You see, when we made that record twenty years ago, we were making it for machines that had a particular characteristic—they were very fuzzy, like playing music through a blanket.

Nowadays an average machine is extremely good and the average CD player is extremely good. So we had to make sure that they were absolutely tuned for a CD player.

I haven't remixed it. I just made sure the EQ is right. And I think it comes over with a great deal of character. I'm very proud of it.

And we expect to have the remainder of the Beatle library on CD by the end of the year, right?

As far as the Beatles are concerned, they are going to have all the albums out on CD by the end of this year. And one I'm particularly looking forward to is getting all those singles together on a good CD album. That's something I want to see happen next year.

I had heard some talk that they might be lumped in with some of the other albums that came out. Will they come out as one whole group?

I think EMI has been very good to issue the albums exactly the way they were issued in this country to begin with. They have got rid of the aberrations that happened all those years ago in different territories. So that throughout the world, the records are now all the same, which is good.

That does mean that the compilations that have been done in the past, without any reference to us by the way, won't be done. And we will now determine what those compilations will be.

It makes sense to me to put out all the singles on a compact disc, and putting on as many as can be done, and give the people the best value for the money. Although I don't know what EMI is going to do. Speaking personally, I'd like to see twenty to thirty tracks on each compact disc. And we'll probably need more than that.

Twenty years ago this week, I got my hands on Sgt. Pepper's Lonely Hearts Club Band *for the very first time. Obviously, the first thing I noticed was the cover. I'd never seen anything like it. I explained it as best I could to the audience, then I put the needle down on Side One and, along with the audience, heard* Pepper *for the first time.*

What's it like for you, and all the memories you must have of those sessions, being back here twenty years later?

Well, it's been a wonderful day, actually. Oddly enough, I haven't listened to *Pepper* a great deal in the past twenty years. And it doesn't seem like twenty years by the way, it seems like yesterday—but I'm not plugging that one!

At the same time, I think that *Pepper* was a special record for me. It was a kind of growth within the boys and the way they wrote their songs. Suddenly they were aware of the potential of the recording studio as an art medium. Before that, they had been making up rock 'n' roll songs for a rock 'n' roll band to perform.

Then gradually, through *Rubber Soul* and *Revolver*, they then realized that they could do more than that. They could paint sound pictures in the studio with me. And that's exactly what we tried to do with *Pepper*.

They had the time. They had stopped touring and had the time to do it. It was very exciting, working on that album.

What were some of the differences in each of the lads within the studio?

John was always clowning and he did some silly things sometimes. He was a very funny bloke, John. He also was very acid sometimes and could be enormously cruel. But he was a most lovable person and, certainly during the *Pepper* times, his wit and humor came through enormously.

They all were, actually. They were all good fun. And whoever wrote the song, whether it was John, Paul, or George, they more or less dictated the style that they were going to go for.

The general routine was that they would sing the song to me, first of all, so I could learn it. Then we would talk about it and see what was required.

Paul was always the most articulate. He had very definite ideas about what he wanted. He would go to the piano or the guitar and play a line that he wanted to have incorporated into the writing of it.

John on the other hand, was much more poetical in his thoughts and much more difficult to read. So I had to get inside his brain and figure out just what he wanted. He would talk in very obscure phrases, like wanting an orange-flavored sound. In the case of "Being for the Benefit of Mr. Kite," he wanted to hear the sawdust on the floor. That was the kind of image he would give to me and I picked up on it.

At what stage of development was George during these sessions? He was fast emerging as a writer. But Within You Without You *is a unique track, especially on this record.*

You know, I never used to give George a great deal of time and I regret that now because he is a fine musician. And of course, I concentrated on the two winners—John and Paul—and George was kind of tolerated.

George's track on this album I thought was boring when we first did it. But hearing it again and hearing the way it was constructed, I think it's a very good track indeed. It's very interesting going back to it after all these years and hearing it.

I remember doing the recordings with the Indian musicians and then having the task of making the same sounds with English musicians in an orchestra. And George was very, very patient.

I think my main objection to it was that it was long and a little bit dirgey, which sometimes happens with that kind of music. But in retrospect, it sounds jolly good.

And of course, a lot of George's later ones were brilliant. "Here Comes the Sun," in some ways is one of the best songs ever written.

Have you had any contact with George lately?

Yes, I spoke with him three or four weeks ago, before he went off to Hawaii. We had a half-an-hour's chat on the phone. We promised to get together when he got back, but now I've been away for the past two weeks. It's just a question of arranging our times so we do meet up.

And you find that he's OK?

George is terrific. He's one of the most together people I know. People forget that he is a very big bloke in the British film industry. He produces fantastic pictures and he keeps it fairly quiet. His Handmade Films has produced some of the best British pictures that we've had in the past few years. Not big ones, but very, very good ones.

A little earlier, I heard Paul field a question about his favorite tracks from Pepper. *He avoided it for a bit, but then admitted that "A Day in the Life" has to rank up there. What are your feelings?*

Well, "A Day in the Life" is probably my favorite track on that album, or certainly one of the favorites. And it wasn't just because it was both John and Paul distinctly [contributing].

It started out being a John song, and then Paul contributed the middle bit which we all know. But Paul contributed a bit more than that too. It was his idea to have the twenty-four bars of silence, which we would then fill in with an orchestra.

So it was a supreme example of the collaboration between the two. Where something like "She's Leaving Home" was purely Paul, and something like "Kite" was purely John. And I think that "A Day in the Life" was a wonderful example of their collaboration.

And then you used several pianos for the finale.

It was fun. It was very easy to do, but it was quite fun. That was just a trick in the studio. We raised the mikes up to the nth degree of volume in the doorway and everybody kept as quiet as church mice. And it worked. We just overdubbed three pianos three times.

The interesting thing was the way the harmonics of the overtones just waved in and out as a phasing affect. But it was just purely acoustic sound.

Do you recall the very beginning of that long recording process, the one that began Sgt. Pepper?

The album began in December of 1966 with the recording of "Strawberry Fields," "When I'm Sixty-Four," and later, "Penny Lane."

I think "Penny Lane" was Paul's answer to John when he wrote "Strawberry Fields," because he was knocked out by it. He thought it was a marvelous song and tried to do something better. And he came up with "Penny Lane," which wasn't bad.

Then we had a break for Christmas and then came back into the studio and started doing more titles. And I really intended that that ["Penny Lane/Strawberry Fields"] was going to be the beginning of the album. But Brian Epstein was anxious to have a single out—he was a bit worried that the Beatles might be slipping in the charts. He wanted a very strong single.

So I said "You couldn't have a stronger one than these two put together—'Strawberry Fields' and 'Penny Lane.'" So we did that.

In those days, we used not to put the single on the album. It was a deliberate policy. We felt that the public shouldn't have to be shortchanged. If they'd already bought the single, they wouldn't have to buy it again on the album. Of course, today it's the opposite.

But we felt very strongly that people should get good value for money. So we kept it off the album. And I'm sorry about that because it really would have been marvelous to have those tracks in addition on the album.

And somebody did bring it up: "Should those songs be put back into the album?" But the decision was right, not to include them.

It was much better to have the album exactly as it was originally issued. And I've no doubt that "Strawberry Fields" and "Penny Lane" will be a part of the compendium that we're going to offer next year.

And what a tremendous single it was. Rare is a single that has so much on both sides.

Well, the nice thing about it was that it was the peak of perfection from each of the boys. John on one side and Paul on the other. Each doing their own thing in a terrific coupling.

The funny thing was that, in this country [England], it didn't make number one in the first week. It was kept out of the charts by Engelbert Humperdinck's "Release Me" which was justice for you! Look at it.

It wasn't as simple as that. In fact, I think we did sell more records than Engelbert. The difficulty and probably my own fault was in that when the dealers listed their returns for the charts they were split. Some of them returned "Strawberry Fields" and some of them reported "Penny Lane."

So while we didn't get as many votes per record we got votes per song, which tended to put it down in the charts. I'm quite sure, in fact, we did sell more.

What does the crystal ball have for George Martin?

Well, I'm going to enjoy myself for a start. I've been in the business a long time and people wonder if I'm still alive.

I started making records in 1950, which is thirty-seven years ago. And it's been a long, long haul. I've made an awful lot of tracks, probably more than anybody else.

So I'm making less records today. I'll probably do another

album in a couple of months. I'm doing more film work. I'm doing more concert work. In fact I'm doing one here with the London Symphony Orchestra.

But above all, I'm enjoying myself. I just built myself a boat in Turkey and I'm kicking around a bit.

I'm not sure I'd like to be back there in that hotel room, twenty-four years ago, all over again—

But you were there! And it's nice to look back on, isn't it?

DAVE CLARK

I think the press made it competitive but there really wasn't any competition between the Beatles and the Dave Clark Five. The Beatles were from Liverpool and it was unheard of that Liverpool would dominate the airwaves. Then all of a sudden the Beatles had their biggest-selling single [at the time], "Please Please Me." And we came out with "Glad All Over." We were selling one-hundred-fifty-thousand copies a day and we were still number two. We were number two for nine weeks and we had to sell a million and a half copies to get to the number one spot. And as you know, the press always likes to build up these things but there was no competition. I think competition is healthy, even today. If you don't have competition, you get complacent. It keeps you on your toes.

CARL PERKINS

CARL
PERKINS

*"Then all of a sudden, when we were
playing in the studio kicking around on
some of the stuff, George Martin said,
'Are we ready to go?' And Ringo cut out
on 'Honey Don't.' And it was a magic
time."*

•

The king of rockabilly, Carl Perkins has influenced a generation of guitarists since his
beginnings more than thirty years ago as a
session player at Sun Records in Memphis.

Perhaps best known for writing Elvis
Presley's signature song, "Blue Suede
Shoes," Perkins' numerous compositions
successfully captured the essence of coming
of age in the fifties. And naturally, the Beatles were all ears once his music made its
way to Liverpool.

Perkins has had a number of marvelous
encounters with the Beatles over the years,
and has maintained close friendships with
both George Harrison and Paul McCartney.

We spoke with Perkins just following the
airing of his 1987 cable TV special, *Carl Perkins and Friends.*

First off, let's talk about the Cinemax special called Carl Perkins and
Friends. *Not only did it feature Eric Clapton, Dave Edmunds, and*

Roseanne Cash, but also a few of your old friends named George Harrison and Ringo Starr. How did that come about?

It started as a dream. I'm fifty-three-and-a-half years old and I was thinking about retiring at the age of fifty-five. So I got to thinking that the business has been mighty good to me for thirty-something years and I never had a TV show or special or anything. I thought, "Why not really try for something big?"

How did you go about getting those folks involved?

I made my own little videos and sent them to these people. Speaking to them was like, "Hi, George. This is your old friend Carl Perkins. I haven't seen you since 1964 but I want to do a TV special and I want to make it the best I possibly can. And I need you, if you'd do it."

And the amazing thing was how quick they got back in touch with me, [saying] that they really wanted to do this. It was one of the most memorable things of my life, playing rockabilly music with some of the giants in the rock world: Ringo, George, Eric, Dave.

It was a magic time in my life. I really did enjoy it. And I think from looking at it and talking to these guys since we did it, they too are proud. I know that Harrison has called me a couple of times and he's really proud that he did that.

Hopefully, he'll get back into the swing; I'd like for that to happen. The world needs that kind of talent. He's a great writer.

How did you decide on what you wanted to do in the show?

We had a rehearsal the first day. So we got started playing and that was it. We were jamming and they wanted to do my old songs.

So the Cinemax people were saying, "Carl, it sounds great and you're all having a lot of fun, but we got a show to rehearse."

And I said, "Well, Hoss, you may be lookin' at the show! I mean, don't this feel good?" And really, that's the way we went with it.

I thought the music on my part certainly could have been tighter—endings and beginnings and so forth. But in doing that, I think we might have lost some of the love that came out visually. It worked better, and really, we never had a rehearsal of a show as such. We got together twice—and the third time the camera went on.

And they caught a bunch of guys doing what artists love to do—get together and play the music, the songs they want to play. That was the magic about it!

There was a great version of "Your True Love."

That was George's idea. He loved that song and he had to teach me the words to my own song! I'd forgotten them, I really had.

He said, "You had a song called 'Your True Love.'" And I said, "Yeah, I did." But when I started doing it, I didn't remember the words. But he remembered every one of them. And I particularly like that song on that session. I think it worked good.

I'll tell you, the camera didn't catch all of the ending. It was such an experience at the end when it was all over. They caught a little of it—you can see Eric Clapton hugging George Harrison. But there was more.

There were dressing room scenes, where the tears were definitely coming from me. Because there is no doubt that I'm one of the luckiest old men in the world to have these guys say, "Hey man, I'd love to make music with you."

So there were some shots that I definitely would like to have had on camera. There were some good-byes that I really felt.

One of the Beatles unanimous highlights was a time they spent with you back in 1964. You all gathered at one of their recording sessions and some very special music happened. Tell us about that.

Well, that was in 1964. I went over to England for the first time I'd ever been, with Chuck Berry. And Chuck had never been to England at that time either.

It was a massive tour and I was in total shock. Every night and everything was packed out. The kids were bopping in the aisles. It was a great time and a great tour.

The last night of that tour, the promoter said, "Carl, I want to take you to a party."

I said, "Man, I'm tired. I'm going back to America in the morning." And I did have a nine o'clock flight, leaving from there. I'd been over there for about a month and I said, "I'm going to have to cancel out on you. I can't, I'm too tired to go."

He said, "I really think you ought to go to this one." So I did. It turned out that the Beatles gave the party for me!

We wound up—John, Paul, George, and Ringo—sitting on a couch and me sitting on a floor with a guitar. And they wanted to know how I kicked off some of those old Sun songs.

That night they invited me to a recording session at Abbey Road for the next night. I almost said that I was going home.

They asked me, "What are you doing tomorrow night?" And maybe one of the best words I ever said was "Nothing." They said, "Well, great. Could you come to a session?" And I said "Yeah!"

So I did. And nothing was said about recording my songs. Then all of a sudden, when we were playing in the studio, kicking around on some of the stuff, George Martin said, "Are we ready to go?" And Ringo cut out on "Honey Don't" and it was a magic time.

Yeah, I was in the studio when they cut "Honey Don't," "Matchbox," and "Everybody's Trying to Be My Baby." And they did a version of "Blue Suede Shoes," which was never released. And it's a honker; it's good!

Were you aware that George used to go by "Carl Harrison," as a stage name back in 1959, in deference to you?

I had heard it. While we were doing the Cinemax special, I was invited out to his home.

So he sent a car for me and my son Greg. The house knocked me out, his wife Olivia, his little boy Dhani. And it's a big massive thing that's a home inside. It's warm.

I walked in the door and there were old Carl Perkins records. And he said, "Now Olivia, tell him I didn't put them on there today."

His juke box is loaded with old Sun records. And she said, "No, he didn't put them on there today; I did. I listen to them all the time."

So we sat on the floor; that's what he wanted to do. We started playing some old songs—me, Dave Edmunds, Ringo, my son Greg—and I said [to George], "Man, you know them all." And I believe it was Dave Edmunds who said, "He ought to—he used to call himself you!"

And I said, "George, really, did that happen? I'd heard that."

And he said, "Shoooo, yes, I certainly did!" And that's a very humbling thing for me. And when he said he did, he did.

You've also collaborated with Paul McCartney on a song named "Get It." How did that materialize?

I was in England a couple of years before that. I was on tour and it was my birthday on April 9. And when I got back to my hotel room, there was a big box with a blue ribbon around it sittin' on a table in the room. I opened it and it was a guitar cake. And it said, "Happy Birthday! We Love You, Paul, Linda, and kids." Well, it really knocked me out because I didn't know he remembered me.

But one day I got a phone call and it was McCartney. He asked what I was doing and I said, "Nothing much." So he said, "I sure would like for you to come to Montserrat. I'm going to do an album. Stevie Wonder's going to be there, Ringo. And I have a song that I'd really like you to do with me on this album."

So I said, "I got one problem and that's all." And he said, "What's that?"

I said, "I don't know where Montserrat is!" And he said, "I'll have my travel agent fix that."

So he sent the tickets and I got on a plane in Nashville and I flew to an island called Antigua, which is as far as you can go commercially.

So a dude was standing there by a private plane and in broken English he said, "Are you Carl Perkins?" I said, "Yeah."

He said, "I come for you. Paul McCartney send me for you." So we climbed in that little airplane and went up over that big blue ocean. And I said, "Hoss, where are we going?" He said, "Montserrat, I'll show you in just a moment." And, in a few minutes, that little dot down there was Montserrat.

Paul and Linda were sitting there waiting after we landed on this little cinder strip. I threw my luggage in the back of their jeep and away we went.

So we went to this beautiful studio called AIR Studios which belongs to George Martin. And I stayed there for eight days.

And that's where you did "Get It"?

Yeah, he sang me this song, "Get It." And he said, "To be truthful, we don't have to do this one if you don't want to. I have others." But he sang it and I loved it. It was a cute song; it really is. So we flew into it, cut it, and it didn't take very long at all.

He's a powerful boy, Paul. He's a great writer and very serious about his music. The initial track was easy to put down. But when you do that with him, you've just started. He'll play all night to get one guitar chord that he wants. He hears what he wants to before it's done. He's a perfectionist. But it was a lot of fun to work on that album.

Now you wrote a song for him entitled "My Old Friend." But it hasn't been released yet. Tell us about it.

That song will be out sometime this year.

The night before I was going to leave I was sitting out with my little cat-gut guitar, knowing I was going to leave the next day and knowing too how much I had enjoyed being down there with Paul and his family.

So I thought that I might just write down how I feel about him, because I might choke up tomorrow and not be able to tell him. And that's exactly what I did.

This song is a personal thing to McCartney, and the title is "My Old Friend."

I sang it for him the next morning, told him that I'd written it the night before. He said, "I love it." Then he called Linda in to hear it and she loved it. He said, "Carl, can you stay another day?" I said, "Yeah, I just have to call my wife."

So I did. He played bass, organ, rhythm guitar, and drums on it. I played a couple of guitar parts and we both sang on the song.

When I left the next day, I thought I had enough on the song. But I got a phone call from him a couple of weeks after, after he got back to England.

He said, "Carl, I'm listening to 'My Old Friend.' Would you mind if I really put a treatment to this song? I hear violins and horns, and I'd really like to make it a big record."

I said, "Hoss, I don't care if you put the queen on there." So he did [the treatment] and I've got the tape and it's beautiful. I've held on to it for a while, because I didn't feel that the time was right. But I think it's very close now. I think it will come out.

ELTON JOHN

*"And even if I'm doing bad things to
myself or if I'm being totally miserable or
morose or being totally unreasonable with
people, I sometimes think, "Oh my God,
John, if there is really a big pearly gate,
you're going to be standing outside of it
and giving me the biggest lecture."*

•

Born Reginald Kenneth Dwight in 1947,
Elton John was a child prodigy on piano,
studying at London's Royal Academy of
Music at the age of eleven. He eventually
garnered attention as a keyboard player in
the groundbreaking British band Bluesology
and later as a solo act in local pubs. After
changing his name, Elton teamed up with
lyricist Bernie Taupin and they set out on a
hit-making career, now over twenty-five
albums long.

Elton first learned of the Beatles while
working as a gofer for Dick James, the band's
original publisher. Elton would often take
Beatles tapes home from work and get a
sneak preview of their latest recording.

Many years later Elton would work with
and get close to John Lennon. He performed
on *Walls and Bridges*, and Lennon made his
last public appearance with Elton on
Thanksgiving night, 1974, at New York's
Madison Square Garden.

Elton and Scott Muni have talked often
throughout his career. However, this partic-

ular conversation is most evocative because
Elton describes the formidable influence
John Lennon had on his music and his life in
general. Elton had a number one song with
the Lennon composition "Lucy in the Sky
with Diamonds," and that's where they
started their talk.

Elton, what prompted you to record "Lucy"?

I said to John, "I'd love to record one of your songs. Which one
would you like me to do?" And he said, "No one's ever done 'Lucy
in the Sky with Diamonds'; no one's ever recorded that ever." I
mean, the Beatles always had cover versions on all their songs but
nobody ever did "Lucy in the Sky with Diamonds." So we did
that one, along with "One Day at a Time," which is on the B
Side, also one of John's.

*The last appearance John Lennon officially made onstage was with you
on Thanksgiving night, 1974, at Madison Square Garden. I've seen a
lot of rock 'n' roll in my life, but I'm hard pressed to remember anything quite like that.*

It was an occasion where grown men, even Scottish road managers who'd seen it all, cried. I've never seen anybody get an ovation like that. No one will ever beat that for me, ever.

I mean, when he walked onstage, it shook him. And I think it
shook the world when he died, just how much reverence people
paid towards John Lennon. Because John Lennon really repre-
sented the rebellious side of the Beatles. He was the one who slept
in the bag with Yoko, or whatever.

And I think it shook a lot of people that when he died that
much reverence was shown towards him. And I'm so glad it was.
Hopefully, he'll have been dancing when he saw it. He deserved
it.

He was physically sick when he came onstage with us that
night. You see, I'd made "Whatever Gets You Through the
Night," and I sang on another track on *Walls and Bridges*, and we
made sort of, well, not a hard bargain that if it got to number one,
he'd come onstage. And he kept his bargain.

He came up to Boston to see us, just to check the show out.

When he saw all the equipment he said, "My God, is this what it's all about?" I came by wearing a chocolate-box cover and nothing else. It was his time with May Pang and he was very happy.

Just to give you an example, he would take my band to the airport and make sure my mother was OK. I've never met anybody more thoughtful. I know you read in some books that John could be cruel and had a very cynical sense of humor, and I've seen that side of him too. I was with him at a particularly crazy time for him and for me. But underneath it all, I never saw anything else but kindness. He is sacred to me.

He is the only person in this business who is absolutely, one hundred percent sacred to me. And even if I'm doing bad things to myself, or if I'm being totally miserable or morose, or being unreasonable with people, I sometimes think, "Oh my God, John, if there is really a big pearly gate, you're going to be standing outside of it and giving me the biggest lecture."

That's because he's the only person in this business that I've ever looked up to, the only person. I've met my equals. I've met people who are great like Mick Jagger and Pete Townshend, who I admire tremendously, but they are not in the same league, I'm sorry.

You were very close to John Lennon. And when the tragedy happened you and Bernie, with words and music, came out with a brilliant tribute called "Empty Garden."

(STAR FILE/BOB GRUEN)

JOHN LENNON AND ELTON JOHN

Yeah. When John died, I couldn't believe it. I was close to John for a year; let's put it on record. And I hung out with him and I loved him. I've never met anybody who impressed me so much as that man.

When he died, we were in Australia and we heard it on the plane. I'm not a religious person particularly, but we did go to the cathedral to have ten minutes of silence to coincide with Yoko's [request]. And it was the least I could do for him.

So later, I wrote an instrumental called "The Man Who Never Died." It's never been released; it's still in the can. That song made me upset when I wrote it. That was my tribute to John.

And then Bernie came up with the lyric to "Empty Garden," which I thought said it all. It was very hard to say in a lyric and a lot easier in an instrumental.

Aren't you Sean's godfather?

Yes, I am. I don't see enough of him as I probably should.

Well, I can tell you that I did see him recently, and he's a very handsome young man. Talented too. He's very active and he's into everything. He's all questions.

Oh, I'm sure he has the brain of someone of twenty-one probably at this age. There are certain reasons why I'm not as close to him as I should be. I just feel that Sean has been a little exploited at some times. But that's not for me to say. I'm not part of the family. I was just lucky enough to know John Lennon for a year and, God, that was one of the happiest years of my life. And "Empty Garden" is the least I could do.

GEORGE
HARRISON

*"We grew up very fast. I mean, the
experiences we had, most people don't get
in a whole lifetime. But the experiences
we had were crammed into those years,
those few years between 1962, when we
first took off, and began recording and
then eventually came to America."*

•

George Harrison has never quite shaken the
label he was given at the height of Beatlemania when he was known as the quiet Beatle.

Although his contributions to Beatle
albums have consistently commanded more
attention over the years, Harrison remains
the most enigmatic member of the band. His
interest in Eastern spirituality has been well
documented and has greatly influenced his
musical career.

Scott Muni most recently met with
George in Los Angeles in September of 1987
and he was eager to discuss his brand new
album *Cloud Nine*. George seemed especially
proud of his effort because it featured many
old friends, including Ringo, Eric Clapton,
and Elton John. And after releasing several
previous solo recordings, he seemed to know
that *Cloud Nine* would indeed be both a popular and critical success.

No longer the quiet Beatle, George even
formed a new band in 1988, the critically ac-

claimed Travelling Wilburys, with fellow musical legends Bob Dylan, the late Roy Orbison, Tom Petty, and Electric Light Orchestra's Jeff Lynne.

As a kid, you had to go and buy the records that you loved. Radio wasn't like it is in America. You didn't get a wide variety of music in those days, did you?

In England, there was the BBC and they played very middle-of-the-road stuff. Then there was one radio station called Radio Luxembourg and I think it was owned by the three record companies in England—EMI, Decca, and Pye. And if anything wasn't on those labels, you never got to hear it.

Sometimes they distributed product for American labels, but there was always a tendency to get a good American hit and give it to one of their own artists. So we always heard the cover versions.

They had something called needle time, where they gave every record a certain amount of time on the air.

Right, that was the BBC. What needle time meant was, say you had a program that was the Top Twenty and they may only have, by the musician's union, a certain amount of time to play the records. That's what they meant by needle time. The rest of the songs were played by what was called The Northern Dance Orchestra, who worked with the BBC. So they'd say, "And number twenty on the hit parade this week is such and such, and here to sing it is Eddy Jones and the NDO."

So you just heard this real crappy version of it.

Back in June, I was in London doing my radio show live via satellite. But on an off-day, I took my second trip to Liverpool. Now obviously, I'm an outsider, but I was very depressed during my trip there. I went to your schools, I went to your neighborhoods, and I went to the pubs and spent time there. It seems that not a lot of good has happened to Liverpool. I still saw the wreckage from World War II.

This is unbelievable, but when we grew up in Liverpool, you could see a whole row of houses, and then there was a bombsite, like a direct hit during the war. And those bombsites were there until I left Liverpool at the age of seventeen, eighteen.

GEORGE HARRISON

Whereas we went from there to Germany—and as you know through the history, we played a lot of times in Hamburg—the Germans had really built the country back.

The main thing they've done for Liverpool and the rest of the cities in England seems to have been to knock down the landmarks and the things you grew up with. Every city is faceless and looks the same—the concrete, and the one-way motor systems. It's terrible. It's very depressing for me to go back and look at Liverpool.

And yet the people are so funny; they're all comedians. But now that you've been there you realize that when we first came to America with the kind of attitude the Beatles had with the press, you saw that we scored really highly on that level. But we did it naturally. We just naturally had that humor and we do to this day.

I like to have a laugh and a sense of humor. They say Liverpool is a great place to be from and everybody in that place is a comedian.

One thing that confirms that came up in a talk I had with George Martin recently. He said the determining factor in his decision to sign the Beatles was your attitude, spirit, and sense of humor.

Yeah, but I nearly got killed by the rest of the band from that first trip to Abbey Road studios when George Martin recorded us. Afterwards, he played it back and he said, "Is there anything that you don't like?"

I just looked at him and said, "Well, I don't like your tie, for a kickoff!" And the others were like "Ohhhh Noooo, we're trying to get a record deal here." But he also had a sense of humor.

George, you been away from the music scene for awhile. Now comes a new album that you've spent a lot of time making. Let's talk about the album and why you've decided to do it now. Were you restless?

I think it is probably been five years since I had the last album out. But in between, I have been busy. It's not like I haven't done anything. For instance, I spent six months of last year writing songs and doing a soundtrack for a movie. And I've got a studio in my home, so I write songs and record them. So I'm constantly composing.

I've done a few things over the years for some other movies too. I did a song for Dave Edmunds for some soundtrack he was doing, and I did a TV show with Carl Perkins. So I've done a few things like that and I haven't exactly been totally out of it. I also have a film company that I'm involved with as well.

But I think the main reason to do a record now is that I've had a number of years away from it. I was just feeling good about the idea of doing a record on the condition that I could find a producer to work with me that would help share the load. And on this album, it's the first time I felt like I felt when it was with John, Paul, and Ringo.

In those days we could all contribute such a lot to each other, as far as ideas go, bouncing them back off one another. Then these things can turn into something different.

There's generally more input than when you're on your own. It can be a little bit difficult. You can stagnate on your own, in terms of writing, producing, and being the artist. Sometimes you need an outside point of view.

When I decided to do this record, which I was feeling ready to make, I decided that I've got to have some production assistance. "Now, who should it be?"

I only ever worked with three people in the past—George Martin, of course; Phil Spector, who I used on one album; and a guy called Russ Titelman from Warner Brothers. But most of the stuff, I've done on my own.

I don't know a great deal of record producers. But I got this idea that turns out to have been really good, and that was [to work with] Jeff Lynne of Electric Light Orchestra. It was because of his music, and that he's from Birmingham, a similar kind of place to Liverpool. He's also a songwriter, and guitar player, and a producer. He's been through all that in his own band.

So I thought that, musically, we could get on really well together. The only thing missing was that I didn't know him. So I had to contact him and, over a period of eighteen months, get to know him. And that's how this came about.

Did you and Jeff make joint decisions on the album's personnel?

Not really. See, Jeff didn't know Ringo or Eric [Clapton]. I think he knew Elton a little bit. He'd never met the sax player, Jim Horn, so really that part was left to me.

I said to him, "I want Ringo to play on some of these tracks, because of Ringo's sound, and because Ringo enjoys a play and hasn't been playing that much." And I thought it would do him good, you know, get him out of the house. And Jeff was really pleased because he, like many of us, is a Beatle fan. So he got to meet Ringo, and Jim Keltner, who is a drummer-friend of mine for a long time now.

So Jeff was more involved just in the overall production, the sounds we got, and some of the songs which we wrote together.

Did anyone else contribute songs to the album besides you and Jeff?

There is only one song that is not my song or a collaboration between Jeff and I. And that is the song they've chosen as the single. "Got My Mind Set on You."

That comes off a very old album I've had in my collection for years. It's written by a guy who I know nothing about, called Rudy Clark. I picked that song up years ago on this album that I bought following a single release of a record by James Ray called "If You're Going to Make a Fool of Somebody." That was a song the Beatles performed a long time ago, [although] we never actually made a recording of it.

And "Got My Mind Set on You" just stuck in the back of my mind over the years. It just sort of came out on these sessions.

What I'd like to do is have you describe some of the songs on the album in whatever way you like. Let's start with Side One, Cut One, the title track. Is there any significance to why you chose that as the album and title?

We just put it there because it seemed a good opener. Now later, after I saw the album cover, which had clouds on it, I just used that song title as the album title. So there's no great significance to it other than the photograph had clouds on it and I had a song called "Cloud Nine."

It's the kind of song that's not expected from me. When I wrote the tune, I heard it as a cross between J. J. Cale and James Brown, if there could be such a thing. Of course I don't sing like James Brown, but it's a very good, bluesy-oriented song.

There's Eric Clapton and myself on that one. I play slide and Eric plays regular guitar. It's got this friend of mine, Jim Horn, an American saxophonist. He's got a horn section on it that sounds a bit like Al Green. So it's a pretty funky track, that one.

The second song on the record is called "If That's What It Takes." Now this is the first song I wrote with Jeff Lynne, so there's a bit of a story to it.

I've written one song with Eric Clapton years ago. I've written one with Bob Dylan, and I've written a lot for Ringo in the sense that I've given him some of my tunes or finished off some of his. But I've never really had a great experience with collaboration with other songwriters.

So this project was interesting for me because Jeff and I again realized that we had a lot in common. We started to write "If That's What It Takes," and we wrote the verse part of that together. Then we went through three or four completely different middle bits.

Jeff was not quite satisfied with that. So, when we started the recording dates, this keyboard [player] friend of mine named Gary Wright was there. So just as a joke, I said, "Gary, got any spare middle bits?" And he said, "Yeah, I've got this chord change here which I've never known what to do with."

So that seemed quite interesting, although it was very strange. Later, we put that into the song, along with another piece Jeff had been keeping which turned [out] to be the chorus.

Anyway, we put all these pieces together and the song is really nice. Musically, it goes through so many changes. And the part that Gary provided, we built upon that, added orchestra parts and all. That turned into a really neat Beach Boys thing. So it has these three really distinctive parts, but together, it all flows well as the one song.

The third song on the album I wrote the night before we started the basic sessions. I wrote it just in the mood of an old rock 'n' roll song. In fact, on this track, I used my old Rickenbacker twelve-string, which was probably last heard on "Ticket to Ride" or "A Hard Day's Night" and all those songs.

So that one has a pretty distinctive sound, and it's called "Fish on the Sand." It was just a phrase I read somewhere that was very descriptive. It says, "If I can't be with you, then I'm not so much a man, I'm like a fish on the sand." It's a real up-tempo rock 'n' roll song, with Ringo playing on drums.

There's a song here called "Just for Today," which is the slow song on this side. I actually wrote it in the winter of '83 or in early '84. I have a couple of friends who were at the house. They had all been to Alcoholics Anonymous and had given up drinking. One of them had this little leaflet that he was showing me that AA gives out to help them get through the day. And it's called "Just for Today." I wrote the song based upon that. It says to try and live through this day and not deal with all of life's problems. So that's what that song's about.

It's done on a piano that I have in this big room in my house, this big oak hall. So it has a very ambient sound. The first part of the song is just me and a piano, and I've not really done that before. It's like being naked.

Then there are backing parts on the song that sound like a Welsh choir. It's Jeff Lynne and myself who made up those parts. So it's very much a mood piece.

I've done this in the past with similar things, where I'll say certain things in a song and if I can help other people, OK. But it's also to remind myself, because we all need a reminder that there's so much happening and we try to deal with all these things. We get worn out, run down, and ratty. It's nice to have that to remind us that [we should] live now, deal with this moment right now, and don't worry about everything else that's going on.

And too often people do that. They run around doing one thing, with a million other things on their minds.

I think that applies to everyone, and if I can use the term, I think it's the sleeper on the album. When you do have something like that, it applies to so many people in their own way. And whether it's their situation or not, they will be able to relate to what you're saying because it's everyone's problem to a degree. So I think it's excellent. And the vocal reminded me a little bit of John.

I said that to Jeff. On some of these vocals I said, "Oh, that just sounded like John!" There's just a certain Liverpoolness, possibly.

I mean, let's face it, we were born in the same place, grew up, and were together. There's a lot of Liverpoolness in the way you say certain words. And I have difficulty pronouncing certain words without the Liverpool accent. There's always one or two words in every song lyric that gives away that I'm from Liverpool.

But it's nice to know that you like that one ["Just for Today"]. There's a tendency to always try to have the fast tunes and the catchy tunes [get more attention]. And the songs that are the nice and soothing songs don't tend to be commercial. It's nice to know that people do want to listen to these types of songs too.

The next song is called "This Is Love." Is that another song you composed with Jeff?

When I decided I was going to work with Jeff Lynne, I said, "Will you write me a tune?" I thought it would be interesting, me singing one of his songs.

So he came back to me with a cassette with the makings of this song. He had the chorus all set, but he had four different versions of the verse part. So it was a matter of playing them and saying, "I think I'd like it to go this way." He could still write another three songs with the bits left over! Very clever, he is!

So that song was basically his, but I helped put it together and write some of the lyrics. To me, that's the catchiest one [on the album]. Not necessarily the one I *like* the most, but I think it's so catchy. And although it's been said many times, these songs about love, but I think this one says it again in a way that is still fresh and original. It also happens to have what I consider the nicest sounding slide guitar part on the whole record.

The last song on Side One is a complete indulgence in nostalgia. Again, it's a song I wrote with Jeff Lynne, based on some idea reminiscent of '67–'68. This song has a couple of very reminiscent chord changes that I've used in previous old Beatle tunes.

And because it's a trip down memory lane, it's also very tongue in cheek. It's supposed to be humorous and it's called "When We Was Fab."

"Fabs," as in referring to the Beatles?

But it's not just meant to be related to the Beatles as the Fabs. It's everybody in that period. Everybody was fab. So I wrote the song to sound like one of those.

Jeff and I got all the little bits that we could think of in there— backwards bits, little phasey bits, crazy backing vocals and cellos. There's even the sitars on the end.

I think it's my favorite because it's the first song I've really written with somebody else that was a total collaboration that we were both really pleased with.

You were in San Francisco at that time. I remember you were the one who walked around Haight-Ashbury. You saw those times up close.

Yeah—it was around that time, with meditation and those things. This is like what you would expect out of a track off a Beatles record from that period. There are things that just hit your ear and make you think of other things. So I think that song was a great success, and it makes me laugh every time I hear it.

One of the best things about this record, and this is why I was pleased that it worked out with Jeff Lynne, [is that] he's somebody that I respect. It had to be somebody I totally respected as a producer and songwriter.

What's the point of having somebody tell me to do certain things? Because if I don't believe what they're telling me, I'm not going to do it.

Likewise, I wanted to have somebody who didn't just want to make a record and put me out of the context that I'm in and forget all about what I've done in the past and where I've come from. So in that respect it's very much my record, but it does have this added little influence.

It's more like the feeling I had in the band in the old days when we bounced ideas backwards and forward. We came up with ideas that we may not have thought of just being on our own.

Side Two of Cloud Nine *kicks off with "Devil's Radio."*

Yeah, Ringo's on drums, so it's very much a rock 'n' roll song. And to my mind, the only thing missing off this song is Bob Dylan singing it. It reminds me very much of something that he would have done, back in the late sixties or seventies.

I passed a little church and on the outside of it was a small billboard. It said: GOSSIP...THE DEVIL'S RADIO. DON'T BE A BROADCASTER. So I took it from there. This song is all about gossip, gossip, gossip. And there's a lot of it going on. There's even little bits in the back going, "Hey, you wouldn't believe what I heard."

Next up is "Someplace Else." But that's a song we've heard before this album, isn't it?

I did the music for *Shanghai Surprise*, a film people may not have seen but surely heard about, due to what happened with the press, Sean Penn, and Madonna.

I wrote some songs for the soundtrack. And since they never came out on a soundtrack album, I recut them for this record. One of them, the love song for the movie, was called "Someplace Else." That's a very nice melodic tune.

The producer of the film, at the time, said, "I want you to write a song like 'Stardust.'" [*Laughing*] And I said "That *would* be nice. Who wouldn't like to write 'Stardust'!"

So this isn't exactly "Stardust," but it was an attempt at a very melodic love song.

What's "The Wreck of the Hesperus" about?

That's a real rock 'n' roll tune with Ringo and Jim [Keltner] playing drums, Elton John on piano, a horn section, and Eric plays solos on it.

The title is from a poem written around Victorian times, which I wasn't that familiar with. But it's an expression my mother used to use: "Oh, look at you, you look like the Wreck of the Hesperus." So it's one of those things that stuck.

It's a tongue-in-cheek lyric about the exaggeration of how I'm supposed to be these days. It says "I'm getting as old as Methuselah, I'm getting old as my mother." It's a good rocker.

If I'm not mistaken, you had a lot of support at home. Didn't your mother buy you your first guitar?

That was one thing that was very nice. My parents both liked music; they used to go out dancing a lot. And when I first wanted a guitar, my mother bought me this very cheap guitar worth three pounds, ten shilling, or about six dollars.

And she didn't mind that I used to stay up until two in the morning polishing my guitar and trying to learn how to play.

Later, when I got to know John and Paul, she used to love having them around singing in the back room. She was very encouraging about that.

You met Paul first.

Yeah, Paul went to school with me. I met him when I was twelve years old. So I had this guitar, the one I just talked about, and Paul had a trumpet for some reason. His father, in his earlier days, had been involved in a little dance band. He was a piano player. So there was a lot of music in Paul's house too.

But when we started hanging out together, that's when Paul realized that he wasn't going to be able to sing and play the trumpet at the same time. So he traded it in and got a guitar.

And somewhere along the line you got introduced to the Quarry Men.

That's right. Paul had a friend who was in his class at school and he lived by John. He took Paul to meet John, and then I met him, and the rest is history!

Except for one little detour, when they caught you underage in Hamburg, and you had to take an exit.

Yeah, they deported me. It was funny really. We were there about three months and every night about ten o'clock, they'd stop the music on the bandstand, put the lights on, and come around and check everybody's IDs. And everybody who was less than eighteen had to get out of the club.

And it took about three months for them to find out that I was in the band and only seventeen. They had no work permits or anything, so they deported me.

Did you have any money, with all the hours you were playing onstage?

Nothing really. Whatever money we had, it cost us just to live, to buy food. So I just got enough money to get a train from Hamburg to a ferry in Holland, then back to England and a train ride back to Liverpool.

The Beatles went through a few different lineups as they came together. But when it all started to gel for you, what were some of the impressions you remember? And did John Lennon have a particular influence?

Anything impressed me in those days, whether it was some flecked sports jacket or some other guy with a guitar. I used to hang out with anybody I saw who played guitar to try and get to know him.

I think a bit more's been written about this than actually took place. I mean, I think a lot's been written out as if John was like the big hero of it. I know Paul certainly said that he [John] was our own Elvis. Well, we certainly liked him and loved him like that. [But] at the same time, we were all kicking too. We were all hot to trot, as they say.

As you know, I was at the airport in 1964 when you guys first came to America. I saw the mop tops and the screaming females. Then just a few years ago I saw a ninety-minute film at Abbey Road that took you from that period all the way up to the end. And the transformation was staggering to see.

I was at this friend's house the other night. He has a son who I was talking about. I said, "How old is he?" And he told me that he was twenty-four.

I thought, "What was I doing when I was twenty-four?—jeez, I was doing *Sgt. Pepper!*"

We grew up very fast. I mean, the experiences we had, most people don't get in a whole lifetime. But the experiences we had were crammed into those years, those few years between 1962, when we first took off and began recording and then eventually came to America.

So there was a lot of experience and we did change a lot, for better or for worse. I suppose because we were so well known, and it's so well documented now, and people related so much to us that you can pick up on it moreso than somebody else.

But most people have gone through all these changes, maybe not as fast or as concentrated as we did.

That's interesting. We talk to people who followed you into music because they related to you. They tell us that they write their own songs because of you and say that if the Beatles didn't happen, they wouldn't be in the business.

It's very nice. Of course, at the time we were doing it, we were just trying to be us and do what we did. I mean, we thought we would become successful because we all had a certain amount of ego or knowledge that we had a certain amount of talent. But it became so overwhelming it became ridiculous.

And as you say, all the different things that it helped to open up—like the recording industry now is enormous, but at that time, it was sort of a small thing. All the new labels that came about and all the different styles of clothing; it's unbelievable to think that we were sort of at the center of that.

But the music industry changed, especially in the writing. If you were a writer, you could now get a break.

It certainly changed; wiped out that Tin-Pan-Alley aspect of music. You know, where these guys would go around selling songs.

And the artists had to record them. You were given your song.

We actually made a recording like that. When we first went to EMI and saw George Martin, he gave us a song. And it was written by some guy who was supposed to be a writer of pop songs. He said, "Here's a song; go back and learn it."

So we went and learned it. It was called "How Do You Do It," which Gerry Marsden recorded later with the Pacemakers.

Well, we did a version of that. But later we said, "Look, we'd rather do our own songs." And we never actually put that song out. That's when we recorded "Please Please Me."

How's fatherhood? How's Dhani, and what's it like raising a child?

Well, when you have a kid, you then relive being a kid. But then, as a father, I realized how my father felt about me. So consciously, you're living three separate identities. It enables you to remember all those different things and relive all those different things at the same time.

The press today seems to give a lot of attention to the fact that rock 'n' roll artists are very involved with charities: Live Aid, Farm Aid, Amnesty International, the Prince's Trust, etc. But as we know you were very active in that mode as far back as 1971 with the concert for Bangladesh.

I suppose the concert for Bangladesh was one of the first shows of that size, although it's dwarfed in size when compared with Live Aid. But there has been a lot of years between the two shows. They had satellite broadcasts and the attitude of people was [that they were] much more inclined to help.

Whereas when I did that concert, nothing like that really happened and it took a lot of talking people into doing that. And I can imagine what Bob Geldof must have gone through, because just with the size of Bangladesh, between getting the show done, and then dealing with it afterwards, took nine years before I finally got it all tidied up.

But if you tap people's charitable instincts, there's a lot of great people and a lot of people who want to help. It's just a question of how to do it and when to do it. Nowadays, people are much more inclined to do that and I think it's a good thing.

Especially if someone's a success in their own right, it's not exactly like they're starving themselves. I think we should all give a little and there wouldn't be so much starvation in the world.

George, your Handmade Films company continues to be a success. Recount its inception and tell us where it's going.

It's actually been nine years since Handmade Films [began]. We first came out with *Monty Python's Life of Brian*, which was quite a controversial film at the time. That was the first Handmade Film. I think over the years we've made about fifteen.

Right now, we have about thirty-five people working for Handmade Films. We have an office in New York now which is our latest addition.

But I don't get that involved, physically, other than if I should decide to go and see the rough cuts and talk about how we want to present the film. And sometimes I get involved with the music in the film.

But I can take that or leave it. I have a very competent company that can do it.

You're also an author. I Me Mine *came out in 1980. Do you have any plans to do another book someday?*

Well, I didn't really intend to write a book as such. Derek Taylor met a guy who was a book publisher. He did these limited edition books which are quite expensive, big leather-bound books. So he asked Derek if I'd be interested in doing something based on this book he gave me, *The Log of HMS Bounty*. It was the log book from the Bounty voyage.

It was reproduced in what they call facsimile, and it was exactly in Captain Cook's handwriting. It had everything in it, like how many tons of potatoes [they brought], everything they sighted, where the journeys led. It was printed on this fabulous paper, a leather-bound collectors' edition, which lasts for hundreds of years.

So he [Derek] said to me, "How about if you do a book that is a facsimile of all the bits of paper that you've written songs on, backs of envelopes, and various things like that?"

So the book was really done just as a limited edition. Later a cheaper edition came out, but I don't remember the circumstances. I was talked into doing that because they said that the average person couldn't afford the big edition.

But when the cheaper edition came out, it had lost a lot. It [the limited edition] had twenty-seven different colors of green. The printers told me that it was the most complicated book they'd ever printed.

Later I was involved with another book by Derek Taylor called *Fifty Years Adrift*, done by the same publisher.

And over the last two years, we've been working on another book which was, again, the publisher's idea based upon his meeting with Keith West, an artist from New Zealand. He's been a botanical artist all his life, illustrating botanical books.

So the publisher had this idea of getting us two together and seeing what it would be like if he illustrated some of my songs.

So that book they're hoping to get out by Christmas. It's quite amazing, really. There's all these songs in there that I actually handwrote the lyrics to. It looked strange having type next to all these great pictures. It looks like an old Victorian book, with the pictures drawn mainly in pencil and watercolors.

There's the song I wrote called "Taxman." When the artist and I sat together and tried to think of ideas of how to illustrate it, I said to him, "How's about having a line of people being mangled, you know, like in the old days when you used to put your washing through the thing with the handles and the two rollers?"

And he came back with this picture that is just sensational. It's got nuclear silos in the back and there's all these military people with guns leading an enormous line of people going into the distance. And the guy in the foreground in front of the queue is halfway through the mangle. It's very symbolic. And there's all this money coming out of his mouth and there are these little gnomes collecting all the money.

So some of the pictures have gotten pretty good. There are a lot of Hieronymus-Bosch-looking things and it's due to come out this Christmas [1987].

Now that the new album has come out, I have to wonder if you've considered touring behind it?

I'm not sure about touring, you know? It's the kind of thing that you have to do all the time. You can't just go from one life-style and jump on a stage. I mean, I can. I did it at the Prince's Trust. But at the same time, if anybody saw that, you can see I'm so nervous and out of practice.

To get a tour going, you need to get all your lighting, the whole road crew, and the band, and rehearsals, and all that. There's so much work involved just gearing up for the first concert that it's hardly worth just doing a few concerts. And the prospects of being on the road for six months or nine months is an idea that I don't really like.

I do like the idea of doing some concerts from time to time. Eric Clapton just told me that Elton John is allegedly forming a band for over-forty-year-olds and that I'm in it!

So I won't say that you won't see us doing anything like that, but at this moment, I'm just happy to have made this album.